BIG QUESTION:

Do Humans Need God?

Matchstick Literary
1-888-306-8885
orders@matchliterary.com

BIG QUESTION:

Do Humans Need God?

E. Asamoah-Yaw

CONTENTS

ACKNOWLEDGEMENT

ALL PUBLISHED WORKS initially pass through several people before leaving the author's hands to the publishers. Proofreading, for instance, is particularly unavoidable, and colleagues are most often willing to read manuscripts with great interest without hesitation. But when the subject matter questions conventional wisdom or religious faith in particular, the immediate shocking reaction of trusted companions seems like someone being shocked by electricity current. Many people appear to be comfortable with status quo and reluctant to read or to listen to opposing views.

There are practically dozens of people whose contribution helped to clarify many issues in this book and therefore must be thanked for their honest opinions. Their names are not mentioned because I offered them the assurance that their names would be concealed if they desire so. I however find it ungrateful to avoid mentioning the following contributors' names for their open-minded critical scrutiny of my entire major themes; without them, this book would have been different. Kwabena Agyemang, popularly known as Nana Osei of Abuakwa, Kumasi; Ms. Mary Kraah, the headmistress of Kumasi Girls Senior High School (2008-13); Mr. Kweku Essamuah of Kumasi; and Mrs. Eno Ntiamoah Asamoah of Atlanta, Georgia, USA. None is accountable for anything in this book. I sincerely yield all the goodness to them. I also humbly accept all faults that may be detected, although none is intentional.

I am very grateful to the publishers. And to you the reader, I am most gratified for choosing to share your precious time with me.

E. A-Y

INTRODUCTION

IT IS A fact that most people use the Bible as a textbook or a reference book. Most people do not read it as a work of fiction or a novel. Most readers, who claim to have read it, have not read the entire *suppose sixty-six books* of the Holy Bible. I said supposed sixty-six books because some of the books are a collection of several books or pamphlets written by several ancient Jewish priests at different times and compiled into single booklets at later dates.

Most experts agree that some of the books cannot be called books. An example of such books are Genesis and Deuteronomy; both are piles of eleven booklets each, with at least twenty anonymous different authors who wrote them at different periods of times. The book of Isaiah contains at least three separate books.

Furthermore, some of the books do not really qualify to be called books in modern conventional sense. For instance, the thirty-first book of the Old Testament (*Obadiah*) has only twenty-one verses. In the New Testament, *2 John* has thirteen verses; *3 John* has fifteen verses; *Jude* and *Philemon* have twenty-five verses each. The five books mentioned above contain ninety-nine verses altogether. In contrast, the nineteenth book of the Old Testament (*Psalms*) has 150 chapters. *Psalms* 119 alone contains 176 verses. But *Psalms* 117 has only 2 verses.

A pertinent question here is 'What is a book and what constitute a chapter?'

Is there a difference between a letter, a pamphlet, and a book? Ancient people obviously did not see any difference between them. The New Testament is popularly known to have twenty-seven books, but twenty-one of them are titled and written as Letters.

Based on these arrangements, it is probably justified to use the Holy Bible as a reference book as many do. But based on its philosophical content, it is imperative that every reader of the Holy Bible reads the book in its entirety for a reasonable understanding of the stories written in the sixty-six books. Textual reading of the Holy Bible gives textual incoherent meaning or pieces of the stories only. Readers can get a full understanding of the whole story when each book is carefully and fully read. For instance, in Job 4: 18, the following is written: 'God does not trust his heavenly servants. He finds fault even with his angels.' A textual reader may use this short extract to say that God of Israel trusts not his personal heavenly people or anybody on planet earth. However, if you read the entire book of Job, you will understand that the statement comes from frustrated Job, the most faithful, richest earthly citizen who had been stripped off his total wealth by God and Satan working as a team to test Job's faith.

As you read along, you will find numerous examples of Bible chapters that are inherently evil and unholy. Some chapters and quotations from the main biblical characters such as the God of Israel in the Old Testament and Jesus Christ in the New Testament do not fit a super-divine entity of their description. In the Old Testament, Yahweh, or God of Israel, is depicted as a God for the Jewish people only. The same books in other chapters narrate God's story as a supreme faultless divine entity that created the whole world and perpetually supervises the *whole* universe, *not just the Jewish* universe.

All the authors of the thirty-nine books in the Old Testament clearly emphasize their concerns repeatedly of the *Jewish universe or the Jewish world* with *its creator* and *its controller* as a *God for the nation of Israel*: for example, Zephaniah 2; 9 this is written; As long as I am the living God of Israel, I swear that Moab and Ammon are going to be destroyed . . . . Those of *my people* who survive will plunder them and take their lands. In these books, the God of Israel does not claim to be the God for Gentiles or any universe of people other than the Jewish world. According to the Old Testament, a Jew is a circumcised Hebrew. Uncircumcised Hebrews and the rest of humanity belong to another world or universe. It will be completely out of context, for instance, for the people of China, India, Europe, Australia, and Africa, America, and Russia or any race of people to assume that the God of Israel is their God. *The Old Testament does not claim the universe of non-Jews as part of his domain.* It is concerned with the twelve nations of Israel or the descendants of Abraham, Isaac, and Jacob only.

The New Testament represents *new* understanding of ancient Jewish prophets, poets, historians, and miracle performers or magicians as portrayed in the Old Testament. The entire twenty-seven books were written to provide evidence that the prophesied Jewish Messiah, Messenger, or Prophet has been born and that he is in the person of the Virgin Mary's first son 'Jesus' the Christ. The books attempt to link *pre*-Christ Judaic cultural religion with that of *Christ era* and *after-Christ era* Jewish religious experiences. The books also attempted to show how Christ-era Jews modified the Old texts to embrace both uncircumcised Jews and circumcised Jews and *in some sense,* the entire human race. The fifth book of the New Testament (Acts) in particular was designed to redefine all Jews and Gentiles as a single race of people with common destiny. This unification was engineered by Saul, a Turkish Jew who became well known in the scriptures as the Apostle Paul. At least seven of the twenty-seven books are generally accepted to have been written by Paul who identified himself in the book of Acts as a true Jew: not necessarily a circumcised unmarried Jew.

Some Major Qualities of God According to the Holy Bible

God is supreme. He is the creator of the universe and all its natural contents. He is spiritually present everywhere every time. He has infinite knowledge and controls destinies of all lives. He possesses both human and spiritual attributes at the same time. He makes and unmakes everything possible.

In the Holy Bible, God and human beings act rationally the same. For instance, the biblical God can lose memory, God can swear, God can say 'as long as I live', God can lose temper, God can love or hate one race more than another, and God can kill the innocent as well as the guilty earthly people. Above all, God can choose to test, to trick, and to trap human beings. There are indeed hundreds of chapters where the biblical God has all the above classic human behaviors.

The question therefore is must there be a definite difference between God and man in terms of knowledge and behaviour or in rationality? If the biblical God is supposed to possess infinite knowledge of the planet earth or the Jewish world events, he must definitely be faultless and just. Human tests of any kind would not be needed by God. He already has all the answers before tests are conducted. A test is necessary among human beings because we possess *limited* knowledge in everything.

God's choice of ancient Jews as *his favorite humans* clearly shows bias nature. Ancient Jews represented far less than 0.1 per cent of world population, and the God's rejection of the remaining 99.9 per cent of humanity becomes seriously questionable: if indeed this biblical God is for all humanity. Micah 4: 5 says, 'Each nation worships and obeys its own God, but we (Jews) will worship and obey the Lord our God of (Israel) forever and ever.' Amos 3; 2, *Of*

all nations on earth, you are the one I have known and cared for: (GNT)
That is what makes your sin so terrible, and that is why I must
punish you for them.

Many ethnic groups currently have a generation of people,
who appear to need a god, but they appear to have lost touch with
their ancestral god or deity; for this reason, the Israelites' God has
been adopted as their almighty sovereign God, but God of Israel
emphatically says that he is for Jews only. He does not claim to
represent non-Jews. I am not by any means saying that human
beings need a God. I am only stating an observation.

Evidently, all human beings possess organic matter called the
'brain' our central nervous system or our organ of thought. This
organ's main function is to capture and store information which it
is exposed to, from birth till death, through our ears, eyes, nose,
mouth, tongue, and nerves. The processed information of the brain
is the actions or behaviour we call *listening* but not hearing, *seeing*
but not looking, *speaking* but not talking, *smelling* but not snorting.
The brain organ has a limited life; it dies when the heart dies.

God as a spiritual entity should possess neither a brain nor
a heart. God and humans must be completely different from each
other by all means. If humans and God are the same organically,
God must exist temporarily as humans. God cannot exist for ever,
as we are commonly nurtured to believe. God as a spirit must live
forever. God must have no time span as humans.

Again, on questions about morality, that is, anything relating to
right and wrong in human behaviour, there seems to be a universal
acceptance of what constitutes good and bad. For instance, sexual
intercourse amongst brothers and sisters, mothers *or* fathers and
their children, knowledge of a fact and deliberately ignoring
the facts and telling different stories, malicious personal assault
of another human, and deliberate killing of innocent people are
regarded as immoral in all human cultures without exception.

Once more, if we examine closely all religions of the world, it is without doubt that the fundamental reasons or purposes for every religion appears to be the promotion of basic human morality as mentioned above, plus of course, the other culturally relevant and prescribed morality within each specific culture.

A detailed account of the Holy Bible reveals numerous violations of common human morality by God of Israel and his agents: for instance, destruction of human life without cause, sexual intercourse among very close blood relatives of biblical most significant characters such as, Adam, Eve, Cain, Enoch, Seth, Enosh: Noah, Abraham, Sara, Isaac, Rebecca, Jacob, Judah, Joseph, Moses, Lot, David, Isaiah, Solomon, Mary, Joseph, Jesus, Mary Magdalene, Paul, etc., etc., etc. None of the above characters is innocent of several gross immoral acts according to Holy Bible.

The Holy Bible clearly condemns and at the same time promotes such behaviors. For instance, Abraham and Sara are from one father, Terah. 'She really is my sister. She is the daughter of my father, but not of my mother, and I married her' (Gen. 20: 12). Abraham married his own father's daughter (Sara). 'Do not have sexual intercourse with any of your relatives' (Lev. 18: 6), yet the above characters are described in details at times with this very unholy behaviour. For instance, the *supposed first-ever two humans on planet earth* (Adam and Eve) are of the same genes or of the same identical blood composition (brother and sister), yet they married.

It is a demonstrable fact that a male gene or a male cell alone cannot produce its kind, all by itself. It requires a female egg or gene (Xx and Yx) to produce humans. As a human male, Adam would possess predominantly Y chromosome. And Eve, like all human females, would possess predominantly X chromosomes. The single rib that was supposedly removed from Adam to form the human female, Eve, would necessarily possess Y chromosome or a genetic material which cannot form another human species by itself. The Jewish God could not invent Eve with a male gene alone. The Yx genetic material of Adam cannot be converted into Xy by magical means. Again there is a huge contradiction of God's invention of Adam as the first son of God. In Exodus 4: 22-23, it is written as 'That, I the Lord say "Israel is my first-born son."' Perhaps 'Lord' is used in reference to *Lord* God of Israel, but not the Genesis' God. Who is Adam? Is he not the first son of Genesis' God? Again, who is this *I the Lord*?

We are told that the biblical God is the most incredible magician ever invented by ancient Jews, but why would God have to go through all these surgical process to invent the first female. By a single stroke or command, he could have made the woman appear from nowhere miraculously.

It is noticed in the Holy Bible that ancient Jews considered females as a natural gift to men or as chattels to be used by men; hence the first female, Eve's invention, must by all means resemble an extraction from a male body. Obviously, the logic of this creation is culturally motivated and too loose to be linked with God 'the creator of all!'

We are further told that Adam married Eve (Gen. 3: 20) and had sexual intercourse: (Gen. 4: 1) by modern definition, this act is incest, an abomination, a sin, and indeed a major crime in most cultures and countries. Why would God initiate the first human family in a sinful manner?

Again we are informed that the first two children of Adam and Eve were Cain and Abel. Both were males. Logically, this means that the first earthly family consisted of only four initial people (Adam, Eve, Cain, and Abel). We are *not* told that there were other humans apart from these four people. Although in Genesis 1: 26, God said in his statement '*We* are going to make humans'. Why *we*? Were there other humans before creation? There ought *not* be any other humans on earth at the time according to the creation story in the book of Genesis; else the biblical God could not be the first inventor of the first human.

The 'first' as an idea in creation as written in the Holy Bible is not convincing. The 'first' as a concept in creation is a biblical idea. People are so used to the 'first notion' to the extent that many are convinced there must be the first in every natural thing. In all aspects, *first* in creation is fundamentally an ancient Jewish concept with no supporting indisputable evidence. Without a proof it is necessarily a fiction.

We are further informed however that Cain's first child was Enoch (Adam and Eve's first grandchild), who was also a male (Gen. 4: 17). Cain is mentioned to have had a *nameless-wife*, definitely a woman from another human family. This implies that there was another woman besides Eve in the universe for Cain to have selected a woman as a wife and had sex and a child with. The book of Genesis is not saying so either because saying so would mean that God did not make the first human being. The only woman so far known, then, to Bible readers is Eve at that time.

Could there be a woman from another human family whose daughter became Cain's wife? If so, then the biblical claim of God's invention of the first human is false, baseless, and a wishful thinking.

Indeed, that is how ancient Jews thought human beings *came* to the planet earth. Every cultural group invents its own idea of how the planet earth was first inhabited by human beings. This biblical version is pure and simple, a Jewish version or Jews explanation of the source of man. Alternatively, logically, if there is going to be any additional human being, it would have to be delivered by the only female citizen (Eve), among the five, who could impregnate a child in her womb.

Mother and son (Eve and Cain) therefore must have had sexual intercourse; 'Eve' became pregnant with her own son 'Cain' and gave birth to Cain's first male child called 'Enoch'. Eve happened to be the only human being on the planet earth at the time that possessed an organ (a womb) that could produce human beings.

There is one other confusing statement in the sixty-fifth book of the Holy Bible—*Jude* containing only twenty-fifth verses—about human genealogy. Jude verse 14, 'It was Enoch, the sixth direct descendant from Adam.' But according to Genesis 4: 17, Enoch was the *fifth* earthly person. By 'the sixth direct descendant,' even if we count from Eve, Cain, Abel, and Seth, Enoch is still the fifth direct descendant *from* Adam according to the Good News Holy Bible. Again if we count by procreation process, Adam and Eve would be the first humans, Cain, Abel, and Seth would be the first biblical descendants. Enoch and the rest of Adam's grandchildren would be the *second* generation direct descendant from Adam.

A glance at the 1934 Cambridge University Press published Holy Bible verse 14 of book of Jude shows Enoch as the *seventh* descendant from Adam. Authors of the Holy Bible intentionally confuse the Bible readers with the hope that none would question the logic of their statements. Which of the three reports should readers believe, Enoch as the fifth, the sixth, or the seventh offspring of Adam?

Can we really rationally rely on this ancient biblical fantasy today—the year 2014—really, God as the inventor of life? No. I don't think so! What do you think, and how about your own cultural ancestral God, if you have not lost it through nurture? Don't you, the reader, have an original ancestors' God, besides this ancient Jewish thing? Must we not think about these stories, as humans?

This logic definitely nullifies Mr. and Mrs. Adam as the first couple who inhabited this planet. The entire biblical creation story is therefore obviously mere hocus-pocus and childish.

The Ashanti people of Ghana still maintain the ancient Ananse story with similar view of creation. In that allegory, the character's wisdom is not different from the allegory of the ancient Jews. And I am certain that all cultures of the world can narrate their unique understanding of how life began. Each culture understands the beginning of life differently. The Holy Bible narrates how ancient Jews understood it.

People of this century however *cannot* blame ancient Jews who lived about 3,000 years ago for believing in the *first creation concept,* because human knowledge at that time and indeed at any given time is always proportionate to the size of human population at the time in question. Fewer people, fewer knowledge of nature, and more people, more knowledge of human understanding of nature. Alternatively, fewer people with lesser knowledge enhance dependency on false notions and superstitions, while many people with more knowledge enhances dependency on superior experimental knowledge or science.

All mysteries in all primitive societies had to be assigned to spiritual realm when human intelligence failed to explain causes of mysteries. Dependency on superstition is the norm in all primitive societies.

Most distinguished biblical historians agree that the book of Genesis was written in about 100 years before Jesus Christ was born. Some experts even believe Genesis was written somewhere around 1445 BC. But no matter how far back we date the book, we cannot deny the fact that superstition was the order of the day. Human knowledge was essentially limited to each culture's boundaries and its experience.

Genesis chapter 5 gives some account of Adam and his descendants. Readers are informed that Adam lived on the planet earth for 930 years. One of his surviving descendants was Noah whose procreation made possible the presently living humans on the planet earth according to the Holy Bible. Nobody knows for sure how ancient Jews of the first century BC calculated years, months, weeks, and days. But if the counting method we use today is what ancient Jews also used, then given the nature of primitive unhygienic conditions at the period, compared to conditions of twenty-first century worldly people, no one would rationally accept Adam's age of 930 years as realistic.

How a real human being could live up to 930 years can be possible *only in fiction books* such as the Holy Bible? A fictional character may live over 1,000 years; yes, but remember it could exist only in fictions, not in reality. There is no record in *actual human history* where a human organ of any kind has survived beyond 170 years.

Thus, the story of man according to ancient Jews, as narrated in the Holy Bible, will fail every logical test, no matter how anyone interprets it. Adam's age by modern human standards is simply not true.

Religious Faith *(GNT; Quotations source)*

Now, let us examine faith. Virtually, every human being is *born into* some kind of religious faith. And most people do not question the viability or authenticity of their born-into-religious-faiths: even when they are grown beyond matured age of eighteen years. Most religious people are faithful in their religions because their parents nurtured them into the faith in which they themselves had possibly been born into. In general, religiosity necessarily begins at home.

It is observed that being born into a faith is different from choosing a faith for oneself when matured. Faith is *not* a choice made by us as individual rational people, *if* it is the same faith we are primarily born into. It is faith decided for us by those who nurtured us from birth to adulthood. The retention of our infancy years' faith cannot be the result of a rational or random selection. Because we are already ingrained with the idea of calling ourselves Christians, Muslim, Buddhist, etc, during our early teens. Our repetitive exposure to our nurtured faith practices as children are intrinsically coded into our long-term memory-lobes or our brain cells; hence, our acquired religious faiths from infancy have necessarily become part of our daily instinct.

We may *rationally* choose to abandon our primary nurtured faith after carefully comparing and examining the other faiths.

Choice comes into the equation when it is between faiths B, C, or D, to the exclusion of our primary faith A.

Again as an example, the choice process is the same as our names, especially maiden names. Names are given to us by our parents, and we grow to accept and use them. We may choose to change them when matured.

Most matured people are incapable of altering or abandoning their primary religious faiths or names because of their mindset. They have unconditionally accepted their parent's religions and outdoor names. It is only a fraction of people who willingly rationalize on the logics of these matters. Selecting a religious faith, as a matured person, from our base faith to a different religious faith, *besides* the one we are born into, must be considered as faith based on personal rational choice. My question therefore is, are we Christians by rational choice or by indoctrination? If the answer is rational choice, can we be honest to say that we have actually read thoroughly Christian's holy book, 'Holy Bible,' page to page, Genesis to Revelation? If not, why not? Fear of change of faith?

Satan *(GNT; Quotation source)*

In the Holy Bible, Satan is a word used to characterize God's adversary, or an entity which does ungodly things. A Satan is a demon, an evil spirit, a wicked person, or a person who opposes good deeds. The opposite of God or Good is Satan or Bad. In the New Testament, Matthew 12: 24 and Luke 11: 15, Satan is called Beelzebub, the chief of the demons. The book of Revelation gives a clear picture of the character that is popularly known as Satan. But there are several chapters in the holy book where God's behaviour is worse than that of Satan. Bear in mind however that the entire book of Revelation is a report of dreams by an unknown person, addressed to someone known as John 'the Devine.' Read this: Rev. 12, 7-9; "Then *war broke out in Heaven*. Michael and his Angels fought against the Dragon that fought back with his Angels; but the Dragon was defeated, and he and his Angels were not allowed to stay in Heaven any longer. The huge Dragon was thrown out - that ancient serpent was thrown to earth, and all his angel went with hm."

Several chapters of the holy book show ambiguous roles of the most powerful characters - God and Satan. And most often it is impossible to determine whether the actor of God is really aware of his supreme global roles. A war among heavenly creatures (Angels), where the "know-all-ahead-of- time" God is the Omni King: is this believable? Can any reasonable person accept this tale: even, every earthly idiot knows God is the ruler in Heaven? Nothing can challenge his authority. Can war really break out there too? If God cannot manage or govern his own kingdom, how can he be expected to control planet earth? On top of that his infamous Satan and his gang of bad angels are thrown down here to live with us on earth. This is insane!

Again, readers of the holy book are informed that everything satanic is repulsive to God. But in the book of Job, for example, God and Satan have come together as good friends to cause harm to God's own very faithful richest earthly person, *Job and his family*. And God's singular reason for this mischief is nothing other than to test Job's faith in him. The God of Israel need not test Job or humans because he is supposed to know everything at all times before the actual human action begins.

I have intentionally chosen God and Satan's unholy alliance drama as a preamble to this discourse. And I hope at the end of Job's story, you will be able to answer the question I have proposed throughout this critique: whether humans really need God.

21

PART 1

The Story of Job: Test of faith?

(GNT; Quotation source)
God and Satan United to Commit a Serious Crime

THIS IS AN allegory of the most faithful and richest man. He had a wife, seven sons, three daughters, plus three friends. One day, God and Satan planned together to test Job's faith in God by making him lose all his wealth, his children, his wife, and his reputation. God deliberately empowered Satan to inflict on Job severe despicable skin disease and finally converted Job to become a destitute living on the street.

The Story

THERE WAS A man named Job, living in the land of Uz, who worshiped God and was faithful to him. He was a good man, careful not to do anything evil. He had seven sons and three daughters, and owned 7,000 sheep, 3,000 camels, 1,000 herd of cattle, and 500 donkeys. He also had a large number of servants and was the richest man on earth.

Job's sons used to take turns in giving feasts, to which all the others would come, and they always invited their three sisters to join them. The morning after each feast, Job would get up early and offer sacrifices for each of his children in order to purify them. He always did this because he thought that one of them might have sinned by insulting God unintentionally.

One day, *several heavenly beings* appeared before the Lord, and *Satan was there among them*. The Lord asked Satan what he had been doing all these years, and Satan answered he had been walking here and there, roaming around the earth. 'Did you come across my servant Job?' the Lord asked. 'There is no one on earth as faithful and good as he is. He worships you and is careful not to do anything evil,' Satan replied. He also added, 'I wander if he would worship you if he got nothing out of it. You have always protected him and his family and everything he owns. You bless everything he does, and you have given him enough cattle to fill the whole country. But suppose you test him by taking away everything he has, I bet he will curse you to your face!' 'All right,' the Lord said to Satan, 'everything Satan has is in your power, but you must not hurt Job himself.' So Satan left.

Note here that there were several heavenly beings, including Satan and God at the meeting, but the conversation was between God and Satan alone. It is interesting to note that Satan asked permission from God for the test to be conducted on Job, and God gladly granted it by saying, 'Everything he has is in your power, but you must not hurt Job himself'.

One day, when Job's children were having a feast at the home of their oldest brother, a messenger came running to Job. 'We were plowing the fields with the oxen,' he said, 'and the donkeys were in a nearby pasture. Suddenly the Sabeans attacked and stole them all. They killed every one of your servants except me. I am the only one who escaped to tell you.' Before he had finished speaking, another servant came and said that lightning struck the sheep and the shepherds and killed them all. I am the only one who escaped to tell you.

Before he had finished speaking, another servant came and said, 'Three bands of Chaldean raiders attacked us, took away the camels, and killed all your servants except me. I am the only one who escaped to tell you.'

Before he had finished speaking, the fourth servant came and said, 'Your children were having a feast at the home of your oldest son, when a storm swept in from the desert. It blew the house down and killed them all. I am the only one who escaped to tell you.'

Job is angry, yet faithful, but he got up and tore his clothes in grief. He shaved his head and threw himself face downward on the ground. He said, 'I was born with nothing, and I will die with nothing. The Lord gave, and now he has taken away. May his name be praised.' In spite of everything that had happened, Job did not sin by blaming God.

Note again that God and Satan's first attempt to make Job unfaithful has failed, although he has lost all his children and thousands of livestock. Job is lamenting that he was born with nothing and he will die with nothing. Big question! If God actually knows the future, then God is supposed to know that all the ten children of Job would be killed in this *test of faith,* or is God not aware that he possesses *infinite knowledge*? How about the biblical text 'Thou shall not kill'? This is part of the Ten Commandments, Exodus 20: 13. Note that God has broken his own law by killing Job's ten children. Even, God and Satan's first meeting is too weird and ungodly.

Satan and God met the second time to finally destroy Job. When the day came for the heavenly beings to appear before the Lord again, Satan was there among them. The Lord asked him, 'Where have you been?' Satan answered, 'I have been walking here and there, roaming around the earth.' 'Did you notice my servant Job?' the Lord asked. Satan answered that there is no one on earth as faithful and good as Job is. He worships and is careful not to do anything evil. God said, 'You persuaded me to let you attack him for no reason at all, but Job is still as faithful as ever.'

Satan successfully persuaded God to allow him to commit murder, and he is still convincing God to grant him another permission to *test* Job again. Satan told God, 'A person will give up everything in order to stay alive. Suppose you hurt his body, he will curse you to your face.' So the Lord said to Satan, 'All right, he is in your power, but you are not to kill him.' God betrays Job by handing him over to Satan.

Notice God's response to Satan's first failed test: 'You persuaded me to let you attack Job for no reason at all.' In the first attempt, God warned Satan not to hurt Job, but now God has authorized Satan to harm but not to kill Job. The question here is, can human beings trust Yahweh God of the Jews, if he is so vulnerable to Satanic influences? Please think about it seriously. Up to this point, moral weaknesses of God and human beings are perfectly identical.

Then Satan left the Lord's presence and made sores break out all over Job's body. Job went and sat by the garbage dump and took a piece of broken pottery to scrape his sores. His wife said to him, 'You are still as faithful as ever, aren't you? Why don't you curse God and die?' Job answered, 'You are talking nonsense! When God sends us something good, we welcome it. How can we complain when he sends us trouble?' Even in all this suffering, Job said nothing against God.

Three of Job's friends, *Eliphaz*, from the city of Teman, *Bildad*, from the land of Shuah, and *Zophar*, from the land of Naamah heard how much Job had been suffering. They decided to go and comfort him. While they were still a long way off, they saw Job, but did not recognize him. When they did, they began to weep and wail, tearing their clothes in grief and throwing dust into the air and on their heads. Then they sat there on the ground with him for seven days and nights without saying a word, because they saw how much he was suffering.

Eliphaz, Job's first friend asked Job, 'Will you be annoyed if I speak? I can't keep quiet any longer. You have taught many people and given strength to feeble hands. When someone stumbled, weak and tired, your words encouraged him to stand. Now it's your turn to be in trouble, and you are too stunned to face it. You worshiped God, and your life was blameless, and so you should have confidence and hope.

'Think back now; name a single case where someone righteous met with disaster. I have seen people plough fields of evil and plant wickedness like seed; now they harvest wickedness and evil.

'Like a storm, God destroys them in his anger. The wicked roar and growl like lions, but God silences them and breaks their teeth.

'Like lions with nothing to kill and eat, they die, and all their children are scattered. Once a message came quietly, and quietly I could hardly hear it. Like a nightmare it disturbed my sleep. I trembled and shuddered; my whole body shook with fear. A light breeze touched my face, and my skin crawled with fright. I could see something standing there; I stared, but couldn't tell what it was. Then I heard a voice out of the silence: "Can anyone be righteous in the sight of God or be pure before his Creator? *God does not trust his heavenly servants; he finds fault even with his angels.* Do you think he will trust a creature of clay, a thing of dust that can be crushed like a moth? We may be alive in the morning, but die unnoticed before evening comes. All that we have is taken away; we die, still lacking wisdom."'

The idea of quoting the Bible in shot verses is detestable, but the above (Job 4: 18) is irresistible: 'God does not trust his heavenly servants; he finds fault even with his angels'. This is a serious blasphemy! How possible? Is God a joke? I hope the reader would think about this statement. The so-called servants and angels in heaven are the only known link between God and earthly people (you and I) and they are not trustworthy? Where is the buckle that links man and the God of Israel, the Genesis' creator God, plus the whole essence of God's spirituality, if his own spiritual beings cannot be trusted?

Job 7

'Human life is like forced army service or like a life of hard manual labor, like a slave longing for cool shade; like a worker waiting to be paid. Month after month I have nothing to live for; night after night bring me grief. When I lie down to sleep, the hours drag; I toss all night and long for dawn. My body is full of worms; it is covered with scabs; pus runs out of my sores. My days pass by without hope. They pass faster than a weaver's shuttle. Remember, O God, my life is only a breath; my happiness has already ended. You see me now, but never again. If you look for me, I'll be gone. Like a cloud that fades and is gone, we humans die and never return; we are forgotten by all who knew us.

'No! I can't be quiet! I am angry and bitter. I have to speak. Why do you keep me under guard? Do you think I am a sea monster? I lie down and try to rest; I look for relief from my pain. But you— you terrify me with dreams; you send me visions and nightmares until I would rather be strangled than live in this miserable body. I give up; I am tired of living. Leave me alone. My life makes no sense. Why are people so important to you? Why pay attention to what they do? You inspect them every morning and test them every minute. Won't you look away long enough for me to swallow my spit? *Are you harmed by my sin? You jailer, why use me for your target practice?* Am I so great a burden to you, God? Can't you ever forgive my sin? Can't you pardon the wrong I do? Soon I will be in my grave, and I'll be gone when you look for me'.

Job completes his commentary of Eliphaz's sorrowful remarks as if he was talking to God face to face. Job realizes that God is using him for a target practice. Job is right. Satan and God are treating Job like a dog with its favorite bone. God himself knows that Job does not deserve the punishment he is going through. Yet because of a 'test of Job's faith' in him, the torture must continue, although God has no doubt of the test result.

Second friend of Job, Bildad, asks Job if he is finally through with his windy speech. God never twists justice; he never fails to do what is right (Job 8: 3). Is it justice for God and Satan to harm Job? If this is not a twist of justice, then I wonder what the above quotation means. Of what significance is God when faithful and innocent earthly people can be harmed by God and Satan, his most wicked adversary, acting together as crooks?

'Children must have sinned against God, and so he punished them as they deserved. But turn now and plead with Almighty God; if you are so honest and pure, then God will come and help you and restore your household as your reward. All the wealth you lost will be nothing compared with what "God will give you then. God will never abandon the faithful or ever give help to evil people"'.

Really! Yes, Satan is supposed to be the king of all evils, and God is supposed to be the father of all goodness, yet God has given Satan the power to make Job and his family suffer as a test of Job's faithfulness to him (for committing no sin whatsoever). God knows all. Why test Job? God already knows the outcome of every test. This is absurd! Job is in a confused state of mind; he is talking to himself like a mad person. Yes, most earthly faithful people will behave the same as Job. God is not expected to be involved in satanic acts.

Job continues, 'Yes, I've heard all that before. But how can a human being win a case against God? How can anyone argue with him? He can ask a thousand questions that no one could ever answer. God is so wise and powerful; no one can stand up against him. Without warning he moves mountains and in anger he destroys them. God sends earthquakes and shakes the ground; he rocks the pillars that support the earth. He can keep the sun from rising and the stars from shining at night. No one helped God spread out the heavens or trample the sea monster's back. God hung the stars in the sky—the Dipper, Orion, the Pleiades, and the stars of the south. We cannot understand the great things he does, and to his miracles, there is no end. God passes by, but I cannot see him. He takes what he wants, and no one can stop him; no one dares ask him, "What are you doing?" God's anger is constant. So how can I find words to answer God? Though I am innocent, all I can do is beg for mercy from God, my judge. Yet even then, if he lets me speak, I can't believe he would listen to me. He sends storms to batter and bruise me without any reason at all. He won't let me catch my breath; he has filled my life with bitterness. Should I try force? Try force on God? Should I take him to court? Could anyone make him go? I am innocent and faithful, but my words sound guilty, and everything I say seems to condemn me. I am innocent, but I no longer care. I am sick of living. Nothing matters; innocent or guilty, God will destroy us. When an innocent person suddenly dies, God laughs. God gave the world to the wicked. He made all the judges blind. And if God didn't do it, who did? My life passes like the swiftest boat, as fast as an eagle swooping down on a rabbit. If I smile and try to forget my pain, all my suffering comes back to haunt me; I know that God does hold me guilty. Since I am held guilty, why should I bother? No soap can wash away my sins. God throws me into a pit with filth, and even my clothes are ashamed of me. If God were human, I could answer him; we could go to court to decide our quarrel. But there is no one to step between us—no one to judge both God and me. Stop punishing me, God! Keep your terrors away! I am not afraid. I am going to talk because I know my own heart.'

Job's third friend (Zophar) tries to comfort him. 'Will no one answer all this nonsense? Does talking so much put you in the right? Job, do you think we can't answer you? That your mocking words will leave us speechless? You claim that what you say is true; you claim you are pure in the sight of God.'

30

Yes, even God himself knows Job is clean, pure, and faithful (Job 1: 1). God's behaviour towards Job is extremely ungodly, extremely satanic, and rather unbefitting a merciful God who is supposed to be the cosmic unblemished spiritual entity.

'How I wish God would answer you! He would tell you there are many sides to wisdom; there are things too deep for human knowledge. God is punishing you less than you deserve. Can you discover the limits and bounds of the greatness and power of God?

The sky is no limit for God, but it lies beyond your reach. God knows the world of the dead, but you do not know it. God's greatness is broader than the earth, wider than the sea. If God arrests you and brings you to trial, who is there to stop him?

'God knows which people are worthless; he sees all their evil deeds. $_{12}$ Stupid people will start being wise when wild donkeys are born tame. $_{13}$ Put your heart right, Job. Reach out to God.

'$_{14}$ Put away evil and wrong from your home. $_{15}$ Then face the world again, firm and courageous. $_{16}$ Then all your troubles will fade from your memory, like floods that are past and remembered no more.

'$_{17}$ Your life will be brighter than sunshine at noon, and life's darkest hours will shine like the dawn. $_{18}$ You will live secured and full of hope; God will protect you and give you rest. $_{19}$ You won't be afraid of your enemies; many people will ask you for help. $_{20}$ But the wicked will look around in despair and find that there is no way to escape. Their only hope is that death will come.'

If God, the supposed Almighty, the one and only single God of the universe can treat Job, the most faithful earthly person, like a piece of shit, then what is the point of humans trying to live a life without a sin. Can there be punishment for righteousness? All the good deeds the Holy Bible has been teaching all the while? God is supposed to know all at all times everywhere even before humans are born. For instance, (Gen. 25: 21-26) the destiny of Jacob and Esau (children of Isaac and his wife Rebecca and grand

31

children of Abraham) were revealed by God before the twins were born. The God of Abraham told Isaac that his wife was pregnant with rival twins with detailed account of how they will live their lives. Why would God need to test Job if he has these superhuman qualities of 'know-all'? All this is because Satan persuaded God for permission to inflict injury to a perfect innocent human being. God himself has testified that Job is faultless, yet God is notoriously ridiculous in punishing a certified righteous person.

It is this kind of biblical chapter that makes the notion of God's existence baseless, useless, and absolute rubbish. How can the good old Lord God plan a wicked act with his most infamous rival, Satan, to punish his most faithful and richest earthly person, (kill all his ten children, make him lose all his wealth, suffer a painful disgraceful skin disease ending up as a destitute living on streets as a beggar): all because God wants to test if Job will continue to be faithful when God placed him in extreme hardship? This behaviour of the supposed God of mankind is exactly opposite to what makes God the God of everything.

Job's friend Zophar continues: 'Everything you say, I have heard before. I understand it all; I know as much as you do. I'm not your inferior. But my dispute is with God, not you; I want to argue my case with him. You cover up your ignorance with lies; you are like doctors who can't heal anyone. Say nothing, and someone may think you are wise! Listen while I state my case. Why are you lying? Do you think your lies will benefit God? Are you trying to defend him? Are you going to argue his case in court? If God looks at you closely, will he find anything good? Do you think you can fool God the way you fool others? Even though your prejudice is hidden, he will reprimand you, and his power will fill you with terror. Your proverbs are as useless as ashes; your arguments are as weak as clay.' Job's Friend (Zophar) is interrupted by Job. Job doesn't care much anymore. He is going to say whatever his heart desires; God can go to hell!

'Be quiet and give me a chance to speak, and let the results be what they will. [I am Job.] I am ready to risk my life. I've lost all hope, so what if God kills me? I am going to state my case to him. It may even be that my boldness will save me, since no wicked person would dare to face God. Job: Now listen to my words of explanation. I am ready to state my case, because I know I am in the right. Are you coming to accuse me, God? If you do, I am ready to be silent and die. Let me ask for two things; agree to them, and I will not try to hide from you: stop punishing me, and don't crush me with terror. Speak first, O God, and I will answer. Or let me speak, and you answer me. What are my sins? What wrongs have I done? What crimes am I charged with? Why do you avoid me? Why do you treat me like an enemy? Are you trying to frighten me? I'm nothing but a leaf; you are attacking a piece of dry straw.

'You bring bitter charges against me, even for what I did when I was young. You bind chains on my feet; you watch every step I take, and even examine my footprints. As a result, I crumble like rotten wood, like a moth-eaten coat.'

Job sounds bold and determined to face God one on one to hear all the charges against him. He knows he has done nothing offensive against God of Israel.

'We are all born weak and helpless. All lead the same short, troubled life. We grow and wither as quickly as flowers; we disappear like shadows. Will you even look at me, God, or put me on trial and judge me? Nothing clean can ever come from anything as unclean as human beings. The length of our lives is decided beforehand—the number of months we will live. You have settled it, and it can't be changed. Look away from us and leave us alone; let us enjoy our hard life—if we can. There is hope for a tree that has been cut down; it can come back to life and sprout.

'Even though its roots grow old, and its stump dies in the ground, with water it will sprout like a young plant. But we die, and that is the end of us; we die, and where are we then? Like rivers that stop running, and lakes that go dry, people die, never to rise. They will never wake up while the sky endures; they will never stir from their sleep. I wish you would hide me in the world of the dead; let me be hidden until your anger is over, and then set a time to remember me. If a man dies, can he come back to life? But I will wait for better times; wait till this time of trouble is ended. Then you will call, and I will answer, and you will be pleased with me, your creature. Then you will watch every step I take, but you will not keep track of my sins. You will forgive them and put them away; you will wipe out all the wrongs I have done.

'There comes a time when mountains fall and solid cliffs are moved away. Water will wear down rocks, and heavy rain will wash away the soil; so you destroy our hope for life.

'You overpower us and send us away forever; our faces are twisted in death. Our children win honour, but we never know it, nor are we told when they are disgraced. We feel only the pain of our own bodies and the grief of our own minds.'

Job is still talking to himself: 'Empty words, Job! Empty words! No one who is wise would talk the way you do or defend himself with such meaningless words! If you had your way, no one would fear God; no one would pray to him.'

'We learned our wisdom from gray-haired people—those born before your father. God offers you comfort; *God is a mere name for comfort.* Can any human being be really pure? Can anyone be right with God?'

Good questions! Even God himself with human image is not and can never be good and pure. Reliance on God merely causes people to live a delusional life with temporal conviction of comfort and safety. Yes 'God is a mere name for comfort,' nothing else!

And if the so-called God of the universe is this same God as portrayed here in the book of Job, then humanity is in serious trouble. The best place for this universal godly notion is a trash basket. Absolute rubbish because goodness and badness are equal in the eyes of the God of Israel.

Why does God not trust even his angels; even they are not pure in his sight. I have heard words like that before; the comfort you give is only torment. *Job is really pissed-off with God!*

'Are you going to keep on talking forever? Do you always have to have the last word? If you were in my place and I in yours, I could say everything you are saying. I could shake my head wisely and drown you with a flood of words. I could strengthen you with advice and keep talking to comfort you. But nothing I say helps, and being silent does not calm my pain. You have worn me out, God; you have let my family be killed. ₈You have seized me; you are my enemy. I am skin and bones, and people take that as proof of my guilt. ₉In anger God tears me limb from limb; he glares at me with hate. ₁₀People sneer at me; they crowd around me and slap my face. ₁₁God has handed me over to evil people.

'I was living in peace, but God took me by the throat and battered me and crushed me. God uses me for target practice and shoots arrows at me from every side—arrows that pierce and wound me—and even then he shows no pity. He wounds me again and again; he attacks like a soldier gone mad with hate. I mourn and wear clothes made of sackcloth, and I sit here in the dust defeated. I have cried until my face is red, and my eyes are swollen and circled with shadows, but I am not guilty of any violence, and my prayer to God is sincere. O Earth, don't hide the wrongs done to me! Don't let my call for justice be silenced! There is someone in heaven to stand up for me and take my side. My friends scorn me; my eyes pour out tears to God. I want someone to plead with God for me, as one pleads for a friend. My years are passing now, and I walk the road of no return.'

Job is terribly angry with God and himself, and appears to be out of words. Job is mad and talking to himself and God at the same time. Job's mind is full of questions. Most people will naturally behave the same as Job.

'Why do you keep tormenting me? Time after time you insult me and show no shame for the way you abuse me. Even if I have done wrong, how does that hurt you? You think you are better than I am, and regard my troubles as proof of my guilt. Can't you see it is God who has done this? *God has set a trap to catch me.* I protest his violence, but no one is listening; no one hears my cry for justice. God has blocked the way, and I can't get through; he has hidden my path in darkness. He has taken away all my wealth and destroyed my reputation. He batters me from every side. He uproots my hope and leaves me to wither and die. God is angry and rages against me; he treats me like his worst enemy. He sends his army to attack me; they dig trenches and lay siege to my tent. ₁₃ God has made my own family forsake me; I am a stranger to those who knew me; my relatives and friends are gone.

'Those who were guests in my house have forgotten me; my servant women treat me like a stranger and a foreigner. When I call a servant, he doesn't answer—even when I beg him to help me.

'My wife can't stand the smell of my breath, and my own brothers won't come near me. ₁₈ Children despise me and laugh when they see me. My closest friends look at me with disgust; those I loved most have turned against me. My skin hangs loose on my bones; I have barely escaped with my life.'

Job has been talking to himself for a while now. He seems to be in trance with lots of invisible people around him, and talking to each one of them and to God at the same time. Job is completely hallucinated. Job is naturally justified. Most rational people will do exactly the same. What is the point of being faithful to God, with God's personal acknowledgement, and instead of being praised; he is punished by God himself for being a good person?

'You are my friends! Take pity on me! The hand of God has struck me down. Why must you persecute me the way God does?

Haven't you tormented me enough? How I wish that someone would remember my words and record them in a book! Or with a chisel carve my words in stone and write them so that they would last forever. But I know there is someone in heaven that will come at last to my defense. Even after my skin is eaten by disease, while still in this body I will see God. I will see him with my own eyes, and he will not be a stranger. My courage failed because you said, "How can we torment him?" You looked for some excuse to attack me. But now, be afraid of the sword—the sword that brings God's wrath on sin, so that you will know there is one who judges.'

There are indeed scores of unbefitting qualities assigned to God of the Israelites and the modern-day Christians' God. God's actions prove clearly that God himself is not aware that he possesses those assigned qualities. Can any reasonable open-minded Bible reader justify Satan and God's wicked machinations against Job and his family, apart from God's test of Job's faithfulness, something which God already knows and therefore unnecessary? With advanced knowledge of human actions of yesterday, today, and tomorrow, God controls everything. God of the universe, by definition, already possess knowledge of the future; hence, a test of any kind is irrelevant and ungodly.

Part 2

God's Unlimited Creative Powers?

(GNT; All quotations source)

BIBLE READERS ARE informed by all the authors of the book that its main character, God, is omnipotent, omnipresent, omniscient, and omnificent; all the four qualities exist in one person at the same time. As part of our inquiry, we are going to find out if Holy Bible authors succeeded in justifying God's omnipresent quality.

First, we are compelled to accept that God is not visible to the naked eyes because God is a spirit, although he has a human male personality. This means that we can see his image in our minds, depending on our acquired knowledge of his nature, particularly as written in the Holy Bible. The reporter or the author of the book of Genesis introduces God to readers as someone who magically commanded from nowhere an earth and a sky to appear. And in seven days and seven evenings, the rest of all things natural come into being. The only time we are told of God's presence was possibly immediately after Adam's invention when God breathed into Adam's nose to begin life. Adam must have seen the shadow of God in the Garden of Eden when God spoke with Adam and Eve in their nakedness.

Genesis

(GNT: Quotation source)

The importance of Genesis as a book in the Holy Bible is its idea of creation or how the universe was created as ancient Jews perceive it. In the first two chapters of the book, readers are informed who and how planet earth was designed. The thirty-one verses of chapter one gives full description of how a character known as God appeared from nowhere and commanded the appearance of the sky and the earth, light, darkness, water and oceans, airborne creatures, waterborne creatures, and land-surface creatures. That God took exactly six days to do all that and rested on the seventh day. At the end of everyday's work, God looks at his own inventions and appreciates himself for what he has accomplished.

Now, it is noted that God created light (verse 3) before creating the Sun, moon, and stars (verse 16): big question! How can there be light without the sun, the moon, and star? Let us assume that the author made an error in reporting God's works in the right sequence. Again, in verses 24 and 25, God decided to create all animals first before creating human[s], (man and female) in verses 26 and 27. At this point, the author has specified that animals were created before human being(s) were made in God's own image. Yes, God was happy to create animals first. He was also happy when he looked at the first man and the first woman he created.

But in chapter 2 verse 7, God decides to make a man again with clay. After this very creation, there existed three human beings in the universe. In verses 21 and 22 of this same chapter 2, God performed another miracle. This time God made the clay-formed-man fall asleep and removed a single rib from him: with that alone he created another female species. It is important to note that in these two chapters, God had invented two men and two women. The names of the last two humans are Adam and Eve. The first two at Genesis 1: 26-27 had no names. Some defenseless Christians attempt to say that the first chapter is an introduction of God's works during the first six days of the week. And that chapter 2 is the description of how he did the inventions. But there is error in this reasoning. Each book of the Holy Bible starts with concise introduction before the main themes commence. The author of the book of Genesis already has an introduction written before chapter 1 starts, and there will be no need to assume chapter 1 as another introductory note. The author is surely trying as much as possible to convince readers that the Jewish God actually created the universe and its contents, but he or she messed up. Chapter 1 contradicts chapter 2 in many ways. Genesis 2: 19 contradict Genesis 1: 20-24. Humans and animals, which one was created first?

Did God form humans and animals alike with earth or only Adam was made of clay? The two chapters disagree.

Authors of the Holy Bible appear desperate in their attempt to make readers believe that our planet earth had an inventor and that creature who created it is by all means a Jewish God, not a Chinese God, not a Japanese God, not an Indian God, not an African God, not a European God, not an American God, or a God of Kosovo. This godly news is simply a mere wishful idea which all cultures of the plant earth possess. The Holy Bible is a book about Jews and their idea of God. God, human beings, and everything natural in the universe must not necessarily originate from Jewish ancestry. It makes every godly idea irrelevant apart from that of the Jews. The real world natural history makes the biblical godly idea null and void. Historically, every culture conceptualizes its own maker and the maker of every natural thing within its human environment.

Now, let us examine just a few chapters of the book of Genesis:

Genesis 27
(GNT)

Husband and Wife: Isaac and Rebecca; Isaac and his wife Rebecca gave birth to twin brothers Esau (elder) and Jacob (junior).

The brothers were rivals before they were born. Isaac has become old and blind. 'He sent for his older son Esau and said to him, "Son!" "Yes," he answered. Isaac said, "You see that I am old and may die soon. Take your bow and arrows, go out into the country, and kill an animal for me. Cook me some of that tasty food that I like, and bring it to me. After I have eaten it, I will give you my final blessing before I die."'

'While Isaac was talking to Esau, Rebecca was listening. So when Esau went out to hunt, she said to Jacob, "I have just heard your father say to Esau, 'Bring me an animal and cook it for me. After I have eaten it, I will give you my blessing in the presence of the Lord before I die.' Now, son," Rebecca continued, "listen to me and do what I say. Go to the flock and pick out two fat young goats, so that I can cook them and make some of that food your father likes so much. You can take it to him to eat, and he will give you his blessing before he dies." But Jacob said to his mother, 'You know that Esau is a hairy man, but I have smooth skin, perhaps my father will touch me and find out that I am deceiving him; in this way, I will bring a curse on myself instead of a blessing." His mother answered, "Let any curse against you fall on me, my son; just do as I say, and go and get the goats for me." So he went to get them and brought them to her, and she cooked the kind of food that his father liked. Then she took Esau's best clothes, which she kept in the house, and put them on Jacob. She put the skins of the goats on his arms and on the hairless part of his neck. She handed him the tasty food, along with the bread she had baked.

'Then Jacob went to his father and said, "Father!" "Yes," he answered. "Which of my sons are you?" Jacob answered, "I am your older son Esau; I have done as you told me. Please sit up and eat some of the meat that I have brought you, so that you can give me your blessing." Isaac said, "How did you find it so quickly, son?" Jacob answered, "The Lord your God helped me find it." [21] Isaac said to Jacob, "Please come closer so that I can touch you. Are

41

you really Esau?" Jacob moved closer to his father, who felt him and said, "Your voice sounds like Jacob's voice, but your arms feel like Esau's arms." He did not recognize Jacob, because his arms were hairy like Esau's. He was about to give him his blessing, but asked again, "Are you really Esau?" "I am," he answered. Isaac said, "Bring me some of the meat. After I eat it, I will give you my blessing." Jacob brought it to him, and he also brought him some wine to drink. Then his father said to him, "Come closer and kiss me, son." As he came up to kiss him, Isaac smelled his clothes—so he gave him his blessing. He said, The pleasant smell of my son is like the smell of a field which the Lord has blessed. May God give you dew from heaven and make your fields fertile! May he give you plenty of grain and wine! May nations be your servants, and may peoples bow down before you. May you rule over all your relatives, and may your mother's descendants bow down before you. May those who curse you be cursed, and may those who bless you be blessed.

'Isaac finished giving his blessing, and as soon as Jacob left, his brother Esau came in from hunting. He also cooked some tasty food and took it to his father. He said, "Please, father, sit up and eat some of the meat that I have brought you, so that you can give me your blessing." "Who are you?" Isaac asked. "Your older son Esau," he answered. Isaac began to tremble and shake all over, and he asked, "Who was it, then, who killed an animal and brought it to me? I ate it just before you came. I gave him my final blessing, and so it is his forever." When Esau heard this, he cried out loudly and bitterly and said, "Give me your blessing also, father!" Isaac answered, "Your brother came and deceived me. He has taken away your blessing." Esau said, "This is the second time that he has cheated me. No wonder his name Jacob translates in Hebrew as 'cheat'. He took my rights as the first-born son, and now he has taken away my blessing. Haven't you saved a blessing for me?" Isaac answered, "I have already made him master over you, and I have made all his relatives his slaves. I have given him grain and wine.

Now there is nothing that I can do for you, son! Esau continued to plead with his father: Do you have only one blessing, father? Bless me too, father!" He began to cry. Then Isaac said to him, No dew from heaven for you, No fertile fields for you. You will live by your sword, but be your brother's slave. Yet when you rebel, you will break away from his control. Esau hated Jacob, because his father had given Jacob the blessing. He thought, "The time to mourn my father's death is near; then I will kill Jacob." But when Rebecca heard about Esau's plan, she sent for Jacob and said, Listen, your brother Esau is planning to get even with you and kill you. Now, son, do what I say. Go at once to my brother Laban in Haran, and stay with him for a while, until your brother's anger cools down and he forgets what you have done to him. Then I will send someone to bring you back. Why should I lose both of my sons on the same day?" Rebecca said to Isaac, "I am sick and tired of Esau's foreign wives. If Jacob also marries one of these Hittites, I might as well die.'"

All famous biblical women from Eve are characterized with deceptions, why? Why should Isaac choose to bless only one of his children, Jacob? Why did Isaac's wife Rebecca betray her husband by making Jacob pretend to be like Esau to receive their father's blessing instead? Is the scripture saying that deception is a good human behaviour? Or are we to learn that dishonesty is sometimes a better choice in life regardless of faith? Jacob's brother, Esau, saw no reason why his father could not bless him too. This is sheer wickedness! Esau could not be blamed for planning to kill his brother. Note that all these are part of biblical teachings. Note that in verse 38, Esau continued to plead with his father: 'Do you have only one blessing, father? Bless me too, father!' He began to cry. How do we judge mother Rebecca, considering her own past history and the history of Isaac himself? The behaviour of such biblical character is revolting. Here, we are with such a character, a calculated liar from infancy, being projected by Jews centuries later as God of Israel's personal embodiment (God of Abraham,

Isaac, and Jacob). Can the behaviour of Isaac and Jacob be seen as godly? Logically, both should be seen as a disgrace to Christianity.

Genesis 28 (GNT)

Isaac called Jacob, greeted him, and told him, 'Don't marry a Canaanite. Go instead to Mesopotamia, to the home of your grandfather Bethuel, and marry one of the young women there, one of your uncle Laban's daughters. May Almighty God bless your marriage and give you many children, so that you will become the father of many nations! May he bless you and your descendants as he blessed Abraham, and may you take possession of this land, in which you have lived and which God gave to Abraham!' Isaac sent Jacob away to Mesopotamia, to Laban, who was the son of Bethuel the Aramean and the brother of Rebecca, the mother of Jacob and Esau. Esau learned that Isaac had blessed Jacob and sent him away to Mesopotamia to find a wife. He also learned that when Isaac blessed him, he commanded him not to marry a Canaanite woman. He found out that Jacob had obeyed his father and mother and had gone to Mesopotamia.

'Esau then understood that his father Isaac did not approve of Canaanite women. So he went to Ishmael son of Abraham and married his daughter Mahalath, who was the sister of Nebaioth.

Jacob left Beersheba and started towards Haran. At sunset he came to a holy place and camped there. He lay down to sleep, resting his head on a stone. *He dreamed that he saw a stairway reaching from earth to heaven, with angels going up and coming down on it. And there was the Lord standing beside him. "I am the Lord, the God of Abraham and Isaac," he said. "I will give to you and to your descendants this land on which you are lying.* They will be as numerous as the specks of dust on the earth. They will extend their territory in all directions, and through you and your descendants I will bless all the nations. Remember, I will be with you and protect you wherever you go, and I will bring you back to this land. I will not leave you until I have done all that I have promised you.'"

Yes, the Lord God of Abraham and Isaac, not the Lord God of anybody else, or humanity as a whole. Yes, this dream character always appears in dreams. There is nothing implicit that this God must by all means be a God for the entire universe. Jacob had a daydream in which God promised to give him and his descendants the land on which he was taking an afternoon nap. Christians everywhere have deliberately taken this ancient Jewish fantasy as a genuine event and ignored the fact that it was primarily a daydream. Did this God of Jacob know that the land was already assigned and occupied by the indigenous people who lived there? Where did God expect the original inhabitants to move to?

'He was afraid and said, "What a terrifying place this is! It must be the house of God; it must be the gate that opens into heaven." Jacob got up early next morning took the stone that was under his head, and set it up as a memorial. Then he poured olive oil on it to dedicate it to God. He named the place Bethel. (The town there was once known as Luz.) Then Jacob made a vow to the Lord: "If you will be with me and protect me on the journey I am making and give me food and clothing, if I return safely to my father's home, then you will be my God. This memorial stone which I have set up will be the place where you are worshiped, and I will give you a tenth of everything you give me."'

Genesis 29 (GNT)

'Jacob asked the shepherds, "My friends, where are you from?" "From Haran," they answered. He asked, "Do you know Laban, grandson of Nahor?" "Yes, we do," they answered. "Is he well?" he asked. "He is well," they answered. "Look, here comes his daughter Rachel with his flock," Jacob said. While Jacob was still talking with them, Rachel arrived with the flock. When Jacob saw Rachel with his uncle Laban's flock, he went to the well, rolled the stone back, and watered the sheep. Then he kissed her and began to cry for joy. He told her, "I am your father's relative, the son of Rebecca." She ran to tell her father; and when he heard the news about his nephew Jacob, he ran to meet him, hugged him and kissed him, and brought him into the house. When Jacob told Laban everything that had happened, Laban said, "Yes, indeed, you are my own flesh and blood." Jacob stayed there a whole month.' Laban told Jacob he shouldn't work for nothing just because he was his relative.

'Laban had two daughters; the older was named Leah, and the younger Rachel. Leah had lovely eyes, but Rachel was shapely and beautiful. Jacob was in love with Rachel, so he decided, he would work seven years for him, if he would let him marry Rachel.

'Laban told Jacob he would rather give her to him than to anyone else. Jacob worked seven years so that he could have Rachel, and the time seemed like only a few days to him, because he loved her. Then Jacob said to Laban, "The time is up; let me marry your daughter." So Laban gave a wedding feast and invited everyone. *But that night, instead of Rachel, he took Leah to Jacob, and Jacob had intercourse with her.* Laban gave his slave woman Zilpah to his daughter Leah as her maid. *Not until the next morning did Jacob discover that it was Leah. He went to Laban and said, "Why did you do this to me? I worked to get Rachel. Why have you tricked me?" Laban answered, "It is not the custom here to give the younger daughter in marriage before the older. Wait until the week's marriage celebrations are over, and I will give you Rachel, if you will work for me another seven years.* Jacob agreed, and when the week of marriage celebrations was over, Laban gave him his daughter Rachel as his wife, and also gave his female slave Bilhah to his daughter Rachel as her maid. *Jacob had intercourse with Rachel also and he loved her more than Leah.* He worked for Laban for another seven years.

'When *the Lord saw* that Leah was loved less than Rachel, he made it possible for her to have children, but Rachel remained childless. Leah became pregnant and gave birth to a son. She said,

"The Lord has seen my trouble, and now my husband will love me; so she named him Reuben. She became pregnant again and gave birth to another son. She said, The Lord has given me this son also, because he heard that I was not loved; so she named him Simeon. Once again she became pregnant and gave birth to another son. She said, now my husband will be bound more tightly to me, because I have borne him three sons; so she named him Levi. Then she became pregnant again and gave birth to another son. She said, this time I will praise the Lord, so she named him Judah. She stopped having children then after.'

With reason therefore, it seems this God of Jacob is not aware of his infinite powers of knowledge. Another bizarre Holy Bible story—Laban has accepted his daughter Rachel to marry Jacob (his sister Rebecca's son) at a grand wedding. Yet at their honeymoon, Laban, the father, deliberately delivered his senior daughter Leah instead of Rachel to sleep with the groom, Jacob because of tradition. The next morning, Jacob realized that he had slept and had sexual intercourse with his bride's senior sister. He could not believe that his father-in-law could be so wicked. How can this Bible chapter be viewed as holy, a tradition unconnected with common human ethics?

Now, let us look at this story from the right perspectives.

In Genesis 29:26, Laban answered, 'It is not the custom here to give the younger daughter in marriage before the older'.

The father, Laban, is clearly telling us that Jewish custom at the time compelled him to deliver the older daughter, Leah, into marriage 'first', although the groom, Jacob, loves to marry the younger sister Rachel. According to custom, therefore, the girls' father is at no fault. But seriously, how do we judge father Laban's human morality in this issue? The God of Abraham, Isaac, and *Jacob* is mute at the event! The father could have informed Jacob before the marriage ceremony of Rachel or convinced his elder daughter, Leah, what custom demands were at the time.

Now, if all such stories in the Holy Bible would be taken as the authors intended them to be as, 'ancient Jewish cultural history,' nobody would question the injustices or the ungodly aspect of the Holy Bible. But these irreligious behaviors become questionable when the Bible is considered as an unquestionable holy document for all cultures on the planet earth. The Holy Bible is a Jewish traditional book written by Jews for Jews. The book is definitely not for non-Jewish people. Everything in the book is clearly Jewish, no matter how you interpret it.

All the stories in the sixty-six books represent the Jews, except probably Ruth, who we are told is a Moabite. 'Ruth' is a biblical book title just because she was the great-grandmother of David, who we are told was the greatest among the kings of Israel.

More than 90 per cent of biblical stories are historically fable or fictitious tales. And even the 10 per cent that are generally considered genuine stories by eminent historians and archaeologist cannot be adequately supported with real historical evidence. There is obviously absolutely nothing holy or universal about the so-called Holy book.

It is unbelievable though that Jacob finally married the two sisters, Rachel and Leah, and had several children with both sisters and also slept and had several children with their maidservants. Certainly, in most cultures, such behaviour would be classified as immoral. Yet it is a behaviour sanctioned by the supposed God of the Jewish universe. I see this behaviour as absurd.

And do remember also that this is the same Jacob who later became one of the characters in God of Abraham, Isaac, and *Jacob* honoured and worshiped by over two billion Christians worldwide.

Well, who am I to judge someone's cultural practices? You may read Genesis chapters 29 and 30 for your own analysis. It was a Jewish custom at the time, and indeed all such practices, plus the entire content of the Bible. They are very Jewish in all aspects.

The whole document is emphatically Jewish and not applicable to mankind as a whole.

Christian leadership has accepted the scriptures for their leaderships' personal and institutional interest without question because their very economic survival is sustained by the manufacture and sale of such spiritual ideas as those of an*cient Jewish myths narrated* here.

Genesis 30 (GNT)

'But Rachel had not borne Jacob any children, and so she became jealous of her sister and said to Jacob, "Give me children, or I will die." Jacob became angry with Rachel and said, "I can't take the place of God. He is the one who keeps you from having children." She said, *"Here is my slave Bilhah; sleep with her, so that she can have a child for me. In this way I can become a mother through her." So she gave Bilhah to her husband, and he had intercourse with her. Bilhah became pregnant and bore Jacob a son.* Rachel said, "God has judged in my favour. He has heard my prayer and has given me a son"; so she named him Dan. Bilhah became pregnant again and bore Jacob a second son. Rachel said, "I have fought a hard fight with my sister, but I have won"; so she named him Naphtali. *When Leah realized that she had stopped having children, she gave her slave Zilpah to Jacob as his wife. Then Zilpah bore Jacob a son.* Leah said, "I have been lucky"; so she named him Gad. Zilpah bore Jacob another son, $_{13}$ and Leah said, "How happy I am! Now women will call me happy"; so she named him Asher. During the wheat harvest Reuben went into the fields and found mandrakes, which he brought to his mother Leah. Rachel said to Leah, "Please give me some of your son's mandrakes." Leah answered, "Isn't it enough that you have taken away my husband? Now you are even trying to take away my son's mandrakes." *Rachel said, "If you will give me your son's mandrakes, you can sleep with Jacob tonight."*

'When Jacob came in from the fields in the evening, Leah went out to meet him and said, "You are going to sleep with me tonight, because I have paid for you with my son's mandrakes." So he had intercourse with her that night. God answered Leah's prayer and she became pregnant and bore Jacob a fifth son.

'Leah said, "God has given me my reward, because I gave my slave to my husband"; so she named her son Issachar. Leah became pregnant again and bore Jacob a sixth son. She said, "God has given me a fine gift. Now *my husband* will accept me, because I have borne him six sons"; so she named him Zebulun.

'Later she bore a daughter, whom she named Dinah. Then *God remembered* Rachel; he answered her prayer and made it possible for her to have children. She became pregnant and gave birth to a son. She said, "God has taken away my disgrace by giving me a son. May the Lord give me another son"; so she named him Joseph. After the birth of Joseph, Jacob said to Laban, "Let me go, so that I can return home. Give me my wives and children that I have earned by working for you, and I will leave."'

In Genesis 30: 22, it is written *God remembered Rachel*. What a remark! Can God really forget anything? Does God possess memory like we humans? Can we really attach sentiments to God's behaviour?

Another Biblical Sexual Malpractice Is Found in Genesis 38 (GNT)

Judah had sexual intercourse and later, a child with his son's wife (Tamar). 'About that time Judah left his brothers and went to stay with a man named Hirah, who was from the town of Adullam. There Judah met a young Canaanite woman whose father was named Shua. He married her, and she bore him a son, whom he named Er. She became pregnant again and bore another son and named him Onan. Again she had a son and named him Shelah.

Judah was at Achzib when the boy was born. For his first son Er, Judah got a wife whose name was Tamar. *Er's conduct was evil, and it displeased the Lord, so the Lord killed him*. Then Judah said to Er's brother Onan, "Go and sleep with your brother's widow. Fulfill your obligation to her as her husband's brother, so that your brother may have descendants." But Onan knew that the children would not belong to him, so when he had intercourse with his brother's widow, *he let the semen spill on the ground, so that there would be no children for his brother. What he did displeased the Lord, and the Lord killed him also*. Then Judah said to his daughter-in-law Tamar, "Return to your father's house and remain a widow until my son Shelah grows up." He said this because he was afraid that Shelah would be killed, as his brothers had been. So Tamar went back home. After some time Judah's wife died. When he had finished the time of mourning, he and his friend Hirah of Adullam went to Timnah, where his sheep were being sheared. Someone told Tamar that her father-in-law was going to Timnah to shear his sheep. So she changed from the widow's clothes she had been wearing, covered her face with a veil, and sat down at the entrance to Enaim, a town on the road to Timnah. As she well knew, Judah's youngest son Shelah was now grown up, and yet she had not been given to him in marriage. When Judah saw her, he thought that she was a prostitute, because she had her face covered. He went over to her at the side of the road and said, 'All right, how much do you charge? He did not know that she was his daughter-in-law. She said, "What will you give me?" He answered, "I will send you a young goat from my flock." She said, "All right, if you will give me something to keep as a pledge until you send the goat." "What shall I give you as a pledge?" he asked. She answered, "Your seal with its cord and the walking stick you are carrying." He gave them to her. Then they had intercourse, and she became pregnant.

'Tamar went home, took off her veil, and put her widow's clothes back on. Judah sent his friend Hirah to take the goat and get back from the woman the articles he had pledged, but Hirah could not find her. He asked some men at Enaim, "Where is the prostitute who was here by the road?" "There has never been a prostitute here," they answered. He returned to Judah and said, "I couldn't find her. The men of the place said that there had never been a prostitute there." Judah said, "Let her keep the things. We don't want people to laugh at us. I did try to pay her, but you couldn't find her." About three months later someone told Judah, "Your daughter-in-law Tamar has been acting like a whore and now she is pregnant." Judah ordered, "Take her out and burn her to death."

'As she was being taken out, she sent word to her: father-in-law: "I am pregnant by the man who owns these things. Look at them and see whose they are—this seal with its cord and this walking stick." Judah recognized them and said, "She is in the right. I have failed in my obligation to her—I should have given her to my son Shelah in marriage." And Judah never had intercourse with her again. When the time came for her to give birth, it was discovered that she was going to have twins. While she was in labor, one of them put out an arm; the midwife caught it, tied a red thread around it, and said, 'This one was born first." But he pulled his arm back, and his brother was born first. Then the midwife said, "So this is how you break your way out!" So he was named Perez. Then his brother was born with the red thread on his arm, and he was named Zerah.'

Can anyone, religious or irreligious, read this Genesis chapter 38, and in particular, verses 6-10 and let it pass without comment? I am very doubtful! The Holy Bible is really full of trash. God killed Judah's elder son (Er) simply because 'God was not pleased with Er's conduct'. Judah asked his younger son Onan (Er's brother) to have sexual intercourse with Tamar, the dead brother's wife, so that when Tamar becomes pregnant with Onan, the children will become descendants of the dead brother Er. And worst of this biblical nonsense, during Onan's sexual intercourse with Tamar, he pulled out his penis to let his semen drop outside her vagina so as not to impregnate his deceased brother's wife. Remember that it was Judah, the father of Er and Onan, who instructed Onan to have sex with his own brother's wife (Tamar the widow). This affair obviously had nothing to do with God. Oman's only sin was that he did not allow his semen drop into the woman to cause a pregnancy he did not want. And God killed Onan for that act only.

As human beings, who are endowed with common sense, do we say nothing about this ugly ungodly act of the so-called Christian biblical God, just because it is presumed to be an unquestionable act of the ancient Jewish God or just because it is written in a book, which has a known history as a Jewish religious document, 'The Holy Bible'?

The saddest part of this biblical God's evil behaviour and that of Judah (the father) is, Judah himself finally had sexual intercourse with his dead son's wife 'Tamar', impregnated her, and had twin children with her. And as already discussed above, other cultures' customary rights cannot be questioned because their ancestors created the customs for their offspring and succeeding generation, purposely to maintain their traditional identity. Obviously this was one of Jewish community's custom. The behaviour of God of the Jews must really be understood within that community only. And needless to say, it is a complete mistake to apply it to the entire world or any cultural community. If indeed this is the God who transformed in the New Testament to become the God for the entire universe, then there is something wrong with our modern thinking. Please read again verses 6-10 of Genesis 38 and judge the story yourself.

Book of Exodus (GNT; source)

This book has been discussed at length in my earlier work *Biography of the Biblical God*, but it seems necessary to highlight the origin of Moses as a link character between Jews and their God as written in chapters 3 and 4.

In chapter 3, the author of Exodus described Moses as a shepherd of his father-in-law, Jethro. That one day when Moses was out to feed the goats and sheep, he saw an angel of the Lord in the form of a burning flame in the bush. He tried to get closer to verify what he was witnessing. Suddenly a voice came from the fire calling his name, 'Moses! Moses!' Moses asked who was calling. A voice answered, I am 'I AM'. Exodus 2: 24 says, 'I have *remembered* my covenant with Abraham, Isaac, and Jacob. I am concerned about their suffering in Egypt, and I am sending you to the king of Egypt because I am concerned about them. You will go and lead my people out of his country to the land of the Canaanites where the land is fertile.' Moses confirmed that he was nobody, never been a good speaker, and hesitant. But the Lord told Moses to go and that he will tell him what to say. Moses still insisted that God select someone else for that assignment.

God gives Moses miraculous powers: Then Moses answered the Lord, 'But suppose the Israelites do not believe me and will not listen to what I say. What shall I do if they say that you God did not appear to me?' So the Lord asked Moses, 'What are you holding?' 'A stick,' he answered. The Lord said, 'Throw it on the ground.' When Moses threw it down, it turned into a snake, and he ran away from it. Then the Lord said to Moses, 'Bend down and pick it up by the tail.' And it became a stick again. The Lord said, 'Do this to prove to the Israelite that the Lord, the God of their ancestors, the God of Abraham, Isaac, and Jacob has appeared to you.' The Lord showed Moses how to perform two additional magic, but

Moses was still not willing to accept the leadership responsibilities of the Israelites.

At this, the Lord became angry with Moses and said, 'What about your brother Aaron, the Levite? I know that he can speak well. In fact he is now coming to meet you and will be glad to see you. You can speak to him and tell him what to say. I will help both of you to speak, and I will tell you both what to do. He will be your spokesman and speak to the people for you. Then you will be like God, telling him what to say. Take this stick with you and with it you will perform miracles.' The above mentioned conversation between God and Moses is in Exodus 4: 10-17.

Part 3

God's Presence: All places, All times?
God's Infinite Knowledge?
God for Israelites or All humans?
(GNT source)

According to Leviticus

YOU MAY HAVE noticed that there have been a lot of repetitions in my comments of the quoted chapters. Yes, you are right. The Holy Bible is essentially about miracles performed by spirits and their visible agents or God and God's messengers. The various acts of these two entities are repeated several times by the various authors to emphasize the significance of miracles in the livelihood of man.

All the thirty-nine Old Testament books attempt to glorify the mysteries of God and that of God-appointed earthly agents. Every author's objective appears to impress readers that God is mysterious and supreme; hence, God's magical performances must be stressed in every book.

The situation is even worse in the twenty-seven New Testament books. Matthew to Revelations are actually built with paraphrases, deliberate misinterpretations, and misquotations of old texts, carefully designed to fit into Christ-era generation. Prominent religious characters such as Moses and the God of Israel are redesigned into Paul and Jesus Christ with similar roles to befit the then new generation's religious agenda. Such characters as Christ do represent God, and Paul represents Moses in the same circumstances. They are designed to fulfil old prophecies and to perform identical mysteries. The recurrence or repetitions of chapter comments in this discourse is simply not avoidable.

Leviticus 1 (GNT)

'The Lord called Moses and spoke to him from the tent of the Lord's presence, saying, "Speak to the people of Israel and say to them, when any one of you brings an offering to the Lord, you shall bring your offering of livestock from the herd or from the flock. If his offering is a burnt offering from the herd, he shall offer a male without blemish. He shall bring it to the entrance of the tent of my presence, that he may be accepted before the Lord. He shall lay his hand on the head of the burnt offering, and it shall be accepted for him to make atonement for him. Then he shall kill the bull before the Lord, and Aaron's sons the priests shall bring the blood and throw the blood against the sides of the altar that is at the entrance of the tent of my presence. Then he shall lay the burnt offering and cut it into pieces, and the sons of Aaron the priest shall put fire on the altar and arrange wood on the fire. And Aaron's sons the priests shall arrange the pieces, the head, and the fat, on the wood that is on the fire on the altar, but its entrails and its legs he shall wash with water. And the priest shall burn all of it on the altar, as a burnt offering, a food offering with a pleasing aroma to the Lord."'

The above words are supposed to be the direct words of the creator of this world; I mean our supposed maker. Please read it again and think about it: Note that all the above are direct instructions from the Lord to the people of Israel through Moses who initially suspected the Jews will not believe that his instructions are from God. The message is addressed to Jewish audience. All the above godly titles must be applicable to Jews only. It sounds confusing, but clearly the above have nothing to do with the rest of humanity who are not Jews. Think carefully about it! The Question then is, can the modern-day understanding of 'Lord God' be matched with this second BC. Leviticus' understanding of God? Common sense dictionary will surely reject it, because the author of Leviticus book is saying that this God is solely responsible for the twelve tribes of Israel only, and indeed at a period, 200 years, before Christ was born. The idea is surely very ancient and very Jewish and definitely not applicable to twenty-first-century world of religiously liberated people.

Leviticus 15 (GNT)

It contains Jewish Laws about bodily discharges.

The Lord spoke to Moses and Aaron with instructions regarding personal hygiene. The message is for the people of Israel that any man who has a discharge from his penis is unclean. 'Whether his body runs with his discharge, or his body is blocked up by his discharge, it is his uncleanness. Every bed on which the one with the discharge lies shall be unclean, and everything on which he sits shall be unclean.

'And anyone who touches his bed shall wash his clothes and bathe himself in water and be unclean until the evening. And whoever sits on anything on which the one with the discharge has sat shall wash his clothes and bathe himself in water and be unclean until the evening. And whoever touches the body of the one with the discharge shall wash his clothes and bathe him in water and be unclean until the evening. And if the one with the discharge spits on someone who is clean, then he shall wash his clothes and bathe him in water and be unclean until the evening. And any saddle on which the one with the discharge rides shall be unclean.

'And whoever touches anything that was under him shall be unclean until the evening. And whoever carries such things shall wash his clothes and bathe him in water and be unclean until the evening. Anyone whom the one with the discharge touches without having rinsed his hands in water shall wash his clothes and bathe himself in water and be unclean until the evening. 12 And an earthenware vessel that the one with the discharge touches shall be broken and every vessel of wood shall be rinsed in water.

'And when the one with a discharge is cleansed of his discharge, then he shall count for himself seven days for his cleansing, and wash his clothes. And he shall bathe his body in fresh water and shall be clean. And on the eighth day he shall take two turtledoves or two pigeons and come before the Lord to the entrance of the tent of my presence and give them to the priest. And the priest shall use them, one for a sin offering and the other for a burnt offering. And the priest shall make atonement for him before the Lord for his discharge.'

When a man has an emission of semen, he shall bathe his whole body in water. He remains unclean until the evening. And every garment and every skin on which the semen comes shall be washed with water and be unclean until the evening.

After sexual intercourse both the man and the woman must have a bath, and they remain unclean until evening. 'When a woman has a discharge, and the discharge in her body is blood, she shall be in her menstrual impurity for seven days, and whoever touches her shall be unclean until the evening. And everything on which she lies during her menstrual impurity shall be unclean. Everything also on which she sits shall be unclean.

'And whoever touches her bed shall wash his clothes and bath himself in water and be unclean until the evening. And whoever touches anything on which she sits shall wash his clothes and bath himself in water and be unclean until the evening. Whether it is the bed or anything on which she sits, when he touches it he shall be unclean until the evening. And if any man lies with her and her menstrual impurity comes upon him, he shall be unclean seven days, and every bed on which he lies shall be unclean. If a woman has a discharge of blood for many days, not at the time of her menstrual impurity, or if she has a discharge beyond the time of her impurity, all the days of the discharge she shall continue in uncleanness. As in the days of her impurity, she shall be unclean.

'But if she is cleansed of her discharge, she shall count for herself seven days, and after that she shall be clean. And on the eighth day she shall take two turtledoves or two pigeons and bring them to the priest, to the entrance of the tent of my presence.

And the priest shall use one for a sin offering and the other for a burnt offering. And the priest shall make atonement for her before the Lord for her unclean discharge. Thus you shall keep the people of Israel separate from their uncleanness, lest they die in their uncleanness by defiling my tabernacle that is in their midst.' This is the law for anyone, male or female, who has a discharge, and for the man who lies with a woman who is unclean.

Again, I am inviting you the reader to reread the chapter again and think about it seriously. Can our God, the supposed designer of our physical biological body, really say these things? Has he forgotten that he is the architect of all the over ten million organic components of our human biological physique, the one He, our 'God', actually manufactured with mere soil and the female with a single male rib? Or may we understand this creation as a mere ancient Jewish fantasy? There is no doubt in my mind that there is no such thing as God of any description. We may perceive the idea in our minds that there is a God, but certainly, it will always remain as an individual's opinion or a mere wishful thinking!

How can we not conclude that 'El' the creator is not the same as 'Yahweh' the God of Israel? Or is this God of Israel not the same as the Genesis God—the inventor—the one who is supposed to have conceptualized and formed the first two humans—Adam and his wife Eve Adam? Indeed if the two are the same, the God of Israel would not need to instruct Moses and Aaron to say to the people of Israel these things. God's communication would be direct, not through a mediator.

Logically, by their narratives, it becomes very clear that these two gods are totally different from each other in every respect. If you and I and Moses and Pastor Aaron are true descendants of Adam and Eve, the God of Israel ought to have known that everything God has made is supposed to be meticulously made in his own image and therefore necessarily perfect; sex organs and sexuality of both male and female cannot be spiritually unclean. Menstrual blood and semen may be unhygienic when it is left to dry on the skin or kept inside the vagina for too long. It may produce foul odor, but they definitely have nothing to do with spirituality or God of Israel. Must there be spiritual link in sex? I hope the reader has an open mind to make rational judgment of issues like this in the Holy Bible. As indeed the human brains' designed purpose is for critical analysis.

Obviously, Moses' instructions to the people of Israel are definitely Moses 'own making. It has nothing to do with God of Israel or God of any kind. Gods, by definition, are invisible entities in peoples' minds. The above is doubtlessly the mind of Moses himself. In the prehistoric days, every mystery such as the monthly menstrual cycle of matured women could not be logically explained; hence, the mystery must be assigned to a God. A primitive mind always turns to spirituality to explain every natural phenomenon which human intelligence fails to explain causes.

In fact, some scholars have concluded that the first five books in the Old Testament were written by Moses himself, because of such utterances as the narratives above. The entire Leviticus instructions are the nurtured hygienic code of behaviour which leaders in Jewish communities at the time considered necessary to let new generations among the Jews know and practice. And of course there is nothing wrong about that, since most cultures around the world did and still do the same thing for their continuous existence or survival as a community of people. In this modern scientific technological world, only primitive-minded people would link sex with spirits.

It is so baffling that the God of Israel could not create a better direct Jewish ethnic link between himself and his beloved Jews, and none other than 'Moses', (Exod. 2: 1-10) someone of a questionable Jewish origin who no ancient history can confirm his lineage—neither an Egyptian nor a Jew to act as God's own favorite personal spokesman for his beloved Jews. I don't get it! Who is kidding who here? Should we ignore common prudence on such ungodly statements? No, we should not. I don't think so because reason is definitely a human duty! You and I evidently have a natural duty to question these stories. We are not religiously required in any rational way to accept every senseless word in the Bible just because the supposed sacred title of the book (holy) implicitly classifies the book as a holy book.

Leviticus 18 *deals with unlawful Sexual affairs among Israelites. The first question that automatically comes to mind is whether it is possible to have a universal law to regulate sexual behaviour. But on a reflection of the previous Leviticus chapters, the best conclusion of course is the already known intention of biblical authors; their unbiased anxiety to perpetuate ancient Jewish culture by any means possible.*

The Lord God of Israel told Moses to tell the people of Israel that he is their Lord God. That they should not behave like they used to do in land of Egypt where they lived before and also not do as the people of Canaan do in that new land to which he is bringing them. They should follow his rules and keep his commandments.

Again *there is nothing explicit or implicit in the above statements* that, this so-called Lord God is, or can be, a God or the God of worldly people which includes the Chinese, the Russians, the

Indians, Africans, Australians, or Europeans or any worldly ethnic people. The entire affair is essentially a Jewish affair. It is essential that Bible readers make notes of this: that the Lord God of Israel is addressing his subjects—the Israelites only! And therefore all those who do not belong to any of the twelve tribes plus the Levis Hebrew families do not interest the God of Israel. Indeed, all biblical prophets make this abundantly clear. The Lord gave the following regulations: Do not have sexual intercourse with any of your relatives. 'You shall not uncover the nakedness of your father, which is the nakedness of your mother; she is your mother, you shall not uncover her nakedness.

'You shall not uncover the nakedness of your father's wife; it is your father's nakedness. You shall not uncover the nakedness of your sister, your father's daughter or your mother's daughter, whether brought up in the family or in another home. You shall not uncover the nakedness of your son's daughter or of your daughter's daughter, for their nakedness is your own nakedness.

'You shall not uncover the nakedness of your father's wife's daughter, brought up in your father's family, since she is your sister.

'You shall not uncover the nakedness of your father's sister; she is your father's relative. You shall not uncover the nakedness of your mother's sister, for she is your mother's relative. You shall not uncover the nakedness of your father's brother, that is, you shall not approach his wife; she is your aunt. You shall not uncover the nakedness of your daughter-in-law; she is your son's wife, you shall not uncover her nakedness. You shall not uncover the nakedness of your brother's wife; it is your brother's nakedness. You shall not uncover the nakedness of a woman and of her daughter, and you shall not take her son's daughter or her daughter's daughter to uncover her nakedness; they are relatives; it is depravity. And you shall not take a woman as a rival wife to her sister, uncovering her nakedness while her sister is still alive. 'You shall not have sexual intercourse with a woman while she is in her menstrual uncleanness. And you shall not lie sexually with your neighbour's wife and so make yourself unclean with her. You shall not give any of your children to offer them to Molech, and so profane the name of your God: I am the Lord. You shall not lie with a male as with a woman; it is an abomination. And you shall not lie with any animal and so make yourself unclean with it; neither shall any woman give herself to an animal to lie with it: it is perversion. Keep my charge. Never practice any of these abominable [customs] that were practiced before you, and never make yourselves unclean by them: I am the Lord your God.'

The whole chapter is the voice of God of Israel according to the author. But it sounds as if the author did not have a chance to read the other biblical texts which carry scores of contradictory statements. For instance, Adam and Eve and their ancestors had sex with their fathers, mothers, sisters, brothers, and other relatives. Adam and Eve are of the same blood, but they got married, had sexual intercourse, and brought forth several children. Adam and Eve's first grandson was Enoch. But who was Enoch's mother? Did Cain not have sex with his own mother (Eve) to give birth to Enoch? Can the author tell the twenty-first-century Bible readers what really happened among the first human family! The author of the book of Leviticus obviously did not read the first book of the Holy Bible 'Genesis', especially chapters 1, 2, 4, 7, 11, 38, and indeed many more such books and chapters.

Leviticus 20 contains God of Israel's rules regarding common immoralities in Jewish communities. The type of punishment attached to each offence is meticulously delegated to the Israelites through Moses. People of Israel or of the strangers who sojourn in Israel who give any of his children to Molech shall surely be put to death. The whole community shall stone him to death.

'I myself will set my face against that man and will cut him off from among his people, because he has given one of his children to Molech, to make my sanctuary unclean and to profane my holy name. And if the people of the land do at all close their eyes to that man when he gives one of his children to Molech, and do not put him to death, then I will set my face against that man and against his clan and will cut them off from among their people, him and all who follow him in whoring after Molech.' If anyone goes for advice to people who consult the spirit of the dead, I will turn against him and will no longer consider him one of my people.

If a man commits adultery with the wife of a fellow Israelite, both the adulterer and the adulteress shall surely be put to death. If a man has sexual intercourse with his father's wife, he has uncovered his father's nakedness; both of them shall surely be put to death, and their blood is upon them.

In view of these sexual laws, Jacob married Rachel, but he had sex with his sister-in-law, Leah, who was Rachel's senior sister (Gen. 28: 23-35). Jacob finally married both sisters and had several children with both, plus having sex and children also with their two maids; all with God of Israel's blessings. Abraham and his wife Sara were of the same father—Terah (Gen. 20: 12).

If a man has sexual intercourse with his daughter-in-law, both of them shall surely be put to death; they have committed perversion, and their blood is upon them.

If a man has sex with a male as with a woman, both of them have committed an abomination; they shall surely be put to death, and their blood is upon them. 'Lot, bring them, the men of Sodom want to have sex with the two men who came here.' (Gen. 19: 5)

'If a man takes a woman and her mother also, it is depravity; he and they shall be burned with fire, that there may be no depravity among you. If a man lies with an animal, he shall surely be put to death, and you shall kill the animal. If a woman approaches any animal and have sex with it, you shall kill the woman and the animal; they shall surely be put to death; their blood is upon them. If a man takes his sister, a daughter of his father or a daughter of his mother, and sees her nakedness, and she sees his nakedness, it is a disgrace, and they shall be cut off in the sight of the children of their people. He has uncovered his sister's nakedness, and he shall bear his iniquity. If a man has sexual intercourse with a woman during her menstrual period, he has made naked her fountain, and she has uncovered the fountain of her blood. Both of them shall be cut off from among their people. You shall not uncover the nakedness of your mother's sister or of your father's sister, for that is to make naked ones relative; they shall bear their iniquity. If a man has sex with his uncle's wife, he has uncovered his uncle's nakedness; they shall bear their sin; they shall die childless. If a man takes his brother's wife, it is impurity. He has uncovered his brother's nakedness; they shall be childless.'

You Shall Be Holy

'You shall therefore keep all my statutes and all my rules and do them that the land where I am bringing you to live may not vomit you out. And you shall not walk in the customs of the nation that I am driving out before you, for they did all these things, and therefore I detested them. But I have said to you, "You shall inherit their land, and I will give it to you to possess, a land flowing with milk and honey." I am the Lord your God, who has separated you from the peoples. You shall therefore separate the clean beast from the unclean, and the unclean bird from the clean. You shall not make yourselves detestable by beast or by bird or by anything with which the ground crawls, which I have set apart for you to hold unclean. You shall be holy to me, for I the Lord am holy and have separated you from the peoples, that you should be mine.'

'Any man or woman who consults the spirits of the dead shall be stoned to death: any person who does this is responsible for his own death.'

The entire chapter is written with the Voice of God of Israel dictating Jewish customary laws to ancient Jewish communities.

Christians all over the world have not only consulted the spirit of the dead, but they have actually worshiped many dead people, if indeed all these dead Jews were real humans like you and I.

Jesus Christ was crucified and killed thousands of years ago. Images of Jesus and his parents (Mary and Joseph) are prominently sculptured in every conceivable material, and strategically exhibited in Catholic churches in Italy and in other European cities and Christian countries all over the world. Indeed, in most 'Christian countries' across globe, these sculptures or images are worshipped every day. Jesus the Christ is dead and Christians worship his spirit. Every one of them including the Pope must therefore be stoned to death according to this last chapter.

What is the relevance of Leviticus 20: 27 as quoted above? ('Any man or woman who consults the spirit of the dead shall be stoned to death') This is plain simple English. And I demand full logical explanation from Christians! Do Holy Bible readers really apply reason to such extreme cruelty and viciousness of the supposed cosmic God? If not, why not? We are all humans!

Paul was supposedly beheaded in a prison cell in Jerusalem about fifty years after Jesus' death and more than 1,500 years past now, but his statues are moulded and displayed in all Catholic churches and are worshiped daily.

Images of all the supposed disciples of Jesus and the later-day saints are crafted in every conceivable material (wood, metal, earth, plastics, ivory, etc.,) and worshiped daily, by their loyal blind followers everywhere.

What then is the purpose or the relevance of the above satanic chapter and its last verse? The author of the book of Leviticus clearly demonstrates his or her knowledge of Jewish traditional faith by showing the entire dos and don'ts of a typical ancient Jewish community, and there is nothing wrong with that if all of us will understand the author as addressing ancient Jewish audience only. The notion is not in any way applicable to contemporary community of any type.

Yesterday's religious ideas are without question, bygone irrelevant ideas. Christian leaders are surely aware of the irrelevance of Leviticus Laws, but because it is a major religious indoctrination tool for retaining Christian fellowship from present to future generation of Christians, they cannot advise followers to ignore the texts. Chapters of this kind, indeed, become questionable when Christians arrogate themselves to apply this particular ethnic cultural practice (Ancient Jewish Customary Laws and behaviour) to entrap the rest of humanity. Christians do present such vile scriptures as direct instructions from a cosmic God even though the Holy Bible makes no mistake by expressly referring to the 'God of Israel' (Yahweh or I am) who does not claim to be a God for any other nation other than the twelve nations of ancient Israel.

If such information is directed to modern-day Jewish audience, readers may not even be justified to question them because it is a Jewish ancestral belief, and who cares, if you are a non-Jew! But these are Biblical quotations: a universally revered book, a tool, which is used daily by more than two billion people for self-deceptions. Some non-Jews (Christians) have developed faith in these Jewish ancient notions and find it almost impossible to live without it.

Must the rest of the world ignore their individual traditional cultural practices and adopt this Leviticus' ancient Jewish moral laws, just because it is written in the Holy Bible? I hereby invite all readers to think and to answer this Christian perplexing question.

Christian leaders are deliberately selfishly misguiding their followers to reject their ancestral cultural deities by adapting to this foreign ancient archaic religious deities or practices in the name of Christianity or a Jewish God as propagated in the Holy Bible. Question is, is this necessary, especially in the twenty-first century?

I am not by any means promoting the worship of ancient cultural gods of any kind. No. All I am saying is this, the worship of any spiritual being, be it the Genesis God, the Leviticus Laws, the God of Israel, Jesus Christ, or any God of any description in the twenty-first century is irrelevant, useless, useless, and useless—useless because all of them are ancient ideas, hoaxes, and grossly illusory. None possesses anything relevant to humanity.

It is demonstrable that human beings actually do better in all things when reliance on human knowledge of our environment or of our planet is adhered to, particularly, when we successfully delete ancient godly illusions from our mindset.

I find it irresistible to constantly remind my readers and readers of the Holy Bible that the content of this third book of the Holy Bible 'Leviticus' is grossly irreligious, ungodly, hypocritical, and absolute rubbish. The book refuses to recognize the existence of more than 7,000 other global cultures and their cultural gods, besides the Jewish Leviticus culture and its God of Israel.

That each culture develops its moral laws to befit its people that you cannot transplant ancient Jewish public morality to another culture without destroying the cultural identity of its indigenous people, unless it is intended to be a tool to control the peoples' livelihood or mentality. This is hypocritical and ungodly.

Such Leviticus topics as 'the Lord's commandments to Moses' regarding Burnt Sacrifices, Grain Offering, Fellowship Offering, Unintentional Sin Offering, Repayment Offering, Rights for Priests, Edible-Animals, Purification of Women after Childbirth, Laws Concerning Skin Diseases, Unclean Bodily Discharges, Atonement Day Observation, Sacred Blood, Forbidden Sexual Practices, Laws of Holiness and Justice, Penalties for Disobedience, Religious Festivals, Passover and Unleavened Bread, New Year Festival, Just and Fair Punishment, Release of Slaves, Blessings and Punishments for Disobedience, Laws Governing Gifts to God are all exclusively utterances of the God of Israel to the people of Israel, through fictionalized Moses and Aaron the priest.

These ideas definitely have nothing to do with anyone who is not a Jew; and more so to any modern person, be the person a Jew or not a Jew. These are, 'ancient' and 'Jewish' religious customary code of conduct, no more, no less. These customs may be similar to some other global cultures. But similarity must not be perceived as a version of inherited ancient Jewish custom.

(GNT)

In Leviticus 24: 10-23, punishment for blasphemy in Jewish communities are listed. 'Now an Israelite woman's son, whose father was an Egyptian, went out among the people of Israel. And the Israelite woman's son and a man of Israel fought in the camp, 11 and the Israelite woman's son blasphemed the Name, and cursed. Then they brought him to Moses. His mother's name was Shelomith, the daughter of Dibri, of the tribe of Dan. And they put him in custody, till the will of the Lord should be clear to them. Then the Lord spoke to Moses, saying, "Bring out of the camp the one who cursed, and let all who heard him lay their hands on his head, and let the entire congregation stone him. And speak to the people of Israel, saying, whoever curses his God shall bear his sin.

Whoever blasphemes the name of the Lord shall surely be put to death. The entire congregation shall stone him. The sojourner as well as the native, when he blasphemes the Name, shall be put to death. Whoever takes a human life shall surely be put to death.

Whoever takes an animal's life shall make it good, life for life. If anyone injures his neighbor, as he has done it shall be done to him, fracture for fracture, eye for eye, tooth for tooth; whatever injury he has given a person shall be given to him. Whoever kills an animal shall make it good, and whoever kills a person shall be put to death. You shall have the same rule for the sojourner and for the native, for I am the Lord your God." So Moses spoke to the people of Israel, and they brought out of the camp the one who had cursed and stoned him to death. Thus the people of Israel did as the Lord commanded Moses.'

If this Lord is the same God who spoke in the book of Genesis, the killer of Judah's two sons (Gen. 38: 7-10) plus several barbaric atrocities, is telling Moses to form an army of men and train them the art of merciless killing is hereby making the sin of blasphemy punishable by death: he must be the first to be called to trial on the supposed Judgment Day for the same offenses inflicted on non-Jewish citizens during the exodus to the so-called Promised Land. All the laws in Genesis 20 were abused on several occasions by the chief legislator (God of Israel) himself.

Leviticus 25: 25-55 has Restoration of Property as its main theme. 'If your brother becomes poor and sells part of his property, then his nearest redeemer shall come and redeem what his brother has sold. If a man has no one to redeem it and then himself becomes prosperous and finds sufficient means to redeem it, let him calculate the years since he sold it and pay back the balance to the man to whom he sold it, and then return to his property. But if he does not have sufficient means to recover it, then what he sold shall remain in the hand of the buyer until the year of jubilee. In the jubilee it shall be released, and he shall return to his property. If a man sells a dwelling house in a walled city, he may redeem it within a year of its sale. For a full year he shall have the right of redemption. If it is not redeemed within a full year, then the house in the walled city shall belong in perpetuity to the buyer, throughout his generations; it shall not be released in the jubilee. But the houses of the villages that have no wall around them shall be classified with the fields of the land. They may be redeemed, and they shall be released in the jubilee. As for the cities of the Levites, the Levites may redeem at any time the houses in the cities they possess. And if one of the Levites exercises his right of redemption, then the house that was sold in a city they possess shall be released in the jubilee. For the houses in the cities of the Levites are their possessions among the people of Israel. But the fields of pastureland belonging to their cities may not be sold, for that is their possession forever.

Kindness for Poor Brothers:

'If your brother becomes poor and cannot maintain himself with you, you shall support him as though he was a stranger and a sojourner, and he shall live with you. Take no interest from him or profit, but fear your God, that your brother may live beside you. You shall not lend him your money at interest, nor give him your food for profit. I am the Lord your God, who brought you out of the land of Egypt to give you the land of Canaan, and to be your God. If your brother becomes poor beside you and sells himself to you, you shall not make him serve as a slave: he shall be with you as a hired worker and as a sojourner. He shall serve with you until the year of the jubilee.

'Then he shall go out from you, he and his children with him, and go back to his own clan and return to the possession of his fathers. For they are my servants, whom I brought out of the land of Egypt; they shall not be sold as slaves. You shall not rule over him ruthlessly but shall fear your God. As for your male and female slaves whom you may have: you may buy male and female slaves from among the nations that are around you.

'You may also buy from among the strangers who sojourn with you and their clans that are with you, who have been born in your land, and they may be your property. You may bequeath them to your sons after you to inherit as a possession forever. You may make slaves of them, but over your brother's the people of Israel you shall not rule, one over another ruthlessly.'

How to Redeem a Poor Man: 'If a stranger or sojourner with you becomes rich, and your brother beside him becomes poor and sells himself to the stranger or sojourner with you or to a member of the stranger's clan, then after he is sold he may be redeemed. One of his brothers may redeem him, or his uncle or his cousin may redeem him, or a close relative from his clan may redeem him. Or if he grows rich he may redeem himself. He shall calculate with his buyer from the year when he sold himself to him until the year of jubilee, and the price of his sale shall vary with the number of years. The time he was with his owner shall be rated as the time of a hired worker. If there are still many years left, he shall pay proportionately for his redemption some of his sale price. If there remain but a few years until the year of jubilee, he shall calculate and pay for his redemption in proportion to his years of service. He shall treat him as a worker hired year by year. He shall not rule ruthlessly over him in your sight. And if he is not redeemed by these means, then he and his children with him shall be released in the year of jubilee. For it is to me that the people of Israel are servants. They are my servants whom I brought out of the land of Egypt: I am the Lord your God.'

Leviticus 27 narrates the Laws about Vows (GNT)

'The Lord spoke to Moses, saying, "Speak to the people of Israel and say to them, If anyone makes a special vow to the Lord involving the valuation of persons, then the valuation of a male from twenty years old up to sixty years old shall be fifty shekels of silver, according to the shekel of the sanctuary. If the person is a female, the valuation shall be thirty shekels.

"'If the person is from five years old up to twenty years old, the valuation shall be for a male twenty shekels, and for a female ten shekels. If the person is from a month old up to five years old, the valuation shall be for a male five shekels of silver, and for a female the valuation shall be three shekels of silver. If the person is sixty years old or over, the valuation for a male shall be fifteen shekels, and for a female it shall be ten shekels. And if someone is too poor to pay the valuation, then he shall be made to stand before the priest, and the priest shall value him; the priest shall value him according to what the avower can afford. If the vow is an animal that may be offered as an offering to the Lord, all of it that he gives to the Lord is holy. He shall not exchange it or make a substitute for it, good for bad, or bad for good; and if he does in fact substitute one animal for another, then both it and the substitute shall be holy. And if it is any unclean animal that may not be offered as an offering to the Lord, then he shall stand the animal before the priest, and the priest shall value it as either good or bad; as the priest values it, so it shall be. But if he wishes to redeem it, he shall add a fifth to the valuation. When a man dedicates his house as a holy gift to the Lord, the priest shall value it as either good or bad; as the priest values it, so it shall stand. And if the donor wishes to redeem his house, he shall add a fifth to the valuation price, and it shall be his. If a man dedicates to the Lord part of the land that is his possession, and then the valuation shall be in proportion to its seed. A homer of barley seed shall be valued at fifty shekels of silver. If he dedicates his field from the year of jubilee, the valuation shall stand $_{18}$ but if he dedicates his field after the jubilee, then the priest shall calculate the price according to the years that remain until the year of jubilee, and a deduction shall be made from the valuation. And if he who dedicates the field wishes to redeem it, then he shall add a fifth to its valuation price, and it shall remain his. But if he does not wish to redeem the field, or if he has sold the field to another man, it shall not be redeemed anymore.

"'But the field, when it is released in the jubilee, shall be a holy gift to the Lord, like a field that has been devoted. The priest shall be in possession of it. If he dedicates to the Lord a field that he has bought, which is not a part of his possession, then the priest shall calculate the amount of the valuation for it up to the year of jubilee, and the man shall give the valuation on that day as a holy gift to the Lord. In the year of jubilee the field shall return to him from whom it was bought, to whom the land belongs as a possession. All prices shall be fixed according to the official standard. But a firstborn of animals, which as a firstborn belongs to the Lord, no man may dedicate; whether ox or sheep, it is the Lord's. And if it is an unclean animal, then he shall buy it back at the valuation, and add a fifth to it; or, if it is not redeemed, it shall be sold at the valuation. But no devoted thing that a man devotes to the Lord, of anything that he has, whether man or beast, or of his inherited field, shall be sold or redeemed; every devoted thing is most holy to the Lord. No one devoted, who is to be devoted for destruction from mankind, shall be ransomed; he shall surely be put to death.

"'Every tithe of the land, whether of the seed of the land or of the fruit of the trees, is the Lord's; it is holy to the Lord. If a man wishes to redeem some of his tithe, he shall add a fifth to it. And every tithe of herds and flocks, every tenth animal of that entire pass under the herdsman's staff, shall be holy to the Lord. One shall not differentiate between good or bad, neither shall he make a substitute for it; and if he does substitute for it, then both it and the substitute shall be holy; it shall not be redeemed." These are the commandments that the Lord commanded Moses for the people of Israel on Mount Sinai.'

What justification is there for modern-day Christians to include the above passage of the book of Leviticus as part of their holy scriptures? As already explained, the book's contents are photocopies of the Torah's second book. Everything about it is strictly intended for Jewish people. Modern Christians obviously have a choice to delete or ignore it. This of course includes the other four Pentateuch books of the Holy Bible and indeed the Holy Bible as whole. Because the remaining parts are also extracts from the same Torah, just that the Hebrew version is retained by the Jews and classified as authentically Judaic scriptures to suit the interests of both Jews and their offspring followers of Christ.

Jesus Christ's image is molded to suit Christians' religious agenda, that is, by separating Christ from Jewish forum onto global multicultural platform. This was the only way Christ could be presented as a heaven-sent individual who came to this world to sacrifice his life for humanity but not for Jews only.

As most readers can sense out, the scant story of biblical Christ does not even go close to portraying him as a Jew. His Jewish ancestry is being transformed as a mere historical incidental metaphor. The supposed heavenly father is supposed to have used Jews as a mere vehicle to create a cosmic redeemer. Christian leadership has done exceptionally well in this respect by nurturing or indoctrinating millions of followers to accept the half-stories written in the Holy Bible about this Jesus and other biblical mystique characters.

The entire history of Jesus the Christ between thirteen years to twenty-nine years of age is missing in both the Holy Bible and in the real world historical records! Is this not something which all of us should really think about? Is the obvious fictitious nature of this guy not clear? Is Christ not a mere notion, a metaphor, a mere imaginary creature like any godly image existing in all cultures? The image of biblical Christ is no different from the perceived image of any idol worshiped in all cultures. Christ is simply a Jewish idol and must be worshiped by Jews if they so choose.

The fourth Book of the Holy Bible 'Numbers' was written about 100 years before the birth of Jesus. The author is informing readers of chapter 18 verses 16 that the Jewish God approved trading in human beings. The Lord God of Israel said to Aaron, 'Children shall be bought at the age of one month for the fixed price of five pieces of silver, according to official standard . . .'

The God of Israel is instructing Aaron the priest to trade in children, the amount to be charged for specific age of a child is dictated by the God of Abraham, Isaac, and Jacob.

Involvement of God of Israel in buying and selling of human beings should not surprise Bible readers if we take it as part of ancient Jewish culture. Women for instance were created for the convenience of man. Genesis 2: 18 says, 'Then the Lord said, it is not good for the man to live alone. I will make a suitable companion to help him.' Verse 22 says, 'He formed a woman out of the rib and brought her to him.' Can this character we have come to know as a God for the Jews really rationally be assumed to be our God, our maker, the spiritual controller of all planetary things and event? So God did not know that it was not good for man to live alone when he was designing Adam? The two verses quoted above are complete rubbish! God was not smart enough to know the possible implications of creating a lone ranger to occupy this huge planet with seven continents for a single Jewish guy to occupy it? This God is not wise, or he must be crazy. With God's supposed infinite knowledge of everything, such things as different climatic conditions of the various continents could have been anticipated. Each continent needed well-designed male and female plus the rest of natural organisms to befit its natural habitat. The initial procreation from Palestine-confined geographical area, while the vast landmarks of the remaining universe exist unpopulated, makes the biblical creation idea rather childish.

According to Numbers (GNT)

Numbers chapter 1 deals with the First Census of Israel. On the first day of the second month in the second year after the people of Israel left Egypt, the Lord spoke to Moses there in the Tent of his presence in the Sinai Desert. He said as follows: 'You and Aaron are to take census of the people of Israel by clans and families. List the names of the men twenty years and older who are fit for military service. Ask one clan chief from each tribe to help you.' Of the twelve tribes, Moses and Aaron registered 603,550 fit strong men of Jewish descent for active military services. These are the families of Reuben, Simeon, Gad, Judah, Issachar, Zebulum, Ephraim, Manasseh, Benjamin, Dan, Asher, and Naphtali. The Levites were not registered with the other tribes because the Lord had said to Moses, 'When you take a census of the men fit for military service, do not include the tribe of Levites. Instead put the Levites in charge of the Tent of my presence and all its equipment. They shall carry it and its equipment, serve in it, and set up their camp round it. Whenever you move your camp, the Levites shall take the Tent down and set it up again at each camping place. Anyone else who comes near the Tent shall be put to death. The rest of the Israelites shall set up camp, company by company each man with his own group and under his own banner. But the Levites shall camp round the Tent to guard it, so that no one may come near and cause my anger to strike the community of Israel.' So the people of Israel did everything that the Lord had commanded Moses.

I like to remind the reader that apart from the first and the last verses, the entire chapter 1 is written with quotation marks. Fifty-two out of the fifty-four verses of the chapter are God's own words according to the author of Moses' narratives. This is supposed to be the exact phraseology or recorded words of the God of Israel, who is probably the transformed Genesis Creator God, and who later transformed again to become our universal God or Jesus the Christ.

It is very important to be reminded that the God of Israel specifically introduces himself as a God for Israelites, not the God for the entire people of the world as the book of Genesis claims. Readers often wishfully link the two gods into a single entity. Exodus 4: 22-3, Numbers 15: 41, Deuteronomy 32: 9, Micah 4: 5, and dozens others clearly states that God of Israel is a God for the Israelites or ancient Jews only. And note, the book of Numbers was written in about 100 years before Christ was born. But here the author is reporting a quoted story which took place millions of years prior to the emergence of Moses era.

Readers of the Holy Bible are required to accept that the recorded words are not Moses' own making, but rather, words uttered by the God of Israel directly through Moses to the Israelites.

The invisible Supreme Commander of the community of ancient Israel 'God of Israel' has issued his well-planned military strategy to his beloved children of Israel through his loyal and well-groomed visible military Commander Moses and his deputy Aaron.

It is also necessary to maintain in memory the primary intent or the declared purpose for God of Israel to organize the Israelites into this military order: the intent and purpose, being to kill and to destroy non-Jews and their properties that will interrupt the Jews along their exodus to the Promised Land of Canaan.

Again, note also that the tribes of Israel consist of more than twelve clans or families. Levites family, for instance, has no representation among the twelve armed forces divisions according to the book of Numbers. Levites are domesticated for Israeli religious and internal affairs. The author is further going to tell readers that Levites clan consists of another 22,000 people, grouped into twelve divisional tribes.

The total number of the people of Israel enrolled in all the divisions, group by group, was 603,550 plus 22,000. As the Lord had commanded Moses to organize the Jews, they camped, each under his own banner, and they marched each with his own clan.

If every word of the Holy Book is considered to be the true word of God, as most Christians think it is, then clearly the above chapter gives the impression that the God of Israel actually created a military force, an army of 603,550 Jewish soldiers at a specific time in human history—about 100 years before Christ's birth. It may interest Bible readers to know that many eminent historians have dedicated their lifetimes in search of supporting facts, but there is no proven historical record beside the Bible that support the above story.

Militarism is by all definitions a violent or an aggressive act. Its main purpose is to train specially selected citizens in all manners for destroying lives and property. Why should God of Israel promote aggression, especially one intended to kill innocent non-Jews, along their way to the so-called Promised Land of Canaan. Unprovoked violence is immoral in all human cultures.

Now, let's examine this closely. It is a common belief that God is a spirit and therefore cannot be seen with human naked eyes; hence, we cannot question the authenticity of his words. But Moses was supposed to be a real human being who according to the Holy Bible really once upon a time lived on this planet which you and I have inherited from our parents. Moses therefore must be a historical figure; but most Hebrew historians of the past and present have toiled in vain for centuries in search of a verifiable historical and archaeological evidence to validate even a fraction of the above story. Some of them have tried to place the entire biblical story or part of the story or some significant aspect of the story in some historical context, but none of their findings match with real past record unquestionably, chronologically, archeologically, geographically, and scientifically, except of course theological conjectures. The content of the above chapter is therefore definitely a fable.

'The Lord said to Moses, "Bring forward the tribe of Levi and appoint them as servants of Aaron the priest. The only responsibility the Levites have is to serve Aaron and his sons. You shall appoint Aaron and his sons to carry out the duties of the priesthood; anyone else who tries to do so shall be put to death."' (Num. 3: 5)

'But if you have committed adultery, may the Lord make a curse among your people. May God cause his *genital organs to shrink and your stomach to swell up:* May this water enter your stomach and cause it to swell and your genital organs to shrink. The woman shall respond, "I agree the Lord may do so." (Num. 5: 20-22. GNT)

Please, my respectful reader, pause for a moment and reflect on the above classic ancient Jewish godly statements. It will surprise the reader to know that from Adam across Jacob to the Apostle Paul, none of the significant characters in the Bible can be holy, if we put all of them into biblical sexual offences test. The above bizarre punishment of 'genital organ shrinkage would make all the Jewish male heroes in the Bible penis-less.

Then the priest shall write this curse down and wash the writing off into the bowl of bitter water. Before he makes the woman drink the water, which may then cause her bitter pain, the priest shall take the offering of flour out of the woman's hands, hold it up in dedication to the Lord, and present it on the altar. Then he shall take a handful of it as a token offering and burn it on the altar. Finally, he shall make the woman drink the water. If she has committed adultery, the water would cause bitter pain; her stomach will swell up and her genitals organs will shrink. Her name will become a curse among her people. But if she is innocent, she will not be harmed and will be able to bear children. This is the law in cases where a man is jealous and becomes suspicious that his wife has committed adultery. The woman shall be made to stand in front of the altar, and the priest shall perform this ritual. The husband shall be free of guilt, but the woman, if guilty, must suffer the consequences.

Any person who is familiar with idol worshipping would conclude that the religious practices among the Jews at the time were not different from those who worshiped idols. They were all voodoo practitioners. Can a real super-spiritual God, the Almighty God who is supposed to be our creator, ask Moses to mix herbs with water for a sex offender to drink? And if found guilty, the medicine shall cause the offender's stomach to swell and also her genital organs to shrink! The Holy Bible is something else!

Numbers 6: 1-3 says 'The Lord commanded Moses to give the following instructions to the people of Israel. Any man or woman who makes a special vow to become a Nazirite and dedicates himself to the Lord shall abstain himself from wine and beer.' Really, but how do you contrast this with Deuteronomy 14: 25-6 where this same God of Israel recommends drinking of beer, wine, hard liqueur, etc. as good for enjoyment in his presence. 'He shall not drink any kind of drink made from grapes or eat any grapes or raisins. As long as he is a Nazirite, he shall not eat anything that comes from a grapevine, not even the seeds or skins of grapes. As long as he is under Nazirite vow, he must not cut his hair or shave. He is bound by the vow for the full time that he is dedicated to the Lord and he shall let his hair and beard grow. His hair is the sign of his dedication to God, and so he must not defile himself by going near a corpse, not even that of his father, mother, brother, or sister. As long as he is a Nazirite, he is consecrated to the Lord'.

If the consecrated hair of a Nazirite is defiled because he is right beside someone who suddenly dies, he must wait seven days and then shave off his hair clean. On the eighth day, he shall bring two doves or two pigeons to the priest at the entrance of the Tent of the Lord's presence. The priest shall offer one as a sin offering and other as a burnt offering, to perform the ritual of purification for him because of his contact with a corpse. On the same day, the man shall consecrate his hair and rededicate to the Lord his time as a Nazirite. The previous period of time doesn't count, because his consecrated hair was defiled. As a repayment offering, he shall bring a one-year-old lamb.

When a Nazirite completes his vow, he shall complete his ritual. He shall go to the entrance of the Tent and present to the Lord two animals without any defects: a year-old-male lamb for a burnt offering, and a ram for a fellowship offering. He shall also offer a basket of bread made without yeast: thick loaves made of flour mixed with olive oil and biscuit brushed with olive oil and in addition, the required offerings of corn and wine.

The priest shall present all these to the Lord and offer the sin offering and the burnt offering. He shall sacrifice the ram to the Lord as a fellowship offering and offer it with the basket of bread; he shall also present the offerings of corn and wine. At the entrance of the Tent, the Nazirite shall shave off his hair and put it on the fire on which the fellowship offering is being burnt.

Then when the shoulder of the ram is boiled, the priest shall take it and put it together with one thick loaf of bread and one biscuit from the basket, into the hands of the Nazirite. Next the priest shall present them as a special gift to the Lord; they are a sacred offering for the priest, in addition to the bread and leg of the ram which by law belong to the priest. After that, the Nazirite may drink wine. These are the regulations for Nazirite, but if a Nazirite promises an offering beyond what his vow requires him to give; he must fulfill exactly the promise he made.

The Lord commanded Moses to tell Aaron and his sons to use the following words in blessing the people of Israel: may the Lord bless you and take care of you; may the Lord be kind and gracious to you; may the Lord look on you with favour and give you peace; the Lord said, if they pronounce my name as a blessing upon the people of Israel, I will bless them.

It is generally accepted that the book of Numbers was written about 100 years before the birth of Jesus (1 BC); thus, all the information in the book date back about 2,100 years, at least counting back from this century. There is no doubt that even in modern times all human communities need to formulate customary laws and regulations to maintain peace and order in their defined geographical territories. Thus these Moses' instructions from the Jewish Lord cannot be judged by modern-day readers as unrealistic. And I am sure that the Jews who lived in the areas then benefited from the above customary laws. Human intelligence at the time dictated to community residents that those customs were necessary for the Israelites common good. Hence, Christians ought to be cautioned that those godly instructions cannot be relevant today, especially to non-Jews. They were meant for those ancient Jewish communities only.

The book of Numbers has a unique quality among all books of the Holy Bible. In every chapter, the author spells out clearly the meaning attached to all biblical ideas of God as understood by Jews and how important was the image given to them. 'God' is shown vividly as an ancient Jewish culturally designed spiritual leader. The emphasis of God of Israel as a God for Jews only is prominently exposed throughout Numbers and the remaining Old Testament books. All the prophets, heroes, kings, and leaders of every description in the Bible receive directives and guidance from him.

Can a real God for all mankind, not a man-made God, ask people to vow to grow facial hair and hair on their head as a token of obedience or faith? Does the Almighty God need offerings of any kind? Does he really need boiled shoulder of ram, corn, bread, wine and burnt-offering as stated in Numbers chapter 5? Is humanity actually expected to accept this ancient Jewish cult norm? Have we really read and thought about these sayings? If the idea of God is a concept which we learn from childhood and the God of Israel's information as written in the book of Numbers represent the same God we are nurtured by our parents and pastors as our maker, then our parents and pastors have a lot to explain. We ask the question again, is this or can this God of Israel be the same God who made the first human being? Or is this how the Jews, as a human group, explain the source of life, and not necessarily true event which actually occurred sometime in human history?

In Numbers chapter 7, the author says on the day Moses finished setting up the Tent of the Lord's presence, he anointed and dedicated the Tent and all its equipment and the altar. Then the clan chiefs who were leaders in the tribes of Israel, the same men who were in charge of the census, brought their offerings to the Lord: six wagons and twelve oxen, a wagon for every two leaders and an ox for each leader. After they had presented them, *the Lord God of Israel said to Moses*, 'Accept these gifts for use in the work to be done for the Tent; give them to the Levites according to the work they have to do.'

So Moses gave the wagons and the oxen to the Levites. He gave two wagons and four oxen to the Gershonites and four wagons and eight oxen to the Merarites. All their work was to be done under the direction of Ithamar son of Aaron. But Moses gave no wagons or oxen to the Kohathites, because the sacred objects they took care of had to be carried on their shoulders.

The leaders also brought offerings to celebrate the dedication of the altar. When they were ready to present their gifts at the altar, the Lord said to Moses, 'Tell them that each day for a period of twelve days one of the leaders is to present his gifts for the dedication of the altar.'

12. They presented their offerings in the following order:
GNT

Day	Tribe	Leader
1	Judah	Nahshon son of Amminadab
2	Issachar	Nethanel son of Zuar
3	Zebulun	Eliab son of Helon
4	Reuben	Elizur son of Shedeur
5	Simeon	Shelumiel son of Zurishaddai
6	Gad	Eliasaph son of Deuel
7	Ephraim	Elishama son of Ammihud
8	Manasseh	Gamaliel son of Pedahzur
9	Benjamin	Abidan son of Gideoni
10	Dan	Ahiezer son of Ammishaddai
11	Asher	Pagiel son of Ochran
12	Naphtali	Ahira son of Enan

The offering each one brought were identical: one silver bowl weighing 1.5 kilograms and one silver basin weighing 800 grams, by the official standard, both of them were full of flour mixed with oil for the grain offering; one gold dish weighing 110 grams, full of incense; one young bull, one ram, and a one-year-old lamb, for the burnt offering; one goat for the sin offering; and two bulls, five rams, five goats, and five 1-year-old lamb for the fellowship offering. The total of the offerings brought by the twelve leaders for the dedication of the altar were as follows:(1) Twelve silver bowls and twelve silver basins weighing a total of 27.6 kilograms. (2) Twelve gold dishes weighing a total of 1.32 kilograms filled with incense. (3) Twelve bulls, twelve rams, twelve 1-year-old lambs, together with the grain offerings that go with them: for the burnt-offerings. (4) Twelve goats for the sin offering. (5) Twenty-four bulls, sixty rams, sixty goats, sixty 1-year-old lambs, and for the fellowship offerings.

When Moses went into the Tent to talk to the Lord, he heard the Lord speaking to him above the lid on the Covenant Box, between the two-winged creatures.

If you and I reflect on the content of the eighty-nine verses of Numbers chapter 7 and then go back to the book's history, a few puzzles pop up. The book of Numbers was written about 100 years before the birth of Christ. At that time in history, there were other nations in the world. At least biblically, there was Egypt, Assyria, Babylon, and the neighboring countries. In Europe, all the modern nations were in existence with different names; for example, France was called Gaul at the time. The planet earth was geographically organized as city states. There were literally thousands of countries in existence then. Israel was tiny and an insignificant nation of Jewish tribes in the Palestine peninsular area. It is beyond belief that a nation of twelve Jewish tribes is projected in the Holy Bible as the source of mankind. The exposition of God of Israel, who plainly states as being a god for ancient Jews, but no other nations' god, is propagated by Christians as the Global God, as well as the inventor of everything natural. How can non-Jews claim God of the Jews to be their God by obeying and practicing ancient Jewish religious practices? Does this make sense? Is twenty-first century not the right time to dump this ancient garbage?

When Jesus Christ came into the biblical scene, he attempted unsuccessfully to reject his own traditional norms by redefining God's people to include uncircumcised people (gentiles). Jesus Christ, as promoted by Paul, failed to achieve that goal, because the gentiles had their own traditional gods. This, incidentally, has always been the facts of humanity: several gods for several ethnicities. The God of Israel has been remolded by New Testament writers to be the one and only God who is most superior among all other planetary gods and at the same time retains his Jewish title of 'God of Israel'. Isn't it incredible?

Numbers 13: 1-15 continues with Lord God of Israel's instruction to Moses to choose one of the leaders from each of the twelve tribes and send them as spies to explore the land of Canaan, which he is going to give to the Israelites. Moses obeyed and from the wilderness of Paran he sent out leaders as follows: Shammua, Shaphat, Caleb, Igal, Hosea, Palti, Gaddiel, Gaddi, Ammiel, Sethur, Nahbi, and Geuel. Each of the twelve tribes is represented. Can anyone imagine that the God for every human being actually commanded a Jewish leader, Moses, to send spies to investigate innocent non-Jewish citizens? At this point, should we all not understand that the God of Israel is solely for Jews? I am sure that all faithful Christians will find excuses to justify this, but their inner guilt will speak loudly to them in private, that indeed God of Israel cannot be the so-called God who created all of us. And neither can the Genesis God be the God of Israel in a single personality. The two are different from each other, and both are fictitious characters.

'These are the spies Moses sent to explore the land. He changed the name of Hoshea, son of Nun to Joshua. When Moses sent them out, he said to them, "Go north from here into the southern part of the land of Canaan and then into the hill country. Find out what kind of country it is, how many people live there, and how strong they are. Find out whether the land is good or bad and whether the people live in open towns or in fortified cities. Find whether the soil is fertile and whether the land is wooded. And be sure to bring back some of the fruits that grow there.'"

They reported what they had seen and showed them the fruits they had brought. They told Moses they explored the land and found it to be fertile, but the people who live there are powerful and their cities are very large and well fortified. They even saw some descendants of the Amalekites' giants live in the southern part of the land. Hittites, Jebusites, and Amorites live in the hill country; and Canaanites live by the Mediterranean Sea and along the River Jordan. Caleb said, 'We should attack now and take the land. We are strong enough to conquer it.' But the men who had gone with Caleb said, 'No we are not strong enough to attack them; the people there are more powerful than we are.' *So they spread* a false *report among the Israelites about the land they had explored.* They said that land does not even produce enough to feed the people who live there.

In Numbers chapter 14, the people complained all night long and cried out in distress. They complained against Moses, Aaron, and said, "It would have been better to die in Egypt or even here in the wilderness! Why is Lord taking us into that land? We will be killed in battle, and our wives and children will be captured. Wouldn't it be better to go back to Egypt?" They planned to choose another leader to take them back to Egypt. Moses and Aaron bowed to the ground in front of all the people. And Joshua son of Nun and Caleb son of Jephunneh, two of the spies tore their clothes in sorrow and said to the people, 'The land we explored is an excellent land. If the Lord is pleased with us, he will take us there and give us to that rich and fertile land. Do not rebel against the Lord, and don't be afraid of the people who live there. We will conquer them easily. The Lord is with us and he has defeated the gods who protected them; so don't be afraid of them.' The whole community was threatening to stone them to death, but suddenly the people saw the dazzling light of the Lord's presence appear over the tent.

Moses prayed for the people. The Lord God of Israel said to Moses, 'How much longer must these people reject me? How much longer will they refuse to trust in me, even though I have performed many miracles among them, but I will make you the father of a nation that is larger and powerful than they are?' But Moses said to the Lord, 'You brought these people out of Egypt by your power. When Egyptians hear what you have done to your people, they will tell it to the people who live in this land. These people have already heard that you, Lord, are with us, that you are plainly seen when your cloud stops over us, and that you go before us in a pillar of fire by night. Now if you kill all your people, the nations who have heard your fame will say that you killed your people in the wilderness because you were not able to bring them into the land you promised to give them. So now Lord, I pray, Show us your power and do what you promised when you said, "I, am not easily angered, and I show great love and faithfulness and forgive sin and rebellion. Yet I will not fail to punish children and grandchildren to the third and fourth generation for the sins of their parents. And now, Lord, according to your unchanging love, and forgiveness, I pray, the sin of these people, just as you have forgiven them ever since they left Egypt."'

The Lord answered them, *'I will forgive them, as you have asked. But I promise that as surely as I live and as surely as my presence fill the earth; none of these people will live to enter that land.* They have seen the dazzling light of my presence and the miracle that I performed in Egypt and in the wilderness, but they have tried my patience over and over again and have refused to obey me. They will never enter the land which I promised their ancestors. None of those who have rejected me will ever enter it. But because my servant Caleb has a different attitude and has remained loyal to me, I will bring him into the land which he explored, and his descendants will possess the land, in whose valleys the Amalekites and the Canaanite now live. Turn back tomorrow and go into the wilderness in the direction of the Gulf of Aqaba.'

Can God really say this *I swear that as surely as I live'*? To whom does God swear? Is there someone else greater than God according to Holy Bible? 'As long as' who, 'God' lives? Isn't he invincible, indestructible, everlasting, the overall Omni? Can God die? Such utterances as stated above clearly show the true picture of biblical authors: they very often forget their chain of thought. Most often they make their own personal opinions sound like that of a God, but often they slip off-track and make God sound and behave like you and I. Can we not see that these writers are forcing to make the impossible nature of God become a real possibility? The author of the book of Numbers goofed! The Almighty God cannot swear. There are too many of this sort of nonsense in the Holy Bible that ought to be exposed to demystify the holiness attached to the book.

'The Lord God of Israel punished the people for complaining. Numbers 14, 26-38 'The Lord asked Moses and Aaron: how much longer are these wicked people going to complain against me? I have heard enough of these complaints! Now give them this answer: I swear that as surely as I live, I will do you just as you have asked. I, the Lord, have spoken. You will die and your corpses will be scattered across this wilderness. Because you have complained against me, none of you over twenty-one years old will enter that land, I promised to let you live there, but not one of you will, except Caleb and Joshua. You said that your children would be captured, but I will bring them into the land that you rejected, and it will be their home. You will die here in the wilderness. Your children will wonder in the wilderness for forty years, suffering for your unfaithfulness, until the last one of you dies. You will suffer the consequences of your sin for forty years, one year for each of the forty days you spent for exploring the land. You will know what it means to have me against you! [I swear] that I will do this to you wicked people who have gathered together against me. Here in the wilderness every one of you will die. I the Lord have spoken.'

This Jewish God of Israel has sworn more than three times. Isn't it amazing? If this author wants us to believe that the above statements are directly from the supposed God of this universe, can we be informed where he or she heard this from, and when? Or we must take it to be one of those words that God is supposed to speak through humans? Where is the proof? What is the true motive of this narrator? Must we not ponder about these ungodly statements? Think! Please let us think!

In verse 36, the men Moses had sent to explore the land brought back a *false report*, which caused the people to complain against the Lord. And so the Lord struck them with a disease, and they died. Why and how couldn't God of Israel detect that the spies lied to him with 'a false report'. Doesn't it diminish this God's ability to know everything before occurrence? Of the twelve spies, only Joshua and Caleb survived.

The first attempt to invade the Land begins in verse 39 when Moses told the Israelites what the Lord had said; they mourned bitterly. Early the next morning, they started out to invade the hill country saying, 'Now we are ready to go to the place which the Lord told us about. We admit that we have sinned.' But Moses said, 'Then why are you disobeying the Lord now? You will not succeed! Don't go. The Lord is not with you, and your enemies will defeat you. When you face the Amalekites and the Canaanites, you will die in battle; the Lord will not be with you, because you have refused to follow him.' Yet they still dare to go up into the hill country, even though neither the Lord's Covenant Box nor Moses left the camp. Then the Amalekites and the Canaanites who lived there attacked and defeated them and pursued them as far as Hormah.

Numbers chapter 15 deals with Laws about Sacrifice: Lord God of Israel gave Moses the following regulations for the people of Israel to observe in the land that he was going to give them. A bull, a ram, a sheep, or a goat, may be presented to the Lord as a burnt offering or as a sacrifice in fulfillment of a vow or as freewill offering or as an offering at your regular religious festival; the smell of these food offering is pleasing to the Lord. Whoever presents a sheep or a goat as a burnt offering to the Lord is to bring with each animal a kilogram of flour mixed with a liter of olive oil as a grain-offering, together with a liter of wine. The smell of these sacrifices is pleasing to the Lord. When a bull is offered to the Lord as a burnt offering, or as a sacrifice in fulfillment of a vow, or as a fellowship offering, a grain offering of three kilograms of flour mixed with two liters of olive oil is to be presented, together with two liters of wine. The smell of this sacrifice is pleasing to the Lord. That is what shall be offered with each bull, ram, sheep, or goat. When more than one animal is offered, the accompanying offering is to be increased proportionately. *Every native Israelite* is to do this when he presents a food offering, a smell pleasing to the Lord. And at anytime a foreigner living among you, whether on a temporary or a permanent basis, makes food offering, a smell that pleases the Lord, he is to observe the same regulations.

For all time to come, the same rules are binding on you and on the foreigners who live among you. You and they are alike in the Lord's sight; the same regulations apply to you and to them. Note that by the behaviour of God of Israel, this statement is not true. God has always been bias in favour of Israelites.

The Lord gave Moses the following regulations for the people of Israel to observe in the Land he was going to give them. When any food produced there is eaten, some of it is to be put aside as a special contribution to the Lord. When you bake bread, the first loaf of the first bread made from the new corn is to be presented as a special contribution to the Lord. This is to be presented in the same way as the special contribution you make from the corn you thresh. For all time to come, this special gift is to be given to the Lord from the bread you bake. But suppose someone unintentionally fails to keep some of these regulations which the Lord has given to Moses. And suppose that in the future the community fails to do everything that the Lord has commanded through Moses. If the mistake was made because of the ignorance of the community, they are to offer a bull as a burnt offering, a smell that pleases the Lord with the proper grain offering and wine offering. In addition, they are to offer a male goat as a sin offering. The priest shall perform the ritual of purification for the community, and they will be forgiven because the mistake was unintentional, and they brought their sin offering as a food offering to the Lord. The whole community of Israel and the foreigners living among them will be forgiven, because everyone was involved in the mistake. If an individual sins unintentionally, he is to offer a one-year-old female goat as a sin offering. At the altar, the priest shall perform the ritual of purification to purify the man from his sin, and he will be forgiven. The same regulation applies to everyone who unintentionally commits a sin, whether he is a native or a foreigner. But any person who sins deliberately, whether he is a native or a foreigner, is treating the Lord contempt, and shall be put to death, because he has rejected what the Lord has said and has deliberately broken one of his commands. He is responsible for his own death.

The Man Who Broke the Sabbath
(GNT)

Once, while the Israelites were in the wilderness, a man was found gathering firewood on the Sabbath. He was taken to Moses, Aaron, and the whole community, and was put under guard, because it was not clear what should be done with him. Then the Lord said to Moses, 'The man must be put to death; the whole community is to stone him to death outside the camp.' *So the whole community took him outside the camp and stoned him to death, as the Lord had commanded.* The Lord commanded Moses to say to the people of Israel: 'Make tassels on the corners of your garments and put a blue cord on each tassel. You are to do this for all time to come. The tassels will serve as reminders and commands and obey them, and then you will not turn away from me and follow your own wishes desires. The tassels will remind you to keep all my commands, and you will belong completely to me. Numbers 15: 41 *says, I am the Lord your God; I brought you out of Egypt to be your God. I am the Lord.*

Really! So the reason why God evacuated the Jews from Egypt is because 'He' 'God' wants to be the Jewish God; a God for the twelve tribes of Israel; the God of Israel for the Israelites? This God is therefore not the God for non-Jews. This God is not the Genesis God who has the powers for creating natural things of our universe. The Genesis creator God would prevent his chosen beloved Jews to be enslaved in Egypt. He would not wait for 430 years, and *suddenly remember* that he had to appoint Moses to redeem them. He would not need 650,000 Jewish soldiers and God-appointed twelve spies to destroy thousands of innocent inhabitants along Jewish exodus to the so-called Promised Land of Canaan. A Supreme God is supposed to possess infinite knowledge and power over everything and everyone. By his actions and pronouncements, this God of Israel has none of the basic qualities of a divine God. He is phony, an absolute junk!

Numbers 15: 33-36 says about death penalty for a man who could not attend Sabbath: The whole community took him outside the camp and stoned him to death, as the Lord God of Israel had commanded.

How about this act of the ancient Jewish community and the God of Israel? Someone may answer that it is a Jewish religious law or practice at the time and hence as a non-Jewish person, it is not my business to comment on it. Yes, you are damn right to say that. Unfortunately, however, it is part of biblical literature; an acclaimed holy sacred book which for more than 2,000 years, millions of humanity have been charmed to accept without question. Yes, you and I have a human duty to question that because there are millions of non-Jews misinformed Christians who consider these ancient Jewish customary Laws in the book of Numbers as binding on them as well. Indeed we, you and I, have a human duty to challenge this notion.

Numbers 16 (GNT)

The Rebellion of Korah, Drathan, and Abiram: Korah son of Izhar had the audacity to rebel against Moses. He was joined by three members of the tribe of Reuben-Dathan and Abiram the son of Eliab, on son of Peleth—and by 250 other Israelites, well-known leaders chosen by the community. *They assembled before Moses and Aaron, and said to them, 'You have gone too far! All the members of the Community belong to the Lord, and the Lord is with us. Why then, Moses, do you set yourself above the Lord's community?'* When Moses heard this, he threw himself on the ground and prayed. Then he said to Korah and his followers, 'Tomorrow the Lord will show us who belongs to him; he will let the one who belongs him, that is, the one he has chosen, approach him at the altar. Tomorrow morning you and your followers take fire pans, put live coals and incense on them, and take them to the altar. Then we will see which of us the Lord has chosen. You Levites are the ones who have gone too far!'

Extract from *Verses 19-30 says*, 'Then Korah gathered the whole community and they stood facing Moses and Aaron at the entrance of the Tent. *Suddenly the dazzling light of the Lord's presence appeared to the whole community, and the Lord said to Moses and Aaron,* "Stand back from these people, and I will destroy them immediately." But Moses and Aaron bowed down with their faces to the ground and said, *"O God, you are the source of all life. When one man sins do you get angry with the whole community?"* The Lord said to Moses, 'Tell the people to move away from the Tents of Korah, Dathan, and Abiram.' Stand away from the Tent of these wicked men and don't touch anything that belongs to them. Otherwise you will be wiped out with them for their sins'. Dathan and Abiram had come out and were standing at the entrance of their Tents with their wives and children. Moses said to the people, 'This is how you will know that the Lord has sent me to do all these things, and that it is not by my own choice that I have done them. If these men die a natural death without some punishment from God, then the Lord did not send me. But if the Lord does something unheard of and the earth opens up and swallows them with all they own, so that they go down alive to the world of the dead, you will know that these men have rejected the Lord.'

As soon as he had finished speaking, the ground under Dathan and Abiram split open and swallowed them and their families, together with all of Korah's followers and their possessions. So they went down alive to the world of the dead, with their possessions. The earth closed over them, and they vanished.

All the people of Israel who were there fled when they heard their cry. They shouted, 'Run, the earth might swallow us too!' Then *the Lord sent a fire that blazed and burnt out the 250 men who had presented the incense.* Then the Lord said to Moses, 'Tell Eleazar son of Aaron the priest to remove the bronze fire pans from the remains of the men who have been burnt, and scatter the coals from the fire pans somewhere else because the fire pans are holy. They became holy when they were presented at the Lord's altar. So take the fire pans of these men who were put to death for their sins, beat them into thin plates to make a covering for the altar. *It will be a warning to the Israelites that no one who was not a descendants of Aaron should come to the altar to burn incense for the Lord.* Otherwise he would be destroyed like Korah and his men.' All this was done as the Lord had commanded Eleazar through Moses.

Aaron Saves the People: The next day, the whole community complained against Moses and Aaron and said, 'You have killed some of the Lord's people.' After they had all gathered to protest to Moses and Aaron, they turned towards the Tent and saw that the cloud was covering it and the dazzling light of the Lord's presence had appeared. Moses and Aaron went and stood in front of the

Tent, and the Lord said to Moses, *'Stand back from these people, and I will destroy them on the spot!'* The two of them bowed down with their faces to the ground, and Moses said to Aaron, 'Hurry! The Lord's anger has already broken out and an epidemic has already begun.' Verse 49 says that the number of people who died was 14,700, not counting those who died in Korah's rebellion.

The Almighty God of Israel in one of his best angry moods destroyed over 14,700 Jews for questioning one of his many ungodly behaviors. I strongly recommend the reader to reread the entire chapter 16. Can any reader tell the difference between satanic behaviour and godly behaviour, as exposed by the author of the book of Numbers? It is rationally very confusing! Are we not yet convinced that this God of Israel (if such a character ever existed) was nothing more than Jewish fantasy or satanic brute?

Numbers 17: (GNT) Lord God of Israel said to Moses, 'Tell the people of Israel to give twelve sticks, one from the leader of each tribe. Write each man's name on his stick and write Aaron's name on the stick representing Levi. There will be one stick for each tribal leader. Take them to the Tent of my presence and put them in front of the Covenant Box, where I meet you. Then the stick of the man I have chosen will sprout. In this way I will put a stop to the constant complaining of these Israelites against you.' The Lord again spoke to Moses saying, 'Put Aaron's stick back in front of the Covenant Box. It is to be kept as a warning to the rebel Israelites that they will die unless their complaining stops.' Moses did as the Lord commanded. In verse 12, the people of Israel said to Moses, 'Then that's the end of us! If anyone who even comes near the Tent must die, then we are all as good as dead.'

Numbers 18: (GNT)

Duties of Priests and Levites: The Lord said to Aaron, 'You, your sons and the Levites must suffer the consequences of any guilt connected with serving in the Tent of my presence, but only you and your sons will suffer the consequence in the services of the priesthood. Bring in your relative, the tribe of Levites to work with you while you and your sons are serving in the Tent. They are to fulfill their duties to you and their responsibilities for the Tent, but they must not have any contact with sacred objects in the Holy Place or with the altar. If they do, both they and you will be put to death. You and your son alone must fulfill the responsibilities of the Holy Place, and the altar, so that my anger will not again break out against the people of Israel. I am the one who has chosen your relative the Levites from among the Israelites as a gift to you. They are dedicated to me so that they can carry out their duties in the Tent. But you and your sons alone shall fulfill all the responsibilities of the priesthood that concern the altar and what is in the Most Holy Place. These things are your responsibility, because I have given you the gift of the priesthood. *Any unqualified person who comes near the sacred objects shall be put to death.'*

The Share of the Priests: *The Lord said to Aaron, 'Remember that I am giving to you all the special contributions made to me that are not burnt as sacrifices. I am giving them to you and your descendants as the part assigned to you forever. Of the most sacred offerings not burnt on the altar, the following belong to you: the grain offerings, the sin offerings, and the repayment offerings. Everything that is presented to me as a sacred offering belongs to you and your sons. You must eat these things in a Holy Place, and only males may eat them, consider them holy. In addition, any other special contribution that the Israelites present to me shall be yours. I am giving them to you, your sons, and your daughters for all time to come.* Every member of your family who is ritually clean may eat them. I am giving you all the best of the first produce which the Israelites give me each year: olive oil, wine, and corn. It all belongs to you. Every member of your family who is ritually clean may eat it. Everything in Israel that has been unconditionally dedicated to me belongs to you.'

The author is reporting an event which occurred in front of a place of worship, the Tent of God's presence. God is assigning to Aaron and his descendants all priesthood duties. God is also assigning to Levites group of families the responsibilities of all works related to the place of worship. It is also noted that all offerings given by Israelites to the God of Israel are to be owned and used by Aaron and children for all time to come. Practically, all thanksgiving items given in the name of God are literally to be consumed by Aaron in person. The irony here is that in the eyes of the gift presenters, God of Israel has been offered some gifts, although in reality the offerings are for the priests.

Verse 15-20 says thus: *The Lord said to Aaron; 'Every first-born child or animal that the Israelites present to me belongs to you.* But you must accept payment to buy back every first-born child, and must also accept payment for every first-born animal that is ritually unclean. Children shall be bought back at the age of one month for the fixed price of five pieces of silver, according to official standard. But the first-born of cows, sheep, and goats are not to be bought back; they belong completely to me and are to be sacrificed.

'Throw their blood against the altar and burn their fat as a food-offering, a smell pleasing to me. The meat from them belongs to you, like the breast, and the right hind leg of the special offering. I am giving to you, your sons, and to your daughters, for all time to come, all the special contributions which the Israelites present to me. This is an unbreakable covenant that I have made with you and your descendants. You will not receive any property that can be inherited, and no part of the land of Israel will be assigned to you. I the Lord am all you need.' *Verse 21-24 says, The Lord said, 'I have given to the Levites every tithe that the people of Israel present to me.* This is in payment for their services in taking care of the Tent of my presence.

'The other Israelites must no longer approach the Tent and in this way bring on themselves the penalty of death. From now on the Levites will take care of the Tent and bear full responsibility for it. This is a permanent rule that apply also to your descendants. The Levites shall have no permanent property in Israel, because I have given them as their possession the tithe which the Israelites present to me as a special contribution. That is why I told them that they would have no permanent property in Israel.'

The author of book of Numbers chapter 18 has formally acknowledged god-worshipping as a vital duty in Israel. That church leaders or founders must be financially rewarded for their services rendered in their communities. The Levites clan family is declared by God officially as responsible for the management of church duties for salaries paid out of tithes or financial contributions made to God of Israel by the Israelites. The birth of a 'Church' as an economic institution is hereby established by the God of Israel as an 'unbreakable covenant'. Numbers 18: 21, the Lord said; "I have given to the Levites *every tithe* that the people of Israel present to me'". Furthermore, Numbers 18: 28 says, 10 per cent of all the tithe collected should be given to Aaron the priest of the Tent of the Lord's Presence, 'the Church,' as salary payable to Aaron as payment for his services to the Lord God of Israel.

Verse 25-32: the Levites' Tithe: 'The Lord commanded Moses to say to the Levites: "When you receive from the Israelites the tithe that the Lord gives you as your possession, you must present a tenth of it as a special contribution to the Lord. This special contribution will be considered as the equivalent of the offering which the farmer makes of new corn and new wine. In this way you also will present the special contribution that belongs to the Lord from all the tithes which you receive from the Israelites. You are to give this special contribution for the Lord to Aaron the priest. Give it from the best that you receive. When you have presented the best part, you may keep the rest, just as the farmer keeps what is left after he makes his offering. You and your families may eat the rest anywhere, because it is your wages for your service in the Tent. You will not become guilty when you eat it, as long as you have presented the best of it to the Lord. But be sure not to profane the sacred gifts of the Israelites by eating any of the gifts before the best part is offered; if you do, you will be put to death.'

Some extracts from Numbers 19 (GNT)

"The Lord commanded Moses and Aaron to give the Israelites the following regulations: 'Bring to Moses and Aaron a red cow which has no defects and which has never been put to work, and give it to Eleazar the priest. It is to be taken outside the camp and killed in his presence'. Then Eleazar is to take some of its blood and with his finger sprinkle it seven times in the direction of the Tent. The whole animal, including skin, meat, blood, and intestines, is to be burnt in the presence of the priest. Then he is to take some cedar wood, a sprig of hyssop, and the red cord and throw them into the fire. After that he is to wash his clothes and pour water over himself, and then he may enter the camp, but he remains ritually unclean until evening.

The man who burnt the cow must also wash his clothes and pour water over himself, but he also remains unclean until evening. Then a man who is ritually clean is to collect the ashes of the cow and put them in a ritually clean place outside the camp, where they are to be kept for the Israelite community to use in preparing the water for removing ritual uncleanness. Ritual is performed to remove sin. The man who collected the ashes must wash his clothes, but he remains unclean until evening. This regulation is valid for all time to come, both for the Israelites and for the foreigners living among them."

The Lord's commandments and regulations to Moses the leader and Aaron the priest of the Israelites in chapter 19 of book of Numbers is a classic example of idol worshipping. The supposed supreme God for all mankind is asking Moses and Aaron to bring a red cow with no defect, to be killed in the presence of Eleazar the priest, its blood to be sprinkled seven times in the direction of the Tent, the whole animal including skin, meat, blood, and intestines to be burnt in the presence of the priest. How do Christians justify this barbaric satanic instruction from their God?

Verse 11-22: Contact with a Corpse:

"Whoever touches a corpse is ritually unclean for seven days. He must purify himself with water for purification on the third day and the seventh day, and then he will be clean. But if he does not purify himself on both the third and the seventh day, he will not be clean.

Whoever touches a corpse and does not purify himself remains unclean because the water for purification has not been thrown over him. He defiles the Lord's Tent, and he will no longer be considered one of God's people. If someone dies in the Tent, anyone who is in the tent at the time of the death, or who enters it, becomes ritually unclean for seven days. Every jar and pot in the tent that has no lid on it also becomes unclean. If someone touches a person who has been killed or has died a natural death outdoors, or someone touches a human bone, or a grave, he becomes unclean for seven days. To remove the uncleanness, some ashes from the red cow which was burnt to remove the sin shall be taken and put in a pot and fresh water added. In the first case, someone who is ritually clean is to take a sprig of hyssop, dip it in the water, and sprinkle the tent, everything in it, and the people who were there.

In the second case, someone who is ritually clean is to sprinkle the water on the man who had touched the human bone or the dead body, or the grave. On the third day and the seventh, the person who is ritually clean is to sprinkle the water on the unclean person. On the seventh day, he is to purify the man, who, after washing his clothes and pouring water over himself, becomes ritually clean after sunset.

Anyone who has become ritually unclean and does not purify himself remains unclean, because the water for purification has not been thrown over him. He defiles the Lord's Tent and will no longer be considered one of God's people. You are to observe this rule for all time to come. The person who sprinkles the water for purification must also wash his cloth; anyone who touches the water remains unclean until evening. Whatever an unclean person touches is unclean, and anyone else who touches it remains unclean until evening.

Events at Kadesh: 'The Lord reprimanded Moses and Aaron. He said, "Because you did not have enough faith to acknowledge my holy power before the people of Israel, you will not lead them into the land that I promised to give them." This happened at Meribah, where the people of Israel complained against the Lord and where he showed them that he was holy.' (Num. 20: 12-13)

Numbers 21.
(GNT)

Victory over Canaanite: 'When the Canaanite king of Arad in the southern part of Canaan heard that the Israelites were coming by way of Atharim; he attacked them and captured some of them. Then the Israelites made a vow to the Lord: "If you let us conquer these people, we will unconditionally dedicate them and their cities to you and destroy them." The Lord heard them and helped them to conquer the Canaanites. So the Israelites completely destroyed them and their cities, and named the place Hormah.

'The Israelites left Mount Hor by the road that leads to the Gulf of Aqaba in order to go around the territory of Edom. But on the way the people lost their patience and spoke against God and Moses. They complained. "Why did you bring us out of Egypt to die in this desert, where there is no food or water? We can't stand any more of this miserable food!" Then the Lord sent poisonous snakes among the people, and many Israelites were bitten and died.

'The people came to Moses and said, "We sinned when we spoke against the Lord and against you. Now pray to the Lord and take these snakes away." So Moses prayed for the people. Then the

Lord told Moses to make a metal snake and put it on a pole, so that anyone who was bitten could look at it and be healed. So Moses made a bronze snake and put it on a pole. Anyone who had been bitten would look at the bronze snake and be healed.' (Num. 21: 1-9) In verse 34, we read about victories over King Sihon and King Og: *The Lord said to Moses*, "Do not be afraid of him. I will give victory over him, all his people, and his land. Do to him what you did to Sihon, the Amorite king who ruled at Heshbon." So the Israelites killed Og, his sons, and all his people, leaving no survivors, and then they occupied his land.'

'The descendants of Israel are like dust—there are too many of them to be counted. Let me end my days like one of God's people' (Num. 23: 10)

'God is not like men, who lie; He is not a human who changes his mind. Whatever he promises, he does. Their king shall be greater than Agag. And his rule shall be extended far and wide. God brought them out of Egypt; he fight for them like a wild ox. They devour their enemies, crush their bones, and smash their arrows' (Num. 23: 19)

'The nation of Israel is like a mighty lion; it does not rest until it has torn and devoured, until it has drunk the blood of those it has killed' (Num. 23: 24)

In Numbers 25: 2-18, we read about *The People of Israel at Peor:* 'These women invited them to sacrificial feast, where the god of Moab was worshipped. The Israelites ate the food and worshiped the god Baal of Peor. *So the Lord was angry with them and said to Moses,* "Take all the leaders of Israel and, and in obedience to me, execute them in broad daylight, and then I will no longer be angry with the people." Moses said to the officials, "Each of you is to kill every man in your tribe who has become a worshipper of Baal of Peor". One of the Israelites took a Midianite woman into his tent in the sight of Moses and the whole community, while they were mourning at the entrance of the Tent of the Lord's presence. When Phinehas, the son of Eleazar and grandson of Aaron the priest saw this, he got up and left the assembly. He took a spear, followed the man and the woman into the tent, and drove the spear through both of them. In this way, the epidemic that was destroying Israel was stopped, but it had already killed twenty-four thousand people. *The Lord said to Moses,* "Because of what Phinehas has done, I am no longer angry with the people of Israel. He refused to tolerate the worship of any god but me, and that is why I did not destroy them in my anger. So tell him that I am making a covenant with him that is valid for all time to come. He and his descendants are permanently established as priests, because he did not tolerate any rivals to me and brought about forgiveness for the people's sin." The name of the Israelite who was killed with the Midianite woman was Zimri son of Salu, the head of the family tribe of Simeon. The woman's name was Cozbi. Zur, her father, was chief of a group of Midianite clans. *The Lord commanded Moses,* "Attack the Midianites and destroy them, *because of* the evil they did to you when they deceived you at Peor, and because of Cozbi, who was killed at the time of the epidemic at Peor.'"

In Numbers 31: 14-18, we read about *The Army Returns:* 'Moses was angry with the officers and the commanders of battalions and companies, who had returned from the war. He asked them, "Why have you kept all the women alive? Remember that it was the women who followed Balaam's instructions and at Peor led the people to be unfaithful to the Lord. That was what brought the epidemic on the Lord's people. *So now kill every boy and kill every woman who has had sexual intercourse, but keep alive for yourselves all the girls and all the women who are virgins.*"'

Make a note that God, who is a spirit, is angry in the same way as Moses, who is a physical human. Humans can naturally express emotional dissatisfaction in the form of anger. How can a spiritual thing express emotions?

In Numbers 32: 10, says, 'The Lord was angry that day and made a promise, "I swear that because they did not remain loyal to me, none of the men twenty years old or older who came out of Egypt will enter the land that I promised to Abraham, Isaac, and Jacob."

Numbers 33 extracts: GNT

'The following account gives the names and places where the Israelites set up camp after they left Egypt in their tribes under the leadership of Moses and Aaron. At the command of the Lord, Moses wrote down the name of the place each time they set up camp. The people of Israel left Egypt on the fifteenth day of the first month of the year, the day after the first Passover. Under the Lord's protection, they left the city of Rameses in full view of the Egyptians, who were burying the first-born sons that the Lord had killed. By doing this, the Lord showed that he was more powerful than the gods of Egypt. The people of Israel left Rameses and set up camp at Sukkoth. Their next camp was at Etham on the edge of the desert. From there they turned back to Pi Hahiroth, east of Baal Zephon, and camped near Migdol. They left Pi Hahiroth and passed through the Red Sea into the desert of Shur; after a three days' march they camped at Marah. From there, they went to Elim, where they camped, because there were twelve springs of water and seventy palm-trees there. They left Elim and camped near the Gulf of Suez. Their next camp was in the desert of Sin. Then they camped at Dophkah, and after that at Alush. Next was Rephidim, where there was no water for them to drink. From Rephidim to Mount Hor they set up camp at the following places: the Sinai Desert, Kibroth Hattaavah (or 'Graves of Craving'), Hazeroth, Rithmah, Rimmon Perez, Libnah, Rissah, Kehelathah, Mount Shepher, Haradah, Makheloth, Tahath, Terah, Mithkah, Hashmonah, Moseroth, Bene Jaakan, Hor Haggidgad, Jotbathah, Abronah, Eziongeber, the wilderness of Zin (that is Kadesh), and Mount Hor, at the edge of the land of Edom.

At the command of the Lord, Aaron the priest climbed Mount Hor. At the age of 123 he died there on the first day of the fifth month of the fortieth year after the Israelites had left Egypt. The king of Arad in southern Canaan heard that the Israelites were coming. From Mount Hor to the plains of Moab, the Israelites set up camp at the following places: Zalmonah, Punon, Oboth, the ruins of Abarim near Mount Nebo, and in the plains of Moab across the River Jordan from Jericho, between Beth Jeshimoth and the valley of Acacia. There were many other camp sites.

'Instructions before Crossing the Jordan: There in the plains of Moab across the Jordan from Jericho, the *Lord gave Moses the following instructions for Israel:* "When you cross the Jordan into the land of Canaan, you must drive out all the inhabitants of the land. Destroy all their stone and metal idols and all their places of worship. Occupy the land and settle in it, because I am giving it to you. Divide the land among the various tribes and clans by drawing lots, giving a large piece of property to a large clan and a small one to a small clan. But if you don't drive out the inhabitants of the land, those that are left will be as troublesome as splinters in your eyes and thorns in your sides, and they will fight against you. If you do not drive them out, I will destroy you, as I planned to destroy them."

Notice the extreme genocides angry tone of Moses and his boss (God of Israel) for not killing innocent women and children who had not caused any provocation to any Jew. And this is the God whom humanity is persuaded to accept as holiest merciful God of the universe. The Lord God of Israel gave Moses instructions to destroy everything and everyone; 'Occupy the land and settle in it, because I am giving it to you' (Num. 33: 51-53; Num. 31: 14-18). Obviously, a God for the Israelites has no sympathy for non-Jews. If there is such a thing as God for the whole mankind, he would certainly show up to defend the non-Jews who have done no wrong and are about to be slaughtered by the Jews and their satanic God of Israel.

Numbers 34 extracts. GNT: The Boundaries of the Land:

'The Lord gave to Moses the following instructions for the people of Israel. "When you enter Canaan, the land which I am giving you, the borders of your territory will be as follows. *The southern border* will extend from the wilderness of Zin along the border of Edom. It will begin on the east at the southern end of the Dead Sea. Then it will turn southward toward Akrabbim Pass and continue on through Zin as far south as Kadesh Barnea. Then it will turn northwest to Hazar Addar and on to Azmon, where it will turn toward the valley at the border of Egypt and end at the Mediterranean. *The western border* will be the Mediterranean Sea. *The northern border* will follow a line from the Mediterranean to Mount Hor and from there to Hamath Pass. It will continue to Zedad and to Ziphron, and will end at Hazar Enan. The eastern border will follow a line from Hazar Enan to Shepham. It will then go south to Harbel, east of Ain, and on to the hills on the eastern shore of Lake Galilee, then south along the Jordan River to the Dead Sea. These will be the four borders of your land." So Moses said to the Israelites, "This is the land that you will receive by drawing lots, the land that the Lord has assigned the nine and a half tribes. The tribes of Rueben and Gad and the eastern half of Manasseh have received their property, divided according to their families, on the eastern side of the Jordan, opposite Jericho."

Numbers 35; GNT: extracts. The Cities assigned to the Levites. 'In the plains of Moab across the Jordan from Jericho the Lord said to Moses. [Verse 6] "You are to give to Levites six cities of refuge to which a man can escape if he kills someone accidentally. In addition, give them forty-two other cities with their pasture lands, making a total of forty-eight. The number of Levite cities in each tribe is to be determined according to the size of its territory".

'The Cities of Refuge: The Lord told Moses to say to the people of Israel: 'When you cross the Jordan River and enter the land of Canaan, you are to choose cities of refuge to which a man can escape if he kills someone accidentally. There he will be saved from the dead man's relative who seeks revenge. A man accused of manslaughter is not to be put to death without a public trial. Choose six cities, three east of Jordan and three in the land of Canaan. These will serve as cities of refuge for Israelites and for foreigners who are temporary or permanent residents. Anyone who kills someone accidentally can escape to one of them. If, however, a man uses a weapon of iron or of stone or wood to kill someone, he is guilty of murder, and is to be put to death. The dead man's nearest relative has the responsibility for putting the murderer to death. When he finds him, he is to kill him. If a man hates someone and kills him by pushing him down or by throwing something at him, or by striking him with his fist, he is guilty of murder and is to be put to death. The dead man's nearest relative has the responsibility for putting the murderer to death. When he finds him, he is to kill him.

'But suppose a man accidentally kills someone he does not hate, whether by pushing him down or by throwing something at him. Or, suppose that, without looking, a man throws a stone that kills someone whom he did not intend to hurt and who was not his enemy. In such cases, the community shall judge in favour of the man who caused the death and in favour of the dead man's relative who is seeking revenge. The community is to rescue the man guilty of manslaughter from the dead man's relative, and they are to return him to the city of refuge to which he had escaped. He must live there until the death of the man who is then High Priest. If the man guilty of manslaughter leaves the city of refuge to which he has escaped and if the dead man's relative finds and kills him, this act of revenge is not murder. The man guilty of manslaughter must remain in the city until the death of the High Priest, but after that he may return home. These rules apply to you and your descendant wherever you may live. A man accused of murder may be found guilty and put to death only on the evidence of two or more witnesses. The evidence of one witness is not sufficient to support an accusation of murder. A murderer must be put to death. He cannot escape this penalty by the payment of money. If a man has fled to a city of refuge, do not allow him to make a payment in order to return home before the death of the High Priest. If you did this, you would defile the land where you are living. Murder defiles the land, and except by the death by the death of the murderer there is no way to perform the ritual of purification for the land where a man has been murdered. Do not defile the land where you are living, because I am the Lord and I live among the people of Israel'.

Numbers 36 extracts. The Inheritance of Married Women:

'The heads of the families in the clan of Gilead, the son of Machir and grandson of Manasseh, son of Joseph, went to Moses and the other leaders. They said, "The Lord commanded you to distribute the land to the people of Israel by drawing lots. He also commanded you to give the property of our relative Zelophehad to his daughters. But remember if they marry men of another tribe, their property will then belong to the tribe, and the total allotted to us will be reduced. In the Year of Restoration, when all property that has been sold is restored to its original owners, the property of Zelophehad's daughters will be permanently added to the tribe into which they marry and will be lost to our tribe". So Moses gave the people of Israel the following command from the Lord. He said, "What the tribe of Manasseh says is right, and so the Lord says that the daughters of Zelophehad are free to marry anyone they wish, but only within their own tribe. The property of every Israelite will remain attached to his tribe. Every woman who inherits property in an Israelite tribe must marry a man belonging to that tribe. In this way each Israelite will inherit the property of his ancestors, and the property will not pass from one tribe to another. Each tribe will continue to possess its' own property." 'So Mahlah, Tirzah, Hoglah, Milcah, and Noah the daughters of Zelophehad did as the

Lord had commanded Moses, and they married their cousins. They married within the clans of the tribe of Manasseh, son of Joseph, and their property remained in their father's tribe. *These are the rules and regulations that the Lord gave the Israelites through Moses in the plains of Moab across the River Jordan from Jericho.'*

The book of Numbers is not different from the books of Leviticus, Exodus, and Deuteronomy when measured by their satanic contents. The best rational conclusion we can draw from these books, certainly, is the failure of the authors to separate human's fallible behaviour from God's infallible behaviour.

If God is not different from mankind, or God is not the Almighty, what then is the essence or the purpose of God to mankind? Do we really, really need God; especially as perceived by ancient Jews in the Holy Bible?

For all those who see a need for a God, I say, look within yourself or within your culture for your particular nature of God. Because rationally speaking, there is no God anywhere outside you than yourself. Believe in yourself, and don't give up when it gets harder to accomplish a goal. The hardest point in every deliberation is when all efforts are exhausted or the time when the best of you is yearning to come out. Godly ideas are mere distractions to progress in life. The behaviour of this Jewish God according to the Holy Bible is more satanic than Satan himself and very, very delusional.

According to Deuteronomy

(GNT Source)

Deuteronomy 1

Verses 3: 'On the first day of the eleventh month of the fortieth year after they had left Egypt, Moses told the people everything the Lord had commanded him to tell them.'

Verses 5-8: 'It was while the people were at the east of the Jordan in the territory of Moab that Moses began to explain God's laws and teachings. He said, "When we were at Mount Sinai, the Lord our God said to us that we have stayed long enough at this mountain. That we should break camp and move on. Go to the hill country of the Amorites and to all the surrounding regions—to the Jordan Valley, to the hill country and the lowlands, to the southern region, and to the Mediterranean coast. Go to the land of Canaan and on beyond the Lebanon Mountains as far as the great Euphrates River. All of this is the land which I, the Lord, promised to give to your ancestors, Abraham, Isaac, and Jacob, and to their descendants. Go and occupy it.' as according to Moses.

Moses still continues from Verses 13-16: 'Choose some wise, understanding, and experienced men from each tribe, and I will put them in charge of each tribe. Some were responsible for a thousand people, some for a hundred, some for fifty, and some for ten. I also appointed other officials throughout the tribes. 16 "At that time I instructed them to listen to the disputes that come up among the people. Judge every dispute fairly, whether it concerns only your own people or involves foreigners who live among you. Show no partiality in your decisions; judge everyone on the same basis, no matter who they are. Do not be afraid of anyone, for the decisions you make come from God. If any case is too difficult for you, bring it to me, and I will decide it." This is a good show of real leadership by Moses as controlled by the Jewish God of Israel.

Verses 34-39: 'The Lord heard your complaints and became angry, and so he solemnly declared that not one of you from this evil generation will enter the fertile land that he promised to give your ancestors.

'And God said only Caleb the son of Jephunneh will enter it because he has remained faithful to him, and he will give him and his descendants the land that he has explored.

'Moses said because of them the Lord also became angry with him and said, "Even I, Moses, will not enter the Promised Land." He rather strengthened the determination of your helper, Joshua

112

son of Nun to lead Israel to occupy the land. The Lord said to all of us, "Your children, who are still too young to know right from wrong, will enter the land. The children you said would be seized by your enemies. I will give the land to them, and they will occupy it."

Big question is, where does God place the indigenous non-Jewish people who lived on the land the same God intend to give to the children of Israel? They too deserve a place to live and also a land for their descendants. They have lived on that land for centuries. That land is their ancestral land. If God is the creator of all humans, God must have placed the original inhabitants there in the first place. Dear reader, please think about it. Don't they deserve a share of this planet earth too? God has a duty of care for all mankind without bias.

In Deuteronomy 2: 22-37, it is said that 'The Lord had done the same thing for the Edomites, the descendants of Esau, who lived in the hill country of Edom. He destroyed the Horites, so that the Edomites took over their land and settled there, where they still live. The land along the Mediterranean coast had been settled by people from the island of Crete. They had destroyed the Avvim, the original inhabitants, and had taken over all their land as far south as the city of Gaza.) 'After we had passed through Moab, the Lord told us, "Now, start out and cross the Arnon River. I am placing in your power Sihon, the Amorite king of Heshbon, along with his land. Attack him, and begin occupying his land. From today on I will make people everywhere afraid of you. Everyone will tremble with fear at the mention of your name. Then I sent messengers from the desert of Kedemoth to King Sihon of Heshbon with the following offer of peace: "Let us pass through your country. We will go straight through and not leave the road. We will pay for the food we eat and the water we drink. All we want to do is to pass through your country, until we cross the Jordan River into the land that the Lord our God is giving us. The descendants of Esau, who live in Edom, and the Moabites, who live in Ar, allowed us to pass through their territory," but King Sihon would not let us pass through his country. The Lord your God had made him stubborn and rebellious, so that we could defeat him and take his territory, which we still occupy. 'Then the Lord said to me, 'Look, I have made King Sihon and his land helpless before you, take his land and occupy it." Sihon came out with all his men to fight us near the town of Jahaz. The Lord our God put him in our power, and we killed him, his sons, and all his men. At the same time we captured and destroyed every town, and put everyone to death, men, women, and children. *We left no survivors. We took the livestock and plundered the towns.* The Lord our God let us capture all the towns from Aroer, on the edge of the Arnon Valley, and the city in the middle of that valley, all the way to Gilead. No town had walls too strong for us. But we did not go near the territory of the Ammonites or to the banks of the Jabbok River or to the towns of the hill country or to any other place where the Lord our God had commanded us not to go.'

'The Lord God of Israel said, "Look, I have made King Sihon stubborn and rebellious I have made him and his land helpless before you. Take his land and occupy it."' Can a God for all mankind, including King Sihon and his subjects, the supposed righteous benevolent God, really say this? God's reason for this wicked act is simply that he needs the land for the Israelites. Please read above verse. The entire text is Unbelievable! Can you, the reader, explain why God should be so wicked? How do we separate biblical satanic behaviour from godly behaviour?

Lord God of Israel continues his diabolic assault on peaceful non-Hebrew inhabitant in Canaan and the surrounding neighbours. Deuteronomy 3: (GNT); 'Next, we moved north toward the region of Bashan, and King Og came out with all his men to fight us near the town of Edrei. But the Lord said to me, "Don't be afraid of him. I am going to give him, his men, and all his territory to you.

Do the same thing to him that you did to Sihon the Amorite king who ruled in Heshbon." ₃ So the Lord also placed King Og and his people in our power, *and we slaughtered them all.*

'At the same time we captured all his towns—there was not one that we did not take. In all we captured sixty towns—the whole region of Argob, where King Og of Bashan ruled. All these towns were fortified with high walls, gates, and bars to lock the gates, and there were also many villages without walls. ₆ *We destroyed all the towns and put to death all the men, women, and children, just as we did in the towns that belonged to King Sihon of Heshbon. We took the livestock and plundered the towns.* At that time we took from those two Amorite kings the land east of the Jordan River, from the Arnon River to Mount Hermon (Mount Hermon is called Sirion by the Sidonians, and Senir by the Amorites.)

'We took all the territory of King Og of Bashan: the cities on the plateau, the regions of Gilead and of Bashan, as far east as the towns of Salecah and Edrei. (King Og was the last of the Rephaim. His coffin, made of stone, was six feet wide and almost fourteen feet long, according to standard measurements. It can still be seen in the Ammonite city of Rabbah.)

'When we took possession of the land, I assigned to the tribes of Reuben and Gad the territory north of the town of Aroer near the Arnon River and part of the hill country of Gilead, along with its towns. To half the tribe of Manasseh I assigned the rest of Gilead and also all of Bashan, where Og had ruled, that is, the entire Argob region. (Bashan was known as the land of the Rephaim. Jair, from the tribe of Manasseh, took the entire region of Argob, that is, Bashan, as far as the border of Geshur and Maacah. He named the villages after himself, and they are still known as the villages of Jair.)

'I assigned Gilead to the clan of Machir of the tribe of Manasseh. ₁₆ And to the tribes of Reuben and Gad I assigned the territory from Gilead to the Arnon River. The middle of the river was their southern boundary, and their northern boundary was the Jabbok River, part of which formed the Ammonite border. On the west their territory extended to the Jordan River, from Lake Galilee in the north down to the Dead Sea in the south and to the foot of Mount Pisgah on the east. At the same time, I gave them the following instructions: *"The Lord our God has given you this land east of the Jordan to occupy. Now arm your fighting men and send them across the Jordan ahead of the other tribes of Israel, to help them occupy their land . . .* Don't be afraid of them, for the Lord your God will fight for you.'" Is the God of Israel, the one who is commanding Moses, the same God for the people who lived in the east and west of Jordan? If they are not part of the children of God, then who created the original inhabitants of that land? Is the Jewish creation idea in Genesis true? All men are supposed to be created equal, but definitely some men are more equal and preferred by God of Israel than others. God of Israel is surely a God, only, for Israelites. All Christians who are desperate for a God must read the above chapters and assess if this ancient Jewish horrible God can be their God by choice.

Deuteronomy 4 (GNT)

'Then Moses said to the people, "Obey all the laws that I am teaching you, and you will live and occupy the land which the Lord, the God of your ancestors, is giving you. Do not add anything to what I command you, and do not take anything away. Obey the commands of the Lord your God that I have given you. You yourselves saw what the Lord did at Mount Peor. He destroyed everyone who worshiped Baal there, but those of you who were faithful to the Lord your God are still alive today. I have taught you all the laws, as the Lord my God told me to do. Obey them in the land that you are about to invade and occupy. Obey them faithfully, and this will show the people of other nations how wise you are. When they hear of all these laws, they will say, 'What wisdom and understanding this great nation has!' No other nation, no matter

116

how great, has a god who is so near when they need him as the Lord our God is to us. He answers us whenever we call for help. No other nation, no matter how great, has laws so just as those that I have taught you today. Be on your guard! Make certain that you do not forget, as long as you live, what you have seen with your own eyes. Tell your children and your grandchildren ₁₀ about the day you stood in the presence of the Lord your God at Mount Sinai, when he said to me, 'Assemble the people. I want them to hear what I have to say, so that they will learn to obey me as long as they live and so that they will teach their children to do the same.'

"'Tell your children how you went and stood at the foot of the mountain which was covered with thick clouds of dark smoke and fire blazing up to the sky. Tell them how the Lord spoke to you from the fire, *how you heard him speaking but did not see him in any form at all.* He told you what you must do to keep the covenant he made with you—you must obey the Ten Commandments, which he wrote on two stone tablets.' The Lord told me to teach you all the laws that you are to obey in the land that you are about to invade and occupy. 'When the Lord spoke to you from the fire on Mount Sinai, you did not see any form. For your own good, then, make certain that you do not sin by making for yourselves an idol in any form; be it a man or woman, animal, bird, reptile, or fish. ₁₉ *Do not be tempted to worship and serve what you see in the sky—the sun, the moon, and the stars. The Lord your God has given these to all other peoples for them to worship . . . Obey his command not to make for yourselves any kind of idol* ₂₄ *because the Lord your God is like a flaming fire; he tolerates no rivals.* Even when you have been in the land a long time and have children and grandchildren, do not sin by making for yourselves an idol in any form at all. This is evil in the Lord's sight, and it will make him angry. I call heaven and earth as witnesses against you today that, if you disobey me, you will soon disappear from the land. You will not live very long in the land across the Jordan that you are about to occupy. You will be completely destroyed. The Lord will scatter you among other nations, where only a few of you will survive. There you will serve gods made by human hands, gods of wood and stone, gods that cannot see or hear, eat or smell. ₂₉ There you will look for the Lord your God, and if you search for him with all your heart, you will find him. When you are in trouble and all those things happen to you, then you will finally turn to the Lord and obey him. He is a merciful God. He will not abandon you or destroy you, and he will not forget the covenant that he himself made with your ancestors."

'Merciful God' indeed to his own beloved ancient Israelites! I hope the reader has followed the consistency of this Jewish God— that he is only for the Jews. Every non-Jew resident of the fertile lands mentioned above must, by force, be surrounded and wiped out, and be occupied by Reverend Moses and his vicious gangsters, because the Almighty God of Israel has commanded it to be so. Moses himself perished during the Exodus. Because he loved your ancestors, he chose you, and by his great power he himself brought you out of Egypt. As you advanced, he drove out nations greater and more powerful than you, so that he might bring you in and give you their land, the land which still belongs to you. ₃₉ So remember today and never forget: the Lord is God in heaven and on earth. There is no other god.

'Obey all his laws that I have given you today and all will go well with you and your descendants. You will continue to live in the land that the Lord your God is giving you to be yours forever.' Moses gave God's laws and teachings to the people of Israel.

Verse 39 says 'heaven and earth.' The author implies the universe as a whole rather than the nations of ancient Jews. Why is it necessary for God to prove to the Israelites and not the whole world that he is the only God in the universe? This universe in question must surely be the ancient Jewish universe and definitely not the cosmic universe which embraces all humanity on planet earth!

Over 2,000 years ago, ancient people's idea of heaven and earth or the universe was limited to each community's horizon. A small hamlet or village was seen as a nation or world. Their idea of the universe was definitely different from what we understand today as a nation or universe or the globe which we call planet earth today. All biblical references to heaven and earth or the universe must be understood to be applicable only in its narrowest ancient view of their little community's horizon.

With all his supposed awesome overall powers, couldn't God just destroy all other gods or prevent humanity from worshipping idols? Why is it that the God of Israel is so jealous of other gods if every earthly thing is his creation or within his control? It must indeed be emphasized here that the choice of a God for the Israelites was *not* made by the Jews themselves. It was unilaterally decided by God himself. (GNT) *Numbers 15, 41;* says, *'I brought you out of Egypt because I the Lord want to be your God.....'* What is God's problem if the people of Israel don't want him to be their God? Or for that matter, what if human beings do not want to worship him as their God? Why must we accept something invisible, a divine thing, as our source of power? Throughout the Old Testament, the Jews have consistently stated that they are comfortable with idol worshipping. God of Israel has always been a nuisance to the people of Israel. Several commandments which God himself abused many times are expected to be obeyed by the Jews.

Deuteronomy 5 (GNT)
The Ten Commandments:
'¹ Moses called together all the people of Israel and said to them, "People of Israel listen to all the laws that I am giving you today. Learn them and be sure that you obey them. ² At Mount Sinai the Lord our God made a covenant, ³ not only with our fathers, but with all of us who are living today. ⁴ There on the mountain the Lord spoke to you face-to-face from the fire. ₅ I stood between you

and the Lord at that time to tell you what he said, because you were afraid of the fire and would not go up the mountain. The Lord said, [6] 'I am the Lord your God, who rescued you from Egypt, where you were slaves. [7] Worship no god but me. [8] Do not make for you images of anything in heaven or on earth or in the water under the earth. [9] Do not bow down to any idol or worship it, for I am the Lord your God and I tolerate no rivals. I bring punishment on those who hate me and on their descendants down to the third and fourth generation. [10] But I show my love to thousands of generations of those who love me and obey my laws. [11] Do not use my name for evil purposes, for I, the Lord your God, will punish anyone who misuses my name.

[12] 'Observe the Sabbath and keep it holy, as I, the Lord your God, have commanded you. [13] You have six days in which to do your work, [14] but the seventh day is a day of rest dedicated to me. On that day no one is to work; not you, your children, your animals, or the foreigners who live in your country are permitted to work. *Your slaves must rest just as you do.* That is why I command you to observe the Sabbath. [16] Respect your father and your mother, as I, the Lord your God, command you, so that all may go well with you and so that you may live a long time in the land that I am giving you. [17] Do not commit murder. [18] Do not commit adultery. [19] Do not steal. [20] Do not accuse anyone falsely. [21] Do not desire another man's wife; do not desire his house, his land, his slaves, his cattle, his donkeys, or anything else that he owns.' [22] "These are the commandments the Lord gave to all of you when you were gathered at the mountain. When he spoke with a mighty voice from the fire and from the thick clouds, he gave these commandments and no others. Then he wrote them on two stone tablets and gave them to me. [29] 'If only they would always feel this way! If only they would always honour me and obey all my commands, so that everything would go well with them and their descendants forever. [30] Go and tell them to return to their tents. [31] But you, Moses, stay here with me, and I will give

you all my laws and commands. Teach them to the people, so that they will obey them in the land that I am giving them.' ₃₂ "People of Israel, be sure that you do everything that the Lord your God has commanded you. Do not disobey any of his laws. ₃₃ Obey them all, so that everything will go well with you and so that you will continue to live in the land that you are going to occupy."'

Note that from verse 7 to verse 21 are a set of fifteen new commandments which are different from the Ten Commandments given to only the people of Israel and they are to be obeyed as long as they continue to live on the Promised Land according to Deuteronomy chapter 5. The laws are not for non-Jews or those who are not residents of the Promised Land.

All the laws were however broken by the same God of Israel in several chapters and verses from Genesis through to Joshua many times over. If the lawmaker breaks his own laws, everyone else will not hesitate to break them. If the total Twenty-five Commandments and the rest of the Israelites' customary laws were actually made by the God of Israel, it is not likely that a universal God will flout them. And if there is punishment for every offence, all those who abuse the law, including the lawmaker must face justice. Generally, lawmakers or legislators are law-abiding people because they know very well that if they themselves break their own laws, others too would disrespect the laws. Indeed the citizens of Israel have demonstrated on numerous occasions their disapproval of the self-styled God of Israel's commandments and regulations. Indeed, the God Israel had not forgotten that he took his beloved Jews out of slavery in Egypt, because he knew servitude was evil and unacceptable. But in Deuteronomy 5, 14-15, he gives directions to his liberated Jews as how to handle people enslaved by Jews.

The God of Israel is indeed a God for the Israelites.

'These are all the laws that the Lord your God commanded me to teach you. Obey them in the land that you are about to enter and occupy. ₂ As long as you live, you and your descendants are to honour the Lord your God and obey all his laws that I am giving you, so that you may live in that land a long time. Listen to them, people of Israel, and obey them! Then all will go well with you, and you will become a mighty nation and live in that rich and fertile land, just as the Lord, the God of our ancestors, has promised. ₄ Israel, remember this! The Lord—and the Lord alone—is our God. ₅ Love the Lord your God with all your heart, with all your soul, and with all your strength. ₆ Never forget these commands that I am giving you today. ₇ Teach them to your children. Repeat them when you are at home and when you are away, when you are resting and when you are working. ₈ Tie them on your arms and wear them on your foreheads as a reminder. ₉ Write them on the doorposts of your houses and on your gates. ₁₀ Just as the Lord your God promised your ancestors, Abraham, Isaac, and Jacob, he will give you a land with large and prosperous cities which you did not build. ₁₁ The houses will be full of good things which you did not put in them, and there will be wells that you did not dig, and vineyards and olive orchards that you did not plant. When the Lord brings you into this land and you have all you want to eat, ₁₂ make certain that you do not forget the Lord who rescued you from Egypt, where you were slaves.

'₁₃ Honour the Lord your God, worship only him, and make your promises in his name alone. ₁₄ Do not worship other gods, any of the gods of the peoples around you. ₁₅ If you do worship other gods, the Lord's anger will come against you like fire and will destroy you completely, because *the Lord your God, who is present with you, tolerates no rivals.*'₁₆ *Do not put the Lord your God to the test*, as you did at Massah.' (GNT).

The main purpose of every test is to prove or disprove the knowledge. The God in Genesis and the God of Israel are very famous in testing humans, although Bible readers are informed of God's extraordinary knowledge of every human action ahead of time. A few examples of these test cases are Adam and Eve's test in the Garden of Eden; the several tests on Moses, Aaron, and Joshua during the Exodus; Abraham's faith test of his son Isaac as a sacrificial lamb; Job's faith tests, Daniel, Jonah, Jesus Christ, Paul, etc. Humans need tests because we are fallible creatures with limited knowledge in everything. A spiritual entity needs no test.

Again, 'the Lord your God tolerates no rivals,' as in verse 15 above, makes no sense. Holy Bible readers are informed many times that God is the Almighty. He possesses infinite powers beyond everyone and everything; hence, there is no reason there should be rival of any kind to challenge him on anything. God is supposed to be invincible. Humans have rivals because we are vulnerable. God should not be afraid of idols competition.

'₁₇ Be sure that you obey all the laws that he has given you. ₁₈ Do what the Lord says is right and good, and all will go well with you. You will be able to take possession of the fertile land that the Lord promised your ancestors, ₁₉ and you will drive out your enemies, as he promised. ₂₀ In times to come your children will ask you, "Why did the Lord our God command us to obey all these laws?"

₂₁ Then tell them, "We were slaves of the king of Egypt, and the Lord rescued us by his great power. ₂₂ With our own eyes we saw him work miracles and do terrifying things to the Egyptians and to their king and to all his officials. ₂₃ He freed us from Egypt to bring us here and give us this land, as he had promised our ancestors he would. ₂₄ Then the Lord our God commanded us to obey all these laws and to honour him. If we do, he will always watch over our nation and keep it prosperous. ₂₅ If we faithfully obey everything that God has commanded us, he will be pleased with us."'

'The Lord your God will bring you into the land that you are going to occupy and he will drive many nations out of it. As you advance, he will drive out seven nations larger and more powerful than you: the Hittites, the Girgashites, the Amorites, the Canaanites, the Perizzites, the Hivites, and the Jebusites. When the Lord your God places these people in your power and you defeat them, you must put them all to death. Do not make an alliance with them or show them any mercy. Do not marry any of them, and do not let your children marry any of them, because then they would lead your children away from the Lord to worship other gods. If that happens, the Lord will be angry with you and destroy you at once. Do this because you belong to the Lord your God. From all the peoples on earth he chose you to be his own special people. ₇ *'The Lord did not love you and choose you because you outnumbered other peoples; you were the smallest nation on earth.* ₈ But the Lord loved you and wanted to keep the promise that he made to your ancestors. That is why he saved you by his great might and set you free from slavery to the king of Egypt. ₉ Remember that the Lord your God is the only God and that he is faithful.

'He will love you and bless you, so that you will increase in number and have many children; he will bless your fields, so that you will have grain, wine, and olive oil; and he will bless you by giving you many cattle and sheep. He will give you all these blessings in the land that he promised your ancestors he would give to you. ₁₄ *No people in the world will be as richly blessed as you.* None of you or any of your livestock will be sterile.'

If millions of Christians over the world view God of Israel as their God as well, what will be this God's excuse for pronouncing that 'No people in the world will be as richly blessed as Jews?' What is so special about Jews that the rest of humanity don't have, that the God of Israel is so determined to make it his business to represent them? Why all agnostic such as me cannot say that this God of Israel cannot be a God for the whole mankind? The God has not even succeeded in convincing the Israelites that he is their God. Why can't I ask Christians to look somewhere else for their cultural ancestral God, if they are so desperate for a God? Even the livestock owned by Jews are also blessed by this God! The author of the book of Deuteronomy sounds very confused.

'The Lord will protect you from all sickness, and he will not bring on you any of the dreadful diseases that you experienced in Egypt, but he will bring them on all your enemies. 16 Destroy every nation that the Lord your God places in your power, and do not show them any mercy. Do not worship their gods, for that would be fatal. Do not tell yourselves that these peoples outnumber you and that you cannot drive them out. 18 Do not be afraid of them; remember what the Lord your God did to the king of Egypt and to all his people. Remember the terrible plagues that you saw with your own eyes, the miracles and wonders, and the great power and strength by which the Lord your God set you free. In the same way that he destroyed the Egyptians, he will destroy all these people that you now fear.

' 20 He will even cause panic among them and will destroy those who escape and go into hiding. 21 So do not be afraid of these people. The Lord your God is with you; he is a great God and one to be feared. 22 Little by little he will drive out these nations as you advance. You will not be able to destroy them all at once, for, if you did, the number of wild animals would increase and be a threat to you. 23 The Lord will put your enemies in your power and make them panic until they are destroyed. 24 He will put their kings in your power. You will kill them, and they will be forgotten. No one will be able to stop you; you will destroy everyone. 25 Burn their idols. Do not desire the silver or gold that is on them, and do not take it for yourselves. If you do, that will be fatal, *because the Lord hates idolatry.* 26 Do not bring any of these idols into your homes, or the same curse will be on you that are on them. You must hate and despise these idols, because they are under the Lord's curse.'

Can other gods or lesser gods really pose a threat to a greater God himself. *Burn all idols. The Lord hates idols. You must hate and despise these idols* Where is the omnipotence qualification of God of Israel? Can our universal God really be powerless to be threatened by lesser God? These questions are very relevant if we see this

Jewish God as our universal God. Is he really fit to be a God for all of us? The so renowned most powerful designer of all! What do you think? Is this not sufficient evidence to dump this ancient Jewish fantasy?

Deuteronomy 8: extract

'₁ Obey faithfully all the laws that I have given you today, so that you may live, increase in number, and occupy the land that the Lord promised to your ancestors. Remember how the Lord your God led you on this long journey through the desert these past forty years, sending hardships to test you, so that he might know what you intended to do and whether you would obey his commands. ₃ He made you go hungry, and then he gave you manna to eat, food that you and your ancestors had never eaten before. He did this to teach you that you must not depend on bread alone to sustain you, but on everything that the Lord says. ₄ During these forty years your clothes have not worn out, nor have your feet swollen up. ₅ Remember that the Lord your God corrects and punishes you just as parents discipline their children. ₆ So then, do as the Lord has commanded you: live according to his laws and obey him. Moses: ₇ The Lord your God is bringing you into a fertile land—a land that has rivers and springs, and underground streams gushing out into the valleys and hills; ₈ a land that produces wheat and barley, grapes, figs, pomegranates, olives, and honey.'

How does God of Israel account for the indigenous people who have lived on the Promised Land for centuries, the thousands he commanded Moses and his assassins to kill? Is God justified in killing all the men, women, children, and livestock, just to secure land for the descendants of Abraham, Isaac, and Jacob?

'There you will never go hungry or ever be in need. Its rocks have iron in them, and from its hills you can mine copper. You will have all you want to eat, and you will give thanks to the Lord your God for the fertile land that he has given you. ₁₁ Make certain that you do not forget the Lord your God; do not fail to obey any of his laws that I am giving you today. ₁₂ When you have all you want to eat and have built good houses to live in ₁₃ and when your cattle and sheep, your silver and gold, and all your other possessions have increased, ₁₄ be sure that you do not become proud and forget the Lord your God who rescued you from Egypt, where you were slaves. ₁₅ He led you through that vast and terrifying desert where there were poisonous snakes and scorpions. In that dry and waterless land, he made water flow out of solid rock for you. ₁₆ In the desert he gave you manna to eat, food that your ancestors had never eaten. *He sent hardships on you to test you, so that in the end he could bless you with good things.'*

If all life is his creation and destiny is under his control, God of Israel should know what will happen ten years from now before the event. Why should 'he send hardship to test' humans and later bless humans 'with good things'? Christians must answer this question.

'₁₇ So then, you must never think that you have made yourselves wealthy by your own power and strength. ₁₈ Remember that it is the Lord your God who gives you the power to become rich. He does this because he is still faithful today to the covenant that he made with your ancestors. 19 Never forget the Lord your God or turn to other gods to worship and serve them. If you do, then I warn you today that you will certainly be destroyed. 20 If you do not obey the Lord, then you will be destroyed just like those nations that he is going to destroy as you advance.'

Sometimes the author of Deuteronomy's choice of words, and sentences, to narrate a story makes it difficult to understand the core meaning of texts, but here in Deuteronomy 9: 1, 'Listen, people of Israel,' the sentence is very simple and explicit. Everything is in reference to Israelites and their God: definitely not every human being and not the voice of our supposed heavenly father, the global singular God either. Christians may be tempted wrongly to apply this simple text to every human being.

Deuteronomy 8: 18 as quoted above says 'It is the Lord *your* God who gives you the power to become rich'. If a curious person sets an inquiry to interview most rich people to find out how they became rich, it is most likely that most will say it is through good business decisions they made, self-confidence, an uncompromising desire to succeed, hard work, and staying focused. God as a spirit has no role in this struggle to become whoever you want to be. If you note the quoted verse carefully, it says "your God". But you can replace the two words with 'your brain,' because at the end of it all, the total stock of information stored in your brain organ from birth to date is what you can use, by either praying to the spiritual God for help or by sorting out the best knowledge you possess in your brain to launch your desire without prayers. We should remember that the information about God which we use in prayers is also part of our knowledge bank. But prudently speaking, we can say that *one* of these information choices, *spiritual power* and *knowledge power*, will be more predictable and dependable than the other. Yes, the brain power can be quantified, predictable, and more dependable in all logical manners. We can therefore logically conclude that success in human life, wealth, power, and fame, are self-created and self- dependent. It has nothing to do with spirit or spiritual ideas.

Focus seriously on a search for quality knowledge, plus faith in the self, and everything will be possible. Success cannot be possible by opening your arms, gazing at the sky, and talking or asking for spiritual help. *Dependence on spiritual power will surely guarantee everlasting decadence and poverty*. Dependence on brain power can surely guarantee success no matter who you are, religious or irreligious.

The danger in spiritual dependency is that it has the potential to divert your focal point to actions which are not predictable and waste of time and your hard-earned resources.

If you notice carefully, you will see that the people of Israel never trusted the God of Israel. God of Israel imposed himself onto the Jews as their God. Numbers 15: 41 says, 'I am the Lord your God. I brought you out of Egypt to be your God.' The Jews never chose to leave Egypt voluntarily or to have a God specifically designed for them. They preferred to do things their own ways. They did not want to rely on the God of Israel because that God proved untrustworthy as compared to their favorite Gods.

Practically, when the Bible makes reference to your Lord God, it is referring to yourself, 'the self', your brain organ which practically makes everything about you possible. That is the reason why the Bible says God is everywhere; yes, everywhere because you cannot be anywhere without your brain. You are your own God. Feed your brain with quality information. Seek quality knowledge, live with a dream, and all dreams can be realized. Spiritual God is needless and counterproductive. Spiritualism blocks the brain's power to process critical ideas.

In Deuteronomy chapter 9, it will be noticed that the author is narrating a lengthy conversation between God of Israel and Moses. It appears the conversation was going on in the presence of all the Israelites, who are possibly assembled in a huge campsite or an auditorium. Moses draws their attention with a summary of the overall significance of their evacuation from Egypt.

"Listen, people of Israel, today you are about to cross the Jordan River and occupy the land belonging to nations greater and more powerful than you. Their cities are large, with walls that reach the sky. $_2$ The people themselves are tall and strong; they are giants, and you have heard it said that no one can stand against them. $_3$ But now you will see for yourselves that the Lord your God will go ahead of you like a raging fire. He will defeat them as you advance, so that you will drive them out and destroy them quickly, as he promised. $_4$ After the Lord your God has driven them out for you, do not say to yourselves that he brought you in to possess this land because you deserved it. No, the Lord is going to drive these people out for you because they are wicked. It is not because you are good and do what is right that the Lord is letting you take their land. *He will drive them out because they are wicked and because he intends to keep the promise that he made to your ancestors, Abraham, Isaac, and Jacob. 6 You can be sure that the Lord is not giving you this fertile land because you deserve it. No, you are a stubborn people. 7 Never forget how you made the Lord your God angry in the desert.* From the day that you left Egypt until the day you arrived here, you have rebelled against him. 8 Even at Mount Sinai you made the Lord angry—angry enough to destroy you. 9 I went up the mountain to receive the stone tablets on which was written the covenant that the Lord had made with you. I stayed there forty days and nights and did not eat or drink anything. 10 Then the Lord gave me the two stone tablets on which he had written with his own hand what he had said to you from the fire on the day that you were gathered there at the mountain. 11 Yes, after those forty days and nights the Lord gave me the two stone tablets on which he had written the covenant. 12 Then the Lord said to me, "Go down the mountain at once, because your people, whom you led out of Egypt, have become corrupt and have done evil. They have already turned away from what I commanded them to do, and they have made an idol for themselves." 13 The Lord also said to me, "I know how stubborn these people are. 14 Don't try to stop me. I intend to destroy them so that no one will remember them any longer. Then I will make you the father of a nation larger and more powerful than they are." 15 So I turned and went down the mountain, carrying the two stone tablets on which the covenant was written. Flames of fire were coming from the mountain. 16 I saw that you had already disobeyed the command that the Lord your God had given you, and that you had sinned against him by making yourselves a metal idol in the form of a bull-calf. 17 So there in front of you I threw the stone tablets down and broke them to pieces. 18 Then once again I lay face downward in the Lord's presence for forty days and nights and did not eat or drink anything. I did this because you had sinned against the Lord and had made him angry. 19 I was afraid of the

Lord's fierce anger, because he was furious enough to destroy you; but once again the Lord listened to me. ₂₀ The Lord was also angry enough with Aaron to kill him, so I prayed for Aaron at the same time. ₂₁ I took that sinful thing that you had made—that metal bull-calf—and threw it into the fire. Then I broke it in pieces, ground it to dust, and threw the dust into the stream that flowed down the mountain. ₂₂ You also made the Lord your God angry when you were at Taberah, Massah, and Kibroth Hattaavah. ₂₃ And when he sent you from Kadesh Barnea with orders to go and take possession of the land that he was giving you, *you rebelled against him; you did not trust the Lord or obey him.* ₂₄ *Ever since I have known you, you have rebelled against the Lord.* And I prayed, 'Sovereign Lord, don't destroy your own people, the people you rescued and brought out of Egypt by your great strength and power. ₂₇ Remember your servants, Abraham, Isaac, and Jacob, and do not pay any attention to the stubbornness, wickedness, and sin of this people. ₂₈ Otherwise, the Egyptians will say that you were unable to take your people into the land that you had promised them. They will say that you took your people out into the desert to kill them, because you hated them. ₂₉ After all, these are the people whom you chose to be your own and whom you brought out of Egypt by your great power and might.'

What makes the Israelites so special from the rest of mankind that the supposed universal *God chooses* them as his favorite human beings? Can this God really be the God for all mankind, at the same time, with this serious prejudice in favour of only one race of people, ancient Jews? Besides, God knows very well that his best chosen people are notoriously bad (Deut. 9: 13), yet these are the race of people which God of Israel finds it irresistible to let alone.

In this chapter, the fallible human Moses is advising the infallible invincible God of Israel on the best action to take. Although the text is written as prayers in verse 27, Moses said, 'Remember your servants, Abraham, Isaac, and Jacob, and do not pay attention to the stubbornness, wickedness, and sin of this people.' In verse 28, Moses continues to say, 'Otherwise the Egyptians will say that you were unable to take your people into the land that you promised them.'

We read in Deuteronomy 10: 15, 'But the Lord's loves for your ancestors were so strong that *he chose you instead of any other people.*' Deuteronomy 10: 17; 'The Lord your God is supreme over all gods and over all powers. He is great and mighty, and he is to be obeyed. *He does not show partiality and he does not accept bribes.*'

Verses 15 and 17 above contradict each other: 'he chose you instead of any other people' and 'he does not show partiality?' If God of Israel is really supreme over all gods and over all powers, why is he so jealous and fearful of other gods which he himself is supposed to have created for other nations to worship (Deut. 14: 19)? Despite all these, the Jews have persistently ignored Moses and his God of Israel throughout ages. Rationally, the author of Deuteronomy is obviously confused.

'Have reverence for the Lord your God and worship only him. Be faithful to him and make your promises in his name alone. Praise him—he is your God, and you have seen with your own eyes the great and astounding things that he has done for you. When your ancestors went to Egypt, there were only seventy of them. But now the Lord your God has made you as numerous as the stars in the sky.' (Deut. 10: 20-22 GNT).

'Remember these commands and cherish them. Tie them on your arms and wear them on your foreheads as a reminder. Teach them to your children. Talk about them when you are at home and when you are away, when you are resting and when you are working. Write them on the doorposts of your houses and on your gates. Then you and your children will live a long time in the land that the Lord your God promised to give to your ancestors. You will live there as long as there is a sky above the earth. Obey faithfully everything that I have commanded you: Love the Lord your God, do everything he commands, and be faithful to him. Then he will drive out all those nations as you advance, and you will occupy the land belonging to nations greater and more powerful than you. All the ground that you march over will be yours. Your territory will extend from the desert in the south to the Lebanon Mountains in the north, and from the Euphrates River in the east to the Mediterranean Sea in the west. Wherever you go in that land, the Lord your God will make the people fear you, as he has promised, and no one will be able to stop you. Today I am giving you the choice between a blessing and a curse—a blessing, if you obey the commands of the Lord your God that I am giving you today; but a curse, if you disobey these commands and turn away to worship other gods that you have never worshiped before. When the Lord brings you into the land that you are going to occupy, you are to proclaim the blessing from Mount Gerizim and the curse from Mount Ebal. (These two mountains are west of the Jordan River in the territory of the Canaanites who live in the Jordan Valley. They are toward the west, not far from the sacred trees of Moreh near the town of Gilgal.) $_{31}$ You are about to cross the Jordan River and occupy the land that the Lord your God is giving you. When you take it and settle there, $_{32}$ be sure to obey all the laws that I am giving you today. (Deut. 11: 18-32)

Deuteronomy 12 GNT.

'Here are *the laws* that you are to obey as long as you live in the land that the Lord, the God of your ancestors, is giving you. Listen to them! In the land that you are taking, destroy all the places where the people worship their gods on high mountains, on hills, and under green trees. Tear down their altars and smash their sacred stone pillars to pieces. Burn their symbols of the goddess Asherah and chop down their idols, so that they will never again be worshiped at those places. Do not worship the Lord your God in the way that these people worship their gods. Out of the territory of all your tribes the Lord will choose the one place where the people are to come into his presence and worship him. There you are to offer your sacrifices that are to be burned and your other sacrifices, your tithes and your offerings, the gifts that you promise to the Lord, your freewill offerings, and the first-born of your cattle and sheep. There, in the presence of the Lord your God, who has blessed you, you and your families will eat and enjoy the good things that you have worked for. When that time comes, you must not do as you have been doing. Until now you have all been worshiping as you please, because you have not yet entered the land that the Lord your God is giving you, where you can live in peace. When you cross the Jordan River, the Lord will let you occupy the land and live there. He will keep you safe from all your enemies, and you will live in peace.

'The Lord will choose a single place where he is to be worshiped, and there you must bring to him everything that I have commanded: your sacrifices that are to be burned and your other sacrifices, your tithes and your offerings, and those special gifts that you have promised to the Lord. Be joyful there in his presence, together with your children, your servants, and the Levites who live in your towns; remember that the Levites will have no land of their own.

'You are not to offer your sacrifices wherever you choose; ₁₄you must offer them only in the one place that the Lord will choose in the territory of one of *your tribes*. Only there are you to offer your sacrifices that are to be burned and do all the other things that I have commanded you. But you are free to kill and eat your animals wherever you live. You may eat as many as the Lord gives you. All of you, whether ritually clean or unclean, may eat them, just as you would eat the meat of deer or antelope. But you must not eat their blood; you must pour it out on the ground like water. Nothing that you offer to the Lord is to be eaten in the places where you live. It includes the following *customs:* the tithes of your grain, your wine, your olive oil, the first-born of your cattle and sheep, the gifts that you promise to the Lord, your freewill offerings, and any other offerings. You and your children, together with your servants and the Levites who live in your towns, are to eat these offerings only in the presence of the Lord your God, in the one place of worship chosen by the Lord your God. And you are to be happy there over everything that you have done. ₁₉ Be sure, also, not to neglect the Levites, as long as you live in your land. ₂₀ When the Lord your God enlarges your territory, as he has promised, you may eat meat whenever you want to. ₂₁ If the one place of worship is too far away, then, whenever you wish, you may kill any of the cattle or sheep that the Lord has given you, and you may eat the meat at home, as I have told you. ₂₂ Anyone, ritually clean or unclean, may eat that meat, just as he would eat the meat of deer or antelope.

'₂₃ Only do not eat meat with blood still in it, for the life is in the blood, and you must not eat the life with the meat. ₂₄ Do not use the blood for food; instead, pour it out on the ground like water. ₂₅ *If you obey this command, the Lord will be pleased, and all will go well for you and* ₂₆*your descendants.* Take to the one place of worship your offerings and the gifts that you have promised the Lord. ₂₇ Offer there the sacrifices which are to be completely burned on the Lord's altar. Also offer those sacrifices in which you eat the meat and pour the blood out on the altar. ₂₈ Obey faithfully everything that I have commanded you, and all will go well for you and your descendants forever, because you will be doing what is right and what pleases the Lord your God. ₂₉ The Lord your God will destroy the nations as you invade their land, and you will occupy it and settle there. ₃₀ After the Lord destroys those nations, *make sure that you don't follow their religious practices, because that would be fatal.* Don't try to find out how they worship their gods, so that you can worship in the same way. ₃₁ Do not worship the Lord your God in the way they worship their gods, for in the worship of their gods they do all the disgusting things that the Lord hates. They even sacrifice their children in the fires on their altars. $_{32}$ *Do everything that I have commanded you; do not add anything to it or take anything from it.'*

A clear understanding of Deuteronomy chapters 11 and 12 would not be possible until we carefully reflect on Moses' background. Briefly, according to Old Testament, Moses was an unwanted abandoned Jewish baby boy. Moses' natural parents are not known. Moses was raised in the Egyptian king's palace under the supervision of the king's daughter who found and named him Moses. Moses in Hebrew means 'I found him'. As an adult, Moses married Zipporah, an Egyptian girl, and moved out of the palace. Moses was once a murderer (Exod. 2: 12). Moses was appointed by a god known as 'I am', or the 'God of Abraham, Isaac, and Jacob' to lead the enslaved Jews out of slavery in Egypt to God of Israel's selected Promised Land: the land was already inhabited by six non-Jewish tribal people. Moses reluctantly accepted God's offer to lead the Jews, (Exod. 3: 1-21) because he saw himself as unfit for leadership. He was induced by God to accept the leadership role.

Before the Exodus trip commenced, the Jews had lived in Egypt for more than 400 years and naturally knew no laws and traditions other than that of Egypt. They however identified themselves as Hebrews, who customarily worshiped idols of various kinds just as what all Egyptians did.

It was Moses who encountered a God known as *I am* and made it known to that generation of Jews, the descendants of Abraham, Isaac, and Jacob. The God later became known as the God of Israel or the God who is projected exclusively as being responsible for Jews and Jewish affairs.

In effect, Moses was a fatherless, motherless mystery person to all the Jews. All his ideas were alien to the Jews. They were not Egyptian ideas or Hebrew ideas. Moses' ideas were supposed to be divinely inspired. In the modern sense, Moses would be described as a revolutionary person who was ordained by divine powers to create a new nation with new institutions and a leadership that could bring everlasting peace and prosperity to Jews at all costs. His requirements were simply total submission of all Jewish religious customs and complete obedience to the divine laws prescribed by Moses.

In some senses the books of Exodus, Numbers, Leviticus, and Deuteronomy project Moses as an ancient Machiavellian who foresaw divine justification for all actions regardless of the means. As a revolutionary, he introduced new institutions, new laws, new code of behaviour, and above all a new religion designed purposely for his Jewish followers.

I wonder if you the reader see Moses with the same lenses as I do. Looking at his overall nature, would it be wrong to conclude that Moses was certainly one of the numerous *fictional ambiguous characters of the Holy Bible*? I personally have no doubt about that. Moses could not be a historical human being. He never existed on planet earth, because there is no recorded history about him anywhere other than ancient Jewish mythology.

Deuteronomy 13 '₁ Prophets or interpreters of dreams may promise a miracle or a wonder, ₂ in order to lead you to worship and serve gods that you have not worshiped before. Even if what they promise comes true, ₃ do not pay any attention to them. *The Lord your God is using them to test you, to see if you love the Lord with all your heart.*' Does a God who knows all everywhere at all times *really need to test people*? Does he know he is supposed to know all everywhere at all times? Must we not question his doubt, his curiosity, and his understanding of his assigned characteristics as God?

'₄ Follow the Lord and honour him; obey him and keep his commands; worship him and be faithful to him. ₅ But put to death any interpreters of dreams or prophets that tell you to rebel against the Lord, who rescued you from Egypt, where you were slaves. Such people are evil and are trying to lead you away from the life that the Lord has commanded you to live. *They must be put to death, in order to rid yourselves of this evil.* ₆ *Even your brother or your son or your daughter or the wife you love or your closest friend may secretly encourage you to worship other gods, gods that you and your ancestors have never worshiped.* ₇ Some of them may encourage you to worship the gods of the people who live near you or the gods of those who live far away. ₈ But do not let any of them persuade you; do not even listen to them. Show them no mercy or pity, and do not protect them. ₉ *Kill them! Be the first to stone them, and then let everyone else stone them too.* ₁₀ *Stone them to death!* They tried to lead you away from the Lord your God, who rescued you from Egypt, where you were slaves. ₁₁ Then all the people of Israel will hear what happened; they will be afraid, and no one will ever again do such an evil thing. Moses: ₁₂ When you are living in the towns that the Lord your God gives you, you may hear 13 that some worthless people of your nation have misled the people of their town to worship gods that you have never worshiped before. ₁₄ *If you hear such a rumor, investigate it thoroughly; and if it is true that this evil thing did happen,* ₁₅ *then kill all the people in that town and all their livestock too. Destroy that town completely.* ₁₆ *Bring together all the possessions of the people who live there and pile them up in the town square. Then burn the town and everything in it as an offering to the Lord your God. It must be left in ruins forever and never again be rebuilt.'*

What do you think of the above satanic verses? This God of Israel is really crazy! God of Israel knows very well that there can be other gods who could be more powerful than himself, hence his extreme fear that Israelites may switch from him to worship others. Why should he impose death penalty for idol worshipers? Has Moses forgotten that his people lived for over 400 years in Egypt worshipping other gods before Moses' idea of God known as 'I am' was introduced by Moses himself to the Israelites? The descendants of Abraham, Isaac, and Jacob who lived in Egypt had long forgotten the beliefs of their forefathers because of God's long silence. Besides, that God too had far too long forgotten, for more than 400 years that there were some Jewish descendants still alive somewhere in a north-east Africa, a country called Egypt. This new generation of Jews can tell Moses and his God of Israel to go to hell; and that is exactly what they did.

'₁₇ Do not keep for yourselves anything that was condemned to destruction, and then the Lord will turn from his fierce anger and show you mercy. He will be merciful to you and make you a numerous people, as he promised your ancestors, ₁₈ *if* you obey all his commands that *I* have given you today, and do what he requires.' The Israelites evidently rarely obeyed Moses' commands. They worshiped gods of their choice and remained stubborn ever-after.

Deuteronomy 14'₂ You belong to the Lord your God; *he has chosen you to be his own people from among all the peoples who live on earth.* ₃ Do not eat anything that the Lord has declared unclean. ₄ You may eat these animals: cattle, sheep, goats, 5 deer, wild sheep, wild goats, or antelopes—₆ any animals that have divided hoofs and that also chew the cud. ₇ But no animals may be eaten unless they have divided hoofs and also chew the cud. You may not eat camels, rabbits, or rock badgers. They must be considered unclean; they chew the cud but do not have divided hoofs. ₈ Do not eat pigs. They must be considered unclean; they have divided hoofs but do not chew the cud. Do not eat any of these animals or even touch their dead bodies. ₉ You may eat any kind of fish that has fins and scales, ₁₀ but anything living in the water that does not have fins and scales may not be eaten; it must be considered unclean. ₁₁ You may eat any clean bird. ₁₂ But these are the kinds of birds you are not to eat: eagles, owls, hawks, falcons; buzzards, vultures, crows; ostriches; seagulls, storks, herons, pelicans, cormorants; hoopoes; and bats.' Verses 13, 14, 15, 16, 17, and 18 missing from the Holy Bible.' All winged insects are unclean; do not eat them. ₂₀ You may eat any clean insect. Do not eat any animal that dies a natural death. You may let the foreigners who live among you eat it, or you may sell it to other foreigners. But you belong to the Lord your God; you are his people. Do not cook a young sheep or goat in its mother's milk.

₂₂ 'Set aside a tithe—a tenth of all that your fields produce each year.

$_{23}$ Then go to the one place where the Lord your God has chosen to be worshiped; and there in his presence eat the tithes of your grain, wine, and olive oil, and the first-born of your cattle and sheep. Do this so that you may learn to honour the Lord your God always. $_{24}$ If the place of worship is too far from your home for you to carry there the tithe of the produce that the Lord has blessed you with, then do this: $_{25}$ *Sell your produce and take the money with you to the one place of worship.* $_{26}$ *Spend it on whatever you want—beef, lamb, wine, and beer—and there, in the presence of the Lord your God, you and your families are to eat and enjoy yourselves.* $_{27}$ Do not neglect the Levites who live in your towns; they have no property of their own. $_{28}$ At the end of every third year bring the tithe of all your crops and store it in your towns. '$_{29}$ This food is for the Levites, since they own no property, and for the foreigners, orphans, and widows who live in your towns. They are to come and get all they need. Do this, and the Lord your God will bless you in everything you do.'

Now compare the narrative from 'The Good News Bible', Deuteronomy 14: 25-26 with that of Cambridge University Press, Holy Bible published in 1934: 'Then thou shall turn it into money, and bind up the money in thine hand, and shall go unto the place which the Lord thy God shall choose: And thy shall bestow that money for whatever thy soul lusteth after; for oxen, or for sheep, or *for wine, or for strong drink, or for whatsoever thy soul desireth: and thy shall eat there before the Lord thy God, and thy shall rejoice,* thou, and thine household'. (Deut. 14: 25-26)

Is it a sin to drink alcohol? Well, God's own beloved servant, Reverend Moses is telling God's beloved people of Israel that it is OK to drink strong drinks before the Lord thy God. Can any Christian question this? I know some Christians will attempt to twist this simple biblical statement, as they always do. But surely, apart from the common knowledge that 'strong drinks' are often poisonous when over drunk, it is among material things most households use for celebrations.

We are still on the same chapter: can anyone explain what happened to verses 13, 14, 15, 16, 17, and 18 of Deuteronomy 14? Is there any reason why these are missing from the Bible? A total of six verses deliberately omitted from this chapter by the author. Did Moses say something which is not worthy of general public knowledge? Or perhaps the God of Israel was in one of his ungodly angry moods and let slip something worthy of deletion from Bible? Isn't it funny?

Deuteronomy 15 '₁ At the end of every seventh year you are to cancel the debts of those who owe you money. ₂ This is how it is to be done. Each of you who have lent money to any Israelite is to cancel the debt; you must not try to collect the money; the Lord himself has declared the debt cancelled. ₃ You may collect what a foreigner owes you, but you must not collect what any of your own people owe you. ₄ 'The Lord your God will bless you in the land that he is giving you. *Not one of your people will be poor ₅ if you obey him and carefully observe everything that I command you today.* ₆ The Lord will bless you, as he has promised. You will lend money to many nations, but you will not have to borrow from any; you will have control over many nations, but no nation will have control over you. ₇ If in any of the towns in the land that the Lord your God is giving you there are Israelites in need, then do not be selfish and refuse to help them. ₈ Instead, be generous and lend them as much as they need. ₉ Do not refuse to lend them something, just because the year when debts are cancelled is near. Do not let such an evil thought enter your mind. If you refuse to make the loan, they will cry out to the Lord against you, and you will be held guilty. 10 Give to them freely and unselfishly, and the Lord will bless you in everything you do. ₁₁ *There will always be some Israelites who are poor and in need, and so I command you to be generous to them.*'

The verse 11 contradicts verse 4 and 5 mentioned above! Even if all Israelites obey the Lord's command, there will always be some Israelites who will be poor and in need without question;

just as any other nation has. $_{12}$. If any Israelites male or female sell themselves to you as slaves, you are to release them after they have served you for six years. When the seventh year comes, you must let them go free. $_{13}$ When you set them free, do not send them away empty-handed. $_{14}$ Give to them generously from what the Lord has blessed you with—sheep, grain, and wine. $_{15}$ Remember that you were slaves in Egypt and the Lord your God set you free. That is why I am now giving you this command. $_{16}$ But your slave may not want to leave. He may love you and your family and be content to stay. $_{17}$ Then take him to the door of your house and there pierce his ear; he will then be your slave for life. Treat your female slave in the same way. $_{18}$ Do not be resentful when you set slaves free; after all, they have served you for six years at half the cost of hired servants. Do this, and the Lord your God will bless you in all that you do. $_{19}$ Set aside for the Lord your God all the first-born males of your cattle and sheep; don't use any of these cattle for work and don't shear any of these sheep. $_{20}$ Each year you and your family are to eat them in the Lord's presence at the one place of worship. $_{21}$ But if there is anything wrong with the animals, if they are crippled or blind or have any other serious defect, you must not sacrifice them to the Lord your God. $_{22}$ You may eat such animals at home. All of you, whether ritually clean or unclean, may eat them, just as you eat deer or antelope. $_{23}$ But do not use their blood for food; instead, you must pour it out on the ground like water.'

This is the true voice of the God of Israel, or more precisely the voice of the God for the Israelites, the Jewish God. This God has spoken to his beloved people in the most legitimate way that pleases him, and of how to treat fellow Jews, as opposed to, how to treat non-Jewish people. The entire chapter 15 of the book of Deuteronomy and several other chapters clearly stress that this biblical God is *only* for Jews, but very strangely every non-Jewish reader of the Holy Bible have also taken this God to be his or her God. And I am yet to be convinced why this God of Israel must be the universal God, while every act of this God emphatically detaches himself from other race of people.

If there must be a single god for humanity, there is no way that universal God can be this God of Israel. He is too full of horror and undeserving as a God of the planet earth. In all the chapters of the Old Testament, the emphasis is very clear and unambiguous. In the New Testament, however, it is noted that the authors have deliberately copied numerous verses from the Old Testament and paraphrased them into universal concepts. The God of Israel and Jewish ideas are converted into God of the Universe or humanity as a whole. A comparative analysis of the book of Isaiah, Psalms, Joel, Genesis, Deuteronomy, and many other Old Testament books and the new books from Matthew throughout to Revelation shows tremendous intentional fabrications of words, phrases, and ideas.

Deuteronomy 18; Verses 1-2: 'The priestly tribe of Levi is not to receive any share of land in Israel; instead, they are to live on the offerings and other sacrifices given to the Lord. They are to own no land, as the other tribes do; their share is the privilege of being the Lord's priests, as the Lord has promised.'

Verses 9-22, 'When you come into the land that the Lord your God is giving you, don't follow the disgusting practices of the nations that are there. 10 Don't sacrifice your children in the fires on your altars; and don't let your people practice divination or look for omens or use spells 11 or charms, and don't let them consult the spirits of the dead. 12 The Lord your God hates people who do these disgusting things, and that is why he is driving those nations out of the land as you advance. 13 Be completely faithful to the Lord. 14 Then Moses said, 'In the land you are about to occupy, people follow the advice of those who practice divination and look for omens, but the Lord your God does not allow you to do this.

'15 Instead, he will send you a prophet like me from among your own people, and you are to obey him. 16 On the day that you were gathered at Mount Sinai, you begged not to hear the Lord speak again or to see his fiery presence anymore, because you were afraid you would die. ₁₇ So the Lord said to me, "They have made a wise request. ₁₈ I will send them a prophet like you from among their own people; I will tell him what to say, and he will tell the people everything I command. ₁₉ He will speak in my name, and I will punish anyone who refuses to obey him. ₂₀ *But if any prophet dares to speak a message in my name when I did not command him to do so, he must die for it, and so must any prophet who speaks in the name of other gods."* ₂₁ *You may wonder how you can tell when a prophet's message does not come from the Lord. ₂₂ If a prophet speaks in the name of the Lord and what he says does not come true, then it is not the Lord's message.* That prophet has spoken on his own authority, and you are not to fear him.'

A prophet can be defined as follows: clairvoyant, forecaster, seer, psychic, diviner, mystic, telepathist, and spiritualist. Deuteronomy 18: 22 says 'If a prophet speaks in the name of the Lord and what he says does not come true, then it is not the Lord's message.' In primitive societies, tricksters, magicians, and articulate people manipulated people's mind with delusional expectations. Science and technology in modern times have made these voodoo practices redundant. Prophets are no more needed in contemporary societies. Modern world cannot depend on magic, tricks, or prophecy of coming events or sickness healing. They are faith-based and not dependable. Although science cannot explain every mystery of the world, it certainly has answers to most causes and effects of phenomenon more than what prophets can do. Trained scientific professionals and scientific equipment which are capable of diagnosing human problems accurately are being invented and improved upon daily in all religiously liberated communities.

Do modern people of twenty-first century need spiritualist to heal sickness when trained medical doctors abound everywhere? Do we need a diviner to look at our faces and palms to diagnose and heal illness when professional medical personnel are available? Do we need a prophet to perform miracles of any type when we know for certain that they are all learnt artistic performances, spiritual idea manufactures, and mere tricksters? Miracles are primitive.

If Moses lived today in any civilized country where religious additions are absent and primitive science is replaced with modern practical scientific knowledge, would he succeed in telling any religiously enslaved group of people that God has appointed him to move them to a Promised Land belonging to another cultural people? Can Moses really be reborn in a twenty-first-century scientific computerized world? The answer can be yes, only, if Moses reveals himself to a twenty-first-century religiously addicted people who are still primitive and refuse to adapt to modernity. The days of Moses, Yahweh, Elohim, God of Abraham, Isaac, Jacob and Christ are past and gone with their miracle performances. This is the age of reason. We must move on by leaving ancient ideas to rust.

Deuteronomy 19 $_1$ After the Lord your God has destroyed the people whose land he is giving you and after you have taken their cities and houses and settled there, $_{2-3}$ divide the territory into three parts, each with a city that can be easily reached. Then any of you that kill will be able to escape to one of them for protection. $_4$ If you accidentally kill someone who is not your enemy, you may escape to any of these cities and be safe. $_5$ For example, if two of you go into the forest together to cut wood and if, as one of you is chopping down a tree, the axe head comes off the handle and kills the other, you can run to one of those three cities and be safe. $_6$ If there were only one city, the distance to it might be too great, and the relative who is responsible for taking revenge for the killing might catch you and angrily kill an innocent person. After all, it was by accident that you killed someone who was not your enemy.

$_7$ This is why I order you to set aside three cities. $_8$ When the Lord your God enlarges your territory, as he told your ancestors he would, and gives you all the land he has promised, $_9$ then you are to select three more cities. (He will give you this land if you do everything that I command you today and if you love the Lord your God and live according to his teachings.) ₁₀ Do this, so that innocent people will not die and so that you will not be guilty of putting them to death in the land that the Lord is giving you.

'₁₁ But suppose you deliberately murder your enemy in cold blood and then escape to one of those cities for protection. ₁₂ In that case, the leaders of your own town are to send for you and hand you over to the relative responsible for taking revenge for the murder, so that you may be put to death. ₁₃ No mercy will be shown to you. Israel must rid itself of murderers, so that all will go well. ₁₄ Do not move your neighbor's property line, established long ago in the land that the Lord your God is giving you. ₁₅ One witness is not enough to convict someone of a crime; at least two witnesses are necessary to prove that someone is guilty. ₁₆ If any of you try to harm another by false accusations, ₁₇ both of you are to go to the one place of worship and be judged by the priests and judges who are then in office. ₁₈ The judges will investigate the case thoroughly; and if you have made a false accusation, ₁₉ you are to receive the punishment the accused would have received. In this way your nation will get rid of this evil. ₂₀ Then everyone else will hear what happened; they will be afraid, and no one will ever again do such an evil thing. ₂₁ In such cases show no mercy; the punishment is to be a life for a life, an eye for an eye, a tooth for a tooth, a hand for a hand, and a foot for a foot.'

As honest responsible Holy Bible readers, can we accept the above chapter as the word of the true God of the universe? Are these the words of the author of Deuteronomy, or Moses, or that of God of Israel? If really, there is such a thing as a single God for all humans, can such words as written in Deuteronomy 19 be God's own words? I very much doubt it. Rationality is commonly accepted as the difference between humans and animals. You and I are rational beings. Can we neglect this important question? I am aware that addiction to these scriptures, or the 'Christian faith', tends to freeze the brain and makes it impossible to rationalise on such issues. Yet, I am still hopeful that you the reader will ponder for some moments on such matters, as above, for critical analysis. Rationality is of course a human duty. How long can we continue to live seventeen and eighteen pretentious lives, just because we are born and nurtured into a foreign faith which is incompatible with adult reasoning?

Deuteronomy 20 ‘₁ When you go out to fight against your enemies and you see chariots and horses and an army that outnumbers yours, do not be afraid of them. The Lord your God, who rescued you from Egypt, will be with you. ₂ Before you start fighting, a priest is to come forward and say to the army, ₃ "Men of Israel listen! Today you are going into battle. Do not be afraid of your enemies or lose courage or panic. ₄ The Lord your God is going with you, and he will give you victory." ₅ Then the officers will address the men and say, "Is there any man here who has just built a house, but has not yet dedicated it? If so, he is to go home. Otherwise, if he is killed in battle, someone else will dedicate his house. ₆ Is there any man here who has just planted a vineyard, but has not yet had the chance to harvest its grapes? If so, he is to go home. Otherwise, if he is killed in battle, someone else will enjoy the wine. ₇ Is there anyone here who is engaged to be married? If so, he is to go home. Otherwise, if he is killed in battle, someone else will marry the woman he is engaged to." 8 The officers will also say to the men, "Is there any man here who has lost his nerve and is afraid? If so, he is to go home. Otherwise, he will destroy the morale of the others." ₉ When the officers have finished speaking to the army, leaders are to be chosen for each unit. ₁₀ When you go to attack a city, first give its people a chance to surrender. ₁₁ If they open the gates and surrender, they are all to become your slaves and do forced labour for you. ₁₂ But if the people of that city will not surrender, but choose to fight, surround it with your army. ₁₃ Then, *when the Lord your God lets you capture the city, kill every man in it.* ₁₄ *You may, however, take for yourselves the women, the children, the livestock, and everything else in the city. You may use everything that belongs to your enemies. The Lord has given it to you.* ₁₅ That is how you are to deal with those cities that are far away from the land you will settle in. ₁₆ But when you capture cities in the land that the Lord your God is giving you, kill everyone. ₁₇ *Completely destroy all the people: the Hittites, the Amorites, the Canaanites, the Perizzites, the Hivites, and the Jebusites, as the Lord ordered you to do. 18 Kill them, so that they will not make you sin against the Lord by teaching you to do all the disgusting things that they do in the worship of their gods.* ₁₉ When you are trying to capture a city, do not cut down its fruit trees, even though the siege lasts a long time. Eat the fruit, but do not destroy the trees; the trees are not your enemies. ₂₀ You may cut down the other trees and use them in the siege mounds until the city is captured.'

Please read the above verses (10-17) again. The God of Israel or our supposed universal God is actually commanding an army of well-trained soldiers to kill innocent citizens who lived peacefully in their cities for no provocation whatsoever. The only fault they have is that they happen to inhabit that portion of planet earth which is fertile, which, of course, is not their fault. They are also known to have committed a first-degree crime of worshipping idols. The God of Israel has mercilessly ordered complete extermination of the indigenous people just because their lands are needed for settlement of Jews and their future descendants. How can any rational human being, Christian or not, justify this satanic act of God who is supposed to represent the entire humanity? Can anyone tell me why I should not call this ancient Jewish God a monster or a sectarian racist bigot? Verses 13, 14, 17, and 18 are evidently open bigotry.

Deuteronomy 21 ₁ Suppose someone is found murdered in a field in the land that the Lord your God is going to give you, and you do not know who killed him. ₂ Your leaders and judges are to go out and measure the distance from the place where the body was found to each of the nearby towns. ₃ Then the leaders of the town nearest to where the body was found are to select a young cow that has never been used for work. ₄ They are to take it down to a spot near a stream that never runs dry and where the ground has never been ploughed or planted, and there they are to break its neck.

'₅ The Leviticus priests are to go there also, because they are to decide every legal case involving violence. The Lord your God has chosen them to serve him and to pronounce blessings in his name. ₆ Then all the leaders from the town nearest the place where the murdered person was found are to wash their hands over the cow ₇ and say, "We did not murder this one, and we do not know who did it. ₈ Lord, forgive your people Israel, whom you rescued from Egypt. Forgive us and do not hold us responsible for the murder of an innocent person." ₉ And so, by doing what the Lord requires, you will not be held responsible for the murder. ₁₀ When the Lord your God gives you victory in battle and you take prisoners, you may see among them a beautiful woman that you like and want to marry.

'₁₂ Take her to your home, where she will shave her head, cut her fingernails, ₁₃ and change her clothes. She is to stay in your home and mourn for her parents for a month; after that, you may marry her. ₁₄ Later, if you no longer want her, you are to let her go free. Since you forced her to have intercourse with you, you cannot treat her as a slave and sell her.

'₁₅ Suppose a man has two wives and they both bear him sons, but the first son is not the child of his favorite wife. ₁₆ When the man decides how he is going to divide his property among his children, he is not to show partiality to the son of his favorite wife by giving him the share that belongs to the first-born son. ₁₇ He is to give a double share of his possessions to his first son, even though he is not the son of his favorite wife. A man must acknowledge his first son and give him the share he is legally entitled to.

'₁₈ Suppose someone has a son who is stubborn and rebellious, a son who will not obey his parents, even though they punish him.

~19~ His parents are to take him before the leaders of the town where he lives and make him stand trial. ~20~ They are to say to them, "Our son is stubborn and rebellious and refuses to obey us; he wastes money and is a drunkard." ~21~ Then the men of the city are to stone him to death, and so you will get rid of this evil. Everyone in Israel will hear what has happened and be afraid.

'~22~ If someone has been put to death for a crime and the body is hung on a post, ~23~ it is not to remain there overnight. It must be buried the same day, because a dead body hanging on a post brings God's curse on the land. Bury the body, so that you will not defile the land that the Lord your God is giving you.'

Most people have in the past, and even at present, concluded that the book of Deuteronomy or the entire first five biblical books were written by Moses and therefore the instructions given by God to Moses are words from Moses himself. Even if this is true, can these words be applicable to mankind as a whole or to a modern-day Jew or a professed Christian? All the twenty-three verses are essentially Jewish traditions or customary practices. Needless to say, this chapter is one of many testimonies in the Holy Bible which emphatically shows that the book is a Jewish book and definitely not intended for any cultural or religious group besides the Israelites. Any other interpretation of biblical texts would be a mere wish.

However, historically some ethnic societies were militarily conquered and colonized by dominant Jewish descendants who lived in medieval Europe. They successfully infested religions of the conquered people with biblical ideas. They also introduced social management methods of Moses and his idea of 'God of Israel' to suppress and control weaker minds in foreign lands. There are more than two billion people on planet earth today whose ancestors have adapted and nurtured themselves with the laws of Moses and its designed by-products, popularly called 'Christianity', to defuse their conscious minds and hard-earned wealth.

Deuteronomy 22 '₁ If you see an Israelite's cow or sheep running loose, do not ignore it; take it back. ₂ But if its owner lives a long way off or if you don't know who owns it, then take it home with you. When its owner comes looking for it, give it to him. ₃ Do the same thing if you find a donkey, a piece of clothing, or anything else that an Israelite may have lost. ₄ If an Israelite's donkey or cow has fallen down, don't ignore it; help him get the animal to its feet again. ₅ Women are not to wear men's clothing, and men are not to wear women's clothing; the Lord your God hates people who do such things. ₆ If you happen to find a bird's nest in a tree or on the ground with the mother bird sitting either on the eggs or with her young, you are not to take the mother bird. ₇ You may take the young birds, but you must let the mother bird go, so that you will live a long and prosperous life.

₈ 'When you build a new house be sure to put a railing around the edge of the roof. Then you will not be responsible if someone falls off and is killed. ₉ Do not plant any crop in the same field with your grapevines; if you do, you are forbidden to use either the grapes or the produce of the other crop. ₁₀ Do not hitch an ox and a donkey together for plowing. ₁₁ Do not wear cloth made by weaving wool and linen together. ₁₂ Sew tassels on the four corners of your clothes.

'₁₃ Suppose a man marries a young woman and later he decides he doesn't want her. ₁₄ So he makes up false charges against her, accusing her of not being a virgin when they got married. ₁₅ If this happens, the young woman's parents are to take the blood-stained wedding sheet that proves she was a virgin, and they are to show it in court to the town leaders. ₁₆ Her father will say to them, 'I gave my daughter to this man in marriage, and now he doesn't want her. ₁₇ He has made false charges against her, saying that she was not a virgin when he married her. *But here is the proof that my* ₁₈ *daughter was a virgin; look at the bloodstains on the wedding sheet!* Then the town leaders are to take the husband and beat him. ₁₉ They are also to fine him a hundred pieces of silver and give the money to the young woman's father, because the man has brought disgrace on an Israelite woman. Moreover, she will continue to be his wife, and he can never divorce her as long as he lives. 20 But if the charge is true and there is no proof that she was a virgin, 21 then they are to take her out to the entrance of her father's house, where the men of her city are to stone her to death. She has done a shameful thing among our people by having intercourse before she was married, while she was still living in her father's house. In this way you will get rid of this evil. 22 If a man is caught having intercourse with another man's wife; both of them are to be put to death. In this way you will get rid of this evil. 23 Suppose a man is caught in a town having intercourse with a young woman who is engaged to someone else. 24 You are to take them outside the town and stone them to death. She is to die because she did not cry out for help, although she was in a town, where she could have been heard. And the man is to die because he had intercourse with someone who was engaged. In this way you will get rid of this evil. 25 Suppose a man out in the countryside rapes a young woman who is engaged to someone else. Then only the man is to be put to death; 26 nothing is to be done to the woman, because she has not committed a sin worthy of death. This case is the same as when one man attacks another man and murders him. 27 The man raped the engaged woman in the countryside, and although she cried for help, there was no one to help her. 28 *Suppose a man is caught raping a young woman who is not engaged.* 29 *He is to pay her father the bride price of fifty pieces of silver, and she is to become his wife, because he forced her to have intercourse with him. He can never divorce her as long as he lives.* 30 No man is to disgrace his father by having intercourse with any of his father's wives.'

All the above are obviously ancient Jewish customs plus of course everything written in the book of Deuteronomy and, therefore, should not be taken as something embracing all humanity. Unfortunately, however, this is one of the 1,189 chapters of the Holy

Book. Chapter 22 is necessarily as sacred as any other in the Holy Bible: A woman is forced to marry a man who has raped her; a proof that my daughter was a virgin; look at the bloodstains on the wedding sheet; men of the city are to stone her to death for having sexual intercourse before she was married; men and women are not permitted to wear same clothing, the Lord your God hates such things.

Well, these citations can go on and on endlessly, but critically speaking, the embedded faith in the Holy Bible among Christians clearly exposes their faith into serious pertinent questions. What is the ultimate worth of this faith?

Deuteronomy 23 Verses 1-2: *'No man who has been castrated or whose penis has been cut off may be included among the Lord's people. No one born out of wedlock or any descendant of such a person, even in the tenth generation, may be included among the Lord's people.'*

Abraham impregnated his Egyptian maidservant 'Hagar' and had his first child with her. The child's name was Ishmael. He was born out of wedlock. Abraham's wife then was Sara; yet one of Ishmael's descendants, Mohamed, became the last prophet of God, according to Muslim religion. A man's penis can be cut off because of sexual offence? Did ancient Jews think of the other use of the penis, as an organ for passing out waste liquid from the body? Unbelievable faith.

Verses 10-23: *'₁₀ If a man becomes unclean because he has had a wet dream during the night, he is to go outside the camp and stay there. ₁₁ Toward evening* he is to wash himself, and at sunset he may come back into camp. ₁₂ You are to have a place outside the camp where you can go when you need to relieve yourselves. ₁₃ Carry a stick as part of your equipment, so that when you have a bowel movement you can dig a hole and cover it up. *₁₇ No Israelite, man or woman, is to become a temple ₁₈ prostitute.* Also, no money earned in this way may be brought into the house of the Lord your God in fulfillment of a vow. *The Lord hates temple prostitutes.* ₁₉ When you lend money or food or anything else to Israelites do not charge them interest. ₂₀ You may charge interest on what you lend to foreigners, but not on what you lend to Israelites. Obey this rule, and the Lord your God will bless everything you do in the land that you are going to occupy. ₂₁ When you make a vow to the Lord your God, do not put off doing what you promised; the Lord will hold you to your vow, and it is a sin not to keep it. ₂₂ It is no sin not to make a vow to the Lord, ₂₃ but if you make one voluntarily, be sure that you keep it.'

It is amazing to read in detail the sex life of Abraham in the book of Genesis, Abraham's sex life with his maid servant Hagar. He had several children with his second wife's maids (Keturah); all of them with God's consent, and God of Israel was pleased with him. How about other Jewish heroes such as Isaac, Jacob, David, Solomon, Isaiah, Judah, etc. in the Old Testament? They were all sexual perverts according to the Holy Bible. Isaac, for instance, had sex with two sisters, married them both, and he also had sex with all their maids and had several children with the maids as well. Solomon had scores of girlfriends, wives, and children unmatched to any Jewish biblical hero. All of them had children outside their wedlock, and indeed, they became the most famous founding fathers of Judaism, Christianity, and Islam. I am saying that none of the most popular religions in the world today is pure and free of sin. The New Testament followed the same pattern. Sex life of Jesus Christ and significant others are completely missing from all the twenty-seven books, yet we are not supposed to find out.

Deuteronomy 27 '₁ Then Moses, together with the leaders of Israel, said to the people, "Obey all the instructions that I am giving you today. ₂ On the day you cross the Jordan River and enter the land that the Lord your God is giving you, you are to set up some large stones, cover them with plaster, ₃ and write on them all these laws and teachings. When you have entered the rich and fertile land that the Lord, the God of your ancestors, promised you, ₄ and you are on the other side of the Jordan, set up these stones on Mount Ebal, as I am instructing you today, and cover them with plaster.

"₅ Build an altar there made of stones that have had no iron tools used on them, ₆ because any altar you build for the Lord your God must be made of uncut stones. *There you are to offer the sacrifices that are to be burned, ₇ and there you are to sacrifice and eat your fellowship offerings and be grateful in the presence of the Lord your God.* ₈ On the stones covered with plaster write clearly every word of God's laws." ₉ Then Moses, together with the Leviticus priests, said to all the people of Israel, "Give me your attention, people of Israel, and listen to me. Today you have become the people of the Lord your God; ₁₀ so obey him and keep all his laws that I am giving you today." ₁₁ Then Moses said to the people of Israel, ₁₂ "After you have crossed the Jordan, the following tribes are to stand on Mount Gerizim when the blessings are pronounced on the people: Simeon, Levi, Judah, Issachar, Joseph, and Benjamin. ₁₃ And the following tribes will stand on Mount Ebal when the curses are pronounced: Reuben, Gad, Asher, Zebulun, Dan, and Naphtali. ₁₄ The Levites will speak these words in a loud voice: ₁₅ *'God's curse on anyone who makes an idol of stone, wood, or metal and secretly worships it;* the Lord hates idolatry.' "And all the people will answer, 'Amen!' This is God's curse on anyone who dishonors his father or mother. And all the people will answer, 'Amen!'

This is God's curse on anyone who moves a neighbor's property line. And all the people will answer, 'Amen!'

This is God's curse on anyone who leads a blind person in the wrong direction. And all the people will answer, 'Amen!' This is God's curse on anyone who deprives foreigners, orphans, and widows of their rights. And all the people will answer, 'Amen!' This is God's curse on anyone who disgraces his father by having intercourse with any of his father's wives. And all the people will answer, 'Amen!' This is God's curse on anyone who has sexual relations with an animal. And all the people will answer, 'Amen!'

This is God's curse on anyone who has intercourse with his sister or half sister. And all the people will answer, 'Amen!' This is God's curse on anyone who has intercourse with his mother-in-law. And all the people will answer, 'Amen!' This is God's curse on anyone who secretly commits murder. And all the people will answer, Amen! This is God's curse on anyone who accepts money to murder an innocent person. And all the people will answer, 'Amen!' 26 And finally, this is *God's curse on anyone who does not obey all of God's laws and teachings. And all the people will answer, 'Amen!'*"

In chapter 27 of Deuteronomy, Moses and his Ministers of State of ancient Israel broadcast to all the Israelites what constitute the most serious offenses everyone must avoid at all times when they finally cross river Jordan to the Promised Land. For the sake of our convenience, it shall be called the '12 God curses on every Jew'; Hopefully Moses' generation of Israelites did not know the history of their primordial ancestors: from Adam and Eve, Cain and Abel, Enoch and Enosh, Abraham, Isaac, Jacob, and beyond; their history is full of murderers, rapist, fornicators, liars, adulterers, idol worshipers, swindlers, and criminals of every description. God of Israel cannot deny knowledge of any of those acts among his beloved race of people, because he was supposed to be with them from the beginning.

Deuteronomy 28 '₁ If you obey the Lord your God and faithfully keep all his commands that I am giving you today, he will make you greater than any other nation on earth. ₂ Obey the Lord your God and all these blessings will be yours: ₃ The Lord will bless your towns and your fields. ₄ The Lord will bless you with many children, with abundant crops, and with many cattle and sheep. ₅ The Lord will bless your grain crops and the food you prepare from them. ₆ The Lord will bless everything you do. ₇ The Lord will defeat your enemies when they attack you. They will attack from one direction, but they will run from you in all directions. ₈ The

Lord your God will bless your work and fill your barns with grain. He will bless you in the land that he is giving you.

₉ 'If you obey the Lord your God and do everything he commands, he will make you his own people, as he has promised.

'[Why?] ₁₀ *Then all the peoples on earth will see that the Lord has* ₁₁ *chosen you to be his own people, and they will be afraid of you.* The Lord will give you many children, many cattle, and abundant crops in the land that he promised your ancestors to give you. ₁₂ He will send rain in season from his rich storehouse in the sky and bless all your work, so that you will lend to many nations, but you will not have to borrow from any. ₁₃ *The Lord your God will make you the leader among the nations and not a follower; you will always prosper and never fail if you obey faithfully all his commands* that I am giving you today. ₁₄ But you must never disobey them in any way, or worship and serve other gods.

₁₅ 'But if you disobey the Lord your God and do not faithfully keep all his commands and laws that I am giving you today, all these evil things will happen to you:

'[Why?] ₁₆ The Lord will curse your towns and your fields. ₁₇ The Lord will curse your grain crops and the food you prepare from them. ₁₈ The Lord will curse you by giving you only a few children, poor crops, and few cattle and sheep. ₁₉ The Lord will curse everything you do. ₂₀ 'If you do evil and reject the Lord, he will bring on you disaster, confusion, and trouble in everything you do, until you are quickly and completely destroyed. ₂₁ He will send disease after disease on you until there is not one of you left in the land that you are about to occupy. ₂₂ The Lord will strike you with infectious diseases, with swelling and fever; he will send drought and scorching winds to destroy your crops. These disasters will be with you until you die.

'[Why?] ₂₃ No rain will fall, and your ground will become as hard as iron. ₂₄ Instead of rain, the Lord will send down dust storms and sandstorms until you are destroyed. ₂₅ The Lord will give your enemies victory over you. You will attack them from one direction, but you will run from them in all directions, and all the people on earth will be terrified when they see what happens to you. $_{26}$ When you die, birds and wild animals will come and eat your bodies, and there will be no one to scare them off $_{27}$ The Lord will send boils on you, as he did on the Egyptians. He will make your bodies break out with sores. You will be covered with scabs, and you will itch, but there will be no cure. $_{28}$ The Lord will make you lose your mind; he will strike you with blindness and confusion. $_{29}$ You will grope about in broad daylight like someone blind, and you will not be able to find your way. You will not prosper in anything you do. You will be constantly oppressed and robbed, and there will be no one to help you. $_{30}$ You will be engaged to a young woman—but someone else will marry her. You will build a house—but never live in it. You will plant a vineyard—but never eat its grapes.

'[Why?] $_{31}$ Your cattle will be butchered before your very eyes, but you will not eat any of the meat. Your donkeys will be dragged away while you look on, and they will not be given back to you. Your sheep will be given to your enemies, and there will be no one to help you.

' $_{32}$ Your sons and daughters will be given as slaves to foreigners while you look on. Every day you will strain your eyes, looking in vain for your children to return. $_{33}$ A foreign nation will take all the crops that you have worked so hard to grow, while you receive nothing but constant oppression and harsh treatment. $_{34}$ Your sufferings will make you lose your mind. $_{35}$ The Lord will cover your legs with incurable, painful sores; boils will cover you from head to foot.

'[Why?] $_{36}$ The Lord will take you and your king away to a foreign land, where neither you nor your ancestors ever lived before; there you will serve gods made of wood and stone. $_{37}$ In the countries to which the Lord will scatter you, the people will be shocked at what has happened to you; they will make fun of you and ridicule you. ₃₈ You will plant plenty of seed, but reap only a small harvest, because the locusts will eat your crops. ₃₉ You will plant vineyards and take care of them, but you will not gather their grapes or drink wine from them, because worms will eat the vines.

'₄₀ Olive trees will grow everywhere in your land, but you will not have any olive oil, because the olives will drop off. ₄₁ You will have sons and daughters, but you will lose them, because they will be taken away as prisoners of war. ₄₂ All your trees and crops will be devoured by insects. ₄₃ 'Foreigners who live in your land will gain more and more power, while you gradually lose yours. ₄₄ They will have money to lend you, but you will have none to lend them. In the end they will be your rulers. ₄₅ All these disasters will come on you, and they will be with you until you are destroyed, because you did not obey the Lord your God and keep all the laws that he gave you. ₄₆ They will be the evidence of God's judgment on you and your descendants forever. ₄₇ The Lord blessed you in every way, but you would not serve him with glad and joyful hearts.

'₄₈ So then, you will serve the enemies that the Lord is going to send against you. You will be hungry, thirsty, and naked—in need of everything. The Lord will oppress you harshly until you are destroyed. ₄₉ The Lord will bring against you a nation from the ends of the earth, a nation whose language you do not know. They will swoop down on you like an eagle. ₅₀ They will be ruthless and show no mercy to anyone, young or old. ₅₁ They will eat your livestock and your crops, and you will starve to death. They will not leave you any grain, wine, olive oil, cattle, or sheep; and you will die. ₅₂ They will attack every town in the land that the Lord your God is giving you, and the high, fortified walls in which you trust will fall. ₅₃ When your enemies are besieging your towns, you will become so desperate for food that you will even eat the children that the Lord your God has given you. ₅₄ Even the most refined man of noble birth will become so desperate during the siege that he will eat some of his own children because he has no other food.

He will not even give any to his brother or to the wife he loves or to any of his children who are left. $_{56}$ Even the most refined woman of noble birth, so rich that she has never had to walk anywhere, will behave in the same way. When the enemy besieges her town, she will become so desperate for food that she will secretly eat her newborn child and the afterbirth as well. She will not share them with the husband she loves or with any of her children.

$_{58}$ 'If you do not obey faithfully all of God's teachings that are written in this book and if you do not honour the wonderful and awesome name of the Lord your God, $_{59}$ he will send on you and on your descendants incurable diseases and horrible epidemics that can never be stopped. $_{60}$ He will bring on you once again all the dreadful diseases you experienced in Egypt, and you will never recover. $_{61}$ He will also send all kinds of diseases and epidemics that are not mentioned in this book of God's laws and teachings, and you will be destroyed.

'$_{62}$ Although you become as numerous as the stars in the sky, only a few of you will survive, because you did not obey the Lord your God. $_{63}$ Just as the Lord took delight in making you prosper and in making you increase in number, so he will take delight in destroying you and in bringing ruin on you. You will be uprooted from the land that you are about to occupy. $_{64}$ The Lord will scatter you among all the nations, from one end of the earth to the other, and there you will serve gods made of wood and stone, gods that neither you nor your ancestors have ever worshiped before.

'$_{65}$ You will find no peace anywhere, no place to call your own; the Lord will overwhelm you with anxiety, hopelessness, and despair. $_{66}$ Your life will always be in danger. Day and night you will be filled with terror, and you will live in constant fear of death. $_{67}$ Your hearts will pound with fear at everything you see. Every morning you will wish for evening; every evening you will wish for morning. $_{68}$ The Lord will send you back to Egypt in ships, even though he said that you would never have to go there again. There you will try to sell yourselves to your enemies as slaves, but no one will want to buy you.'

Why is God of Israel so desperate to be worshiped and so much afraid that his so-called loved people can possibly disobey him? Why does he need to be obeyed? If his so-called powers are supreme, why should he not give the Israelites different brain organs that will make them worship only the God of Israel alone? At this point, I wonder if the reader does not see the senselessness of the entire 'god' concept in the Holy Bible. God of Israel has issued scores of deadly threats for the Israelites who refuse to listen and to obey his orders, but none has been respected for over forty years in the wilderness.

The final solution to this stubbornness is not punishment but by changing the mindset of the ancient Jews. If this God is the same God who formed Adam with mere soil and Eve with a single male rib, it seems quite easy to replace every Jew's brain with submissive brain tissue that will have no option but to disobey his Almighty God's commandments. The idea of sending the Jews back to Egypt in ship loads will not alter behaviour. God's power has been challenged consistently all these years by the Israelites. God has emphatically proven to be a powerless, useless fantasy and a mere comforting word used by Moses and primitive minds which are still looking for miracles to solve human problems. Human problems are solvable only by humans with critical minds and not by invoking spiritual non-verifiable entities. Those who refuse to change or adapt to new ways of doing things are historically always left behind in human progress.

Deuteronomy 30: '$_{11}$ The command that I am giving you today is not too difficult or beyond your reach. $_{12}$ It is not up in the sky. You do not have to ask, "Who will go up and bring it down for us, so that we can hear it and obey it?" $_{13}$ nor is it on the other side of the ocean. You do not have to ask, "Who will go across the ocean and bring it to us, so that we may hear it and obey it?" $_{14}$ No, it is here with you. You know it and can quote it, so now obey it. $_{15}$ Today I am giving you a choice between good and evil, between life and death. $_{16}$ If you obey the commands of the Lord your God, which I give you today, if you love him, obey him, and keep all his laws, then you will prosper and become a nation of many people. The Lord your God will bless you in the land that you are about to occupy. $_{17}$ But if you disobey and refuse to listen, and are led away to worship other gods, $_{18}$ you will be destroyed—I warn you here and now. You will not live long in that land across the Jordan that you are about to occupy. $_{19}$ I am now giving you the choice between life and death, between God's blessing and God's curse, and I call heaven and earth to witness the choice you make. Choose life. $_{20}$ Love the Lord your God, obey him and be faithful to him, and then you and your descendants will live long in the land that he promised to give your ancestors, Abraham, Isaac, and Jacob.'

Now let us determine whose voice is behind Deuteronomy chapter $_{30}$. Is it the Author, Moses, or God of Israel? Who is doing the talking? In some verses, it sounds like Moses; in those with quotation marks, it appears to be the voice of the Jewish God. But the author's narratives indicate that he or she is reporting an event which occurred in his presence.

In verses 15 and 19, the author writes, 'You have a choice between good and bad; between life and death; and between God's blessing' or God's curse; in their decision to accept and obey or to disrespect God's commandments. Then at end of nineteenth verse, a choice is made for the Israelite to 'choose life' and remain faithful to God because of the degree of God's viciousness if they choose the opposite.

A close examination of all the previous chapters to Deuteronomy 30 visibly reads that the author or Moses or the God of Israel or both are forcing the Israelites with every conceivable threat to make Moses' description of God their choice by force. You can also see that during the exodus, the Israelites detest the idea of being coerced by Moses and Aaron not to worship a God of their choice. God of Israel as the spiritual head has evidently proven to be ineptitude and unwanted. His love affair with the supposed enslaved Jews had always been one-sided and unconvincing.

Needless to say, Moses' miracle-based religious ideas up to the present time, represent a major foundation in Christianity; his Ten Commandments, his numerous moral laws, his exodus management skills, his dream image of a supreme God for the Israelites, and his law enforcement techniques make the man a unique genius worthy of praises. There is, however one major caveat: Someone asked Moses a question in Exodus 2: 14: 'Who made you our leader and our Judge?' This question still remains unanswered. But according to Hebrews 11: 3, 24, 27, the question is not, and cannot, be answered because of faith. According to the book of Hebrews, 'Faith' can transform peoples' fantasies into reality, particularly a primitive superstitious mind, religiously speaking. But human experience and logics shows that what counts most is faith in the individual's self-acquired quality knowledge, not spiritual faith.

Deuteronomy 31$_1$ Moses continued speaking to the people of Israel, $_2$ and said, "I am now a hundred and twenty years old and am no longer able to be your leader. And besides this, the Lord has told me that I will not cross the Jordan. $_3$ The Lord your God himself will go before you and destroy the nations living there, so that you can occupy their land; and Joshua will be your leader, as the Lord has said. $_4$ The Lord will destroy those people, just as he defeated Sihon and Og, kings of the Amorites, and destroyed their country. $_5$ The Lord will give you victory over them, and you are to treat them exactly as I have told you. $_6$ Be determined and confident. Do not be afraid of them. Your God, the Lord himself, will be with you. He will not fail you or abandon you." $_7$ Then Moses called Joshua and said to him in the presence of all the people of Israel, "Be determined and confident; you are the one who will lead these people to occupy the land that the Lord promised to their ancestors." ₁₄ Then the Lord said to Moses, "You do not have much longer to live. Call Joshua and bring him to the Tent, so that I may give him his instructions." Moses and Joshua went to the Tent, ₁₅ and the Lord appeared to them there in a pillar of cloud that stood by the door of the Tent. ₁₆ The Lord said to Moses, "You will soon die, and after your death the people will become unfaithful to me and break the covenant that I made with them. They will abandon me and worship the pagan gods of the land they are about to enter.'" Yes, Lord God of Israel has predicted that his beloved Israelites will abandon him when Moses dies. Good. But if God loves the Jews so much, why couldn't he use his supernatural powers to freeze the Israelites' minds to make them remain obedient to him forever? Surely with all his assigned supremacy, he need not wait for them to sin and then punish them for what he already knew would happen in the first place. If God cannot make the Jews worship him alone, how can he expect the rest of the world to worship him? God has already confessed he knows how stubborn, unfaithful, and deceitful the ancient Jews were. He is supposed to possess powers to control everyone everywhere every time! There is something inherently very wrong with this ancient Jewish guy.

'₁₇ When that happens, I will become angry with them; I will abandon them, and they will be destroyed. Many terrible disasters will come upon them, and then they will realize that these things are happening to them because I, their God, am no longer with them. ₁₈ And I will refuse to help them then, because they have done evil and worshiped other gods. ₁₉ Now, write down this song. Teach it to the people of Israel, so that it will stand as evidence against them. ₂₀ I will take them into this rich and fertile land, as I promised their ancestors. There they will have all the food they want and they will live comfortably. But they will turn away and worship other gods. They will reject me and break my covenant, ₂₁ and many terrible disasters will come on them. But this song will still be sung, and it will stand as evidence against them. Even now, before I take them into the land that I promised to give them, I know what they are thinking." ₂₂ That same day Moses wrote down the song and taught it to the people of Israel. ₂₃ Then the Lord spoke to Joshua son of Nun and told him, "Be confident and determined. You will lead the people of Israel into the land that I promised them, and I will be with you." ₂₄ Moses wrote God's Law in a book, taking care not to leave out anything. ₂₅ When he finished, he said to the Leviticus priests, who were in charge of the Lord's Covenant Box, ₂₆ "Take this book of God's Law and place it beside the Covenant Box of the Lord your God, so that it will remain there as a witness against his people. ₂₇ I know how stubborn and rebellious they are. They have rebelled against the Lord during my lifetime, and they will rebel even more after I am dead. ₂₈ Assemble all your tribal leaders and officials before me, so that I can tell them these things; I will call heaven and earth to be my witnesses against them. ₂₉ *I know that after my death the people will become wicked and reject what I have taught them.* And in time to come, they will meet with disaster, because they will have made the Lord angry by doing what he has forbidden." ₃₀ Then Moses recited the entire song while all the people of Israel listened.'

Moses and God of Israel are both aware of the wickedness and unfaithfulness of this selected few, less than 1 per cent of total world population. The ancient Jews were lucky that God loved them more than any race of people on earth. In fact, this whole story is a mere fiction. And I am sorry to repeat this same question over and over in various areas of this discourse. I repeat them because the Holy Bible consistently repeats itself in several chapters on the same issue. Why can't God use his ultimate powers to make the Jews do as he pleases? By the tone of the narrative, God of Abraham, Isaac, and Jacob is scared of his role among the Israelites. Notice that the Lord has been angry many times because of his people's stubbornness. God's instincts and decisions are not different from those of normal humans. His assigned unique spiritual characteristics appear to be missing in the book of Deuteronomy. In this book, God is spiritually powerless, phony, and a mere wishful perception. The central idea of G O D is completely missing.

A spiritual being that can make humans, as the fictional God in Genesis did, must possess spiritual powers to control all human actions. That is what makes God a God. God of Israel must therefore be seen as Moses' own imagination of God, or rather as a management tool created by Moses or the author of the book to manipulate the Jews.

Indeed, Moses was aware that ancient Jews were superstitious. They worshiped idols like the Egyptians before the time of exodus and that an idea of a Super Idol or Super God which is the most powerful compared to all idols or gods would be feared and welcomed by circumcised Jews. But if you notice carefully, you will realize that the Jews were consistently skeptical of Moses' links with the Super Idol, Super God or God of Israel all the time.

Deuteronomy 32 '₁ Earth and sky, hear my words, listen closely to what I say. ₂ My teaching will fall like drops of rain and form on the earth like dew. My words will fall like showers on young plants, like gentle rain on tender grass. ₃ I will praise the name of the Lord, and his people will tell of his greatness. *₄ The Lord is your mighty defender, perfect and just in all his ways; Your God is faithful and true; he does what is right and fair. ₅ but you are unfaithful, unworthy to be his people, a sinful and deceitful nation. ₆ Is this the way you should treat the Lord, you foolish, senseless people? He is your father, your Creator;* he made you into a nation. ₇ Think of the past, of the time long ago; ask your parents to tell you what happened, ask the old people to tell of the past. ₈ The Most High assigned nations their lands; he determined where peoples should live. He assigned to each nation a heavenly being, ₉ but Jacob's descendants he chose for himself. ₁₀ He found them wandering through the desert, a desolate, wind-swept wilderness. He protected them and cared for them, as he would protect himself.

'11 Like an eagle teaching it's young to fly, catching them safely on its spreading wings, the Lord kept Israel from falling. 12 The Lord alone led his people without the help of a foreign god. 13 He let them rule the highlands, and they ate what grew in the fields. They found wild honey among the rocks; their olive trees flourished in stony ground. 14 Their cows and goats gave plenty of milk; they had the best sheep, goats, and cattle, the finest wheat, and the choicest wine. 15 The Lord's people grew rich, but rebellious; they were fat and stuffed with food. They abandoned God their Creator and rejected their mighty savior. 16 *Their idolatry made the Lord jealous; the evil they did made him angry.* 17 They sacrificed to gods that are not real, new gods their ancestors had never known, gods that Israel had never obeyed. 18 They forgot their God, their mighty saviour, the one who had given them life. 19 When the Lord saw this he was angry and rejected his sons and daughters. 20 "I will no longer help them," he said; "then I will see what happens to them, those stubborn, unfaithful people. 21 With their idols they have made me angry, jealous with their so-called gods, gods that are really not gods. So I will use a so-called nation to make them angry; I will make them jealous with a nation of fools. 22 My anger will flame up like fire and burn everything on earth. It will reach to the world below and consume the roots of the mountains. 23 I will bring on them endless disasters and use all my arrows against them. 24 They will die from hunger and fever; they will die from terrible diseases. I will send wild animals to attack them, and poisonous snakes to bite them. 25 War will bring death in the streets; terrors will strike in the homes. Young men and young women will die; neither babies nor old people will be spared. 26 I would have destroyed them completely, so that no one would remember them. 27 But I could not let their enemies boast that they had defeated my people, when it was I myself who had crushed them. 28 *Israel is a nation without sense; they have no wisdom at all.* 31 *Their enemies know that their own gods are weak, not mighty like Israel's God.* 34 *The Lord remembers* what their enemies have done; he waits for the right time to punish them. ₃₅ The Lord will take revenge and punish them; the time will come when they will fall; the day of their doom is near. ₃₆ The Lord will rescue his people when he sees that their strength is gone. He will have mercy on those who serve him, when he sees how helpless they are. ₃₇ Then the Lord will ask his people, "Where are those mighty gods you trusted? ₃₈ You fed them the fat of your sacrifices and offered them wine to drink. Let them come and help you now; let them run to your rescue.

₃₉ "'I, and I alone, am God; no other god is real. I kill and I give life, I wound and I heal, and no one can oppose what I do". ₄₀ as surely as I am the living God, I raise my hand and I vow ₄₁ that I will sharpen my flashing sword and see that justice is done. I will take revenge on my enemies and punish those who hate me. ₄₂ My arrows will drip with their blood, and my sword will kill all who oppose me. I will spare no one who fights against me; even the wounded and prisoners will die." ₄₃ Nations, you must praise the Lord's people—he punishes all who kill them. He takes revenge on his enemies and forgives the sins of his people.'

Is the above song of Moses a sign of God of Israel's feeling of insecurity, the possibility that his chosen people may one day abandon him forever for another God? Why would God vow and threaten to kill his fellow Jews any time he suspects Israelites may oppose his commands?

Can the real creator of this planet earth really think and behave as this God of Israel? The answer is emphatically no! It is quite apparent up to this point that the story of God and his supposed creation of the universe, Adam and Eve, all living organisms, Moses and Israelites, Ten Commandments, Abraham, Isaac, and Jacob, all of them sound fictitious or unreal stories, indeed, wishful thinking. None is real. I hope all Christians will find time to read the Holy Bible thoroughly and rationalize on these fantasy stories in the book. Your faithful opinion cannot be different from my faithless mind if you read the Bible.

'₄₄ Moses and Joshua son of Nun recited this song, so that the people of Israel could hear it. ₄₅ When Moses had finished giving God's teachings to the people, ₄₆ he said, "Be sure to obey all these commands that I have given you today. Repeat them to your children, so that they may faithfully obey all of God's teachings.

'"₄₇ These teachings are not empty words; they are your very life. Obey them and you will live long in that land across the Jordan that you are about to occupy." ₄₈ That same day the Lord said to Moses, ₄₉ "Go to the Abarim Mountains in the land of Moab opposite the city of Jericho; climb Mount Nebo and look at the land of Canaan that I am about to give the people of Israel. ₅₀ You will die on that mountain as your brother Aaron died on Mount Hor, ₅₁ because both of you were unfaithful to me in the presence of the people of Israel. When you were at the waters of Meribah, near the town of Kadesh in the wilderness of Zin, you dishonored me in the presence of the people. ₅₂ You will look at the land from a distance, but you will not enter the land that I am giving the people of Israel.'"

The reader is humbly invited to read chapter 32 again by giving special attention to verses 4, 6, 8, 16, 28, 31, and 39-43. After reading it over, please think about the words, the sentences, the tone, and the mood of the speeches; I mean the idea behind the whole script.

We are *expected to know* that every statement out there is God's own words. The Almighty Super Powerful God who created the universe and all human beings actually said all that. Let us assume that God was spiritually speaking through his faithful messenger Prophet Moses to the Israelites, although it is clear that the story is being told or written by an unknown author of the book of Deuteronomy. Which of these three characters involved here (God, Moses, and the author) should we accept as real, reliable and authentic?

Now let us examine some verses closely: first, verse 39, 'I and I alone am God; no other God is real'. The second is verses 8 and 9; 'He assigns to each nation a heavenly being, but Jacob's descendants he chose for himself.' Note that Jacob's offspring means Joseph's children and their succeeding generations who made Egypt their motherland. In some verses and chapters, they alone are referred to as the Israelites, although Abraham's first child Ishmael had already made Egypt a home for his children. In the earlier chapters, however, 'Israel' was used as a generic word to represent descendants of Abraham, Isaac, and Jacob. The author is saying in plain words that God chose Jacob's children as his beloved people.

In verses 5, 6, 28, however, God is saying that these people he has voluntarily chosen for himself are not worthy to be in that position because they are unfaithful, sinful, deceitful, foolish, senseless, and without wisdom. If this God of Jacob is the Almighty, perfect, and just in every way as mentioned in verse 4, isn't it puzzling that God the Almighty complains about these people whose minds are supposed to be under his control? It was God himself who chose to serve these people as their Supreme God. Jacob's descendants have repeatedly shown their reluctance to accept this God for whatever he claims to be. And God too knows very well that these (verse 5) people are unfaithful, unworthy, foolish, and senseless to him. What is God's reason for insisting to be accepted as the Jewish God? Who is foolish here, God or Jacob's descendants?

Deuteronomy 34 'Moses went up from the plains of Moab to Mount Nebo, to the top of Mount Pisgah east of Jericho, and there the Lord showed him the whole land: the territory of Gilead as far north as the town of Dan; the entire territory of Naphtali; the territories of Ephraim and Manasseh; the territory of Judah as far west as the Mediterranean Sea; the southern part of Judah; and the plain that reaches from Zoar to Jericho, the city of palm trees.

'₄ Then the Lord said to Moses, "This is the land that I promised Abraham, Isaac, and Jacob I would give to their descendants. I have let you see it, but I will not let you go there." So Moses, the

Lord's servant, died there in the land of Moab, as the Lord had said he would. The Lord buried him in a valley in Moab, opposite the town of Bethpeor, but to this day no one knows the exact place of his burial. Moses was a hundred and twenty years old when he died; he was as strong as ever, and his eyesight was still good. The people of Israel mourned for him for thirty days in the plains of Moab. ₉ Joshua son of Nun was filled with wisdom, because Moses had appointed him to be his successor. *The people of Israel obeyed Joshua and kept the commands that the Lord had given them through Moses.* ₁₀ *There has never been a prophet in Israel like Moses; the Lord spoke with him face-to-face.* ₁₁ *No other prophet has ever done miracles and wonders like those that the Lord sent Moses to perform against the king of Egypt, his officials, and the entire country.* ₁₂ *No other prophet has been able to do the great and terrifying things that Moses did in the sight of all Israel.'*

Moses, the architect of a god, known as 'I am' nicknamed as 'God of Abraham, Isaac, and Jacob'; and frequently called 'God of Israel', sometimes referred to as God of Jacob. Moses initiated and formalized magic in Judaic religious practices. Moses introduced mystery performance of later-years church leaders as a necessary tool to win followers' support. Moses used God's name to perform magic before and during the exodus to demonstrate God's presence and God's power. He used magic as a major religious tool in his attempt to manage the Israelites throughout the exodus. Moses attempted unsuccessfully to merge the Genesis Creator God with his idea of 'God of Israel'. Moses did not achieve his goal of making the Israelites accept him as their God-chosen leader or their judge; Exodus 2: 14 says, 'who made you our leader or our judge.'

The five spiritual enigmas or mystery characters are glued together into a single organization: a primitive form of government, a tool for making laws, executing laws, and enforcing obedience of Jewish public morality. The pentagon here referred to are (1) Genesis' *'Creator God'*; (2) Exodus' Moses with his God *'I am'*; (3) Leviticus to Malachi's *'God of Israel'*; (4) New Testament's *'Jesus*

Christ and the Holy Trinity'; and (5) Apostle Paul's *famous 'Christology protagonist'*. None of the above five pillars of ancient faiths can claim a minimum of 5% authentic real human history. Records of them can be found only in Jewish history. There is none in other cultures' historical records. They are essentially primitive Jewish conjectures.

According to 2 King
(GNT)

In 2 Kings 10, it is written, 'There were seventy descendants of King Ahab living in the city of Samaria. Jehu wrote a letter and sent copies to the rulers of the city, to the leading citizens, and to the guardians of Ahab's descendants. The letter read: "You are in charge of the king's descendants, and you have at your disposal chariots, horses, weapons, and fortified cities. So then, as soon as you receive this letter, you are to choose the best qualified of the king's descendants, make him king, and fight to defend him." The rulers of Samaria were terrified, they said, "How can we oppose Jehu, when neither King Joram nor King Ahaziah could?" So the officer in charge of the palace and the official in charge of the city, together with the leading citizens and the guardians, sent this message to Jehu: "We are your servants, and we are ready to do anything you say. But we will not make anyone king; do whatever you think well." 6 Jehu wrote them another letter: "If you are with me and are ready to follow my orders, bring the heads of King Ahab's descendants to me at Jezreel by this time tomorrow." The seventy descendants of King Ahab were under the care of the leading citizens of Samaria, who were bringing them up.

'7 *When Jehu's letter was received, the leaders of Samaria killed all seventy of Ahab's descendants, put their heads in baskets, and sent them to Jehu at Jezreel.* 8 When Jehu was told that the heads of Ahab's descendants had been brought, he ordered them to be piled up in two heaps at the city gate and to be left there until the following morning. ₉ In the morning he went out to the gate and said to the people who were there, "I was the one who plotted against King Joram and killed him; you are not responsible for that. But who killed all these? ₁₀ This proves that everything that the Lord said about the descendants of Ahab will come true. The Lord has done what he promised through his prophet Elijah." ₁₁ *Then Jehu put to death all the other relatives of Ahab living in Jezreel, and all his officers, close friends, and priests; not one of them was left alive.* ₁₂ Jehu left Jezreel to go to Samaria. On the way, at a place called "Shepherds' Camp," ₁₃ he met some relatives of the late King Ahaziah of Judah and asked them, "Who are you?" "Ahaziah's relatives," they answered. "We are going to Jezreel to pay our respects to the children of Queen Jezebel and to the rest of the royal family." ₁₄ Jehu ordered his men, "Take them alive!" They seized them, and he put them to death near a pit there. There were forty-two people in all, and not one of them was left alive. ₁₅ Jehu started out again, and on his way he was met by Jonadab son of Rechab. Jehu greeted him and said, "You and I think alike. Will you support me?" "I will," Jonadab answered. "Give me your hand, then," Jehu replied. They clasped hands, and Jehu helped him up into the chariot, ₁₆ saying, "Come with me and see for yourself how devoted I am to the Lord." And they rode on together to Samaria. ₁₇ *When they arrived there, Jehu killed all of Ahab's relatives, not sparing even one. This is what the Lord had told Elijah would happen.* ₁₈ Jehu called the people of Samaria together and said, "King Ahab served the god Baal a little, but I will serve him much more. Call together all the prophets of Baal, all his worshipers, and all his priests. No one is excused; I am going to offer a great sacrifice to Baal, and whoever is not present will be put to death." (This was a trick on the part of Jehu by which he meant to kill all the worshipers of Baal.) Then Jehu ordered, "Proclaim a day of worship in honour of Baal!" The proclamation was made, and Jehu sent word throughout all the land of Israel. All who worshiped Baal came; not one of them failed to come. They all went into the temple of Baal, filling it from one end to the other. Then Jehu ordered the priest in charge of the sacred robes to bring the robes out and give them to the worshipers. After that, Jehu himself went into the temple with Jonadab son of Rechab and said to the people there, "Make sure that only worshipers of Baal are present and that no worshiper of the Lord has come in." ₂₄ Then he and Jonadab went in to offer sacrifices and burnt offerings to Baal. He had stationed eighty men outside the temple and had instructed them: *You are to kill all these people; anyone who lets one of them escapes will pay for it with his life!* ₂₅ As soon as Jehu had presented the offerings, he said to the guards and officers, *"Go in and kill them all; don't let anyone escape!" They went in with drawn swords, killed them all, and dragged the bodies outside. Then they went on into the inner sanctuary of the temple,* ₂₆ *brought out the sacred pillar that was there, and burned it.* ₂₇ *So they destroyed the sacred pillar and the temple, and turned the temple into a latrine—which it still is today.* ₂₈ That was how Jehu wiped out the worship of Baal in Israel. But he imitated the sin of King Jeroboam, who led Israel into the sin of worshiping the gold bull-calves he set up in Bethel and in Dan. ₃₀ *the Lord said to Jehu, "You have done to Ahab's descendants everything I wanted you to do. So I promise you that your descendants, down to the fourth generation, will be kings of Israel."* But Jehu did not obey with all his heart the Law of the Lord, the God of Israel; instead, he followed the example of Jeroboam, who led Israel into sin. At that time the Lord began to reduce the size of Israel's territory. King Hazael of Syria conquered all the Israelite territory ₃₃ east of the Jordan, as far south as the town of Aroer on the Arnon River—this included the territories of Gilead and Bashan, where the tribes of Gad, Reuben, and East Manasseh lived. ₃₄ Everything else that Jehu did, including his brave deeds, is recorded in *The History of the Kings of Israel.* He died and was buried in Samaria, and his son

Jehoahaz succeeded him as king. ₃₆ Jehu had ruled in Samaria as king of Israel for twenty-eight years.'

'In the above verse 34, it says *The History of the King[s] of Israel*; do such histories actually exist in real human earthly experience? I doubt it. Is this a summary of the extent of the God of Israel's horrific atrocities against anyone who disrespects his commandments, especially, worshipers of other gods such as the Baal?

Even if this history is real, what is its significance in a Holy Book such as the Holy Bible?

This is certainly a clear display of wickedness unmatched in any ancient fiction writing.

Twenty-eight years of continuous massacre without provocation by God of Israel's appointed assassin-Jehu and the rest. All of us have been converted by the Bible to accept this satanic God of Israel as our God too! Humanity is in serious dilemma! This God does not qualify to be the creator of this massive complex planet. He does not come close to be a father or mother of anyone or anything. He cannot claim to be a special God for Jews and at the same time act as God for all mankind with these kinds of bias behaviour in favour of just a single ethnic group out of over 7,000 world cultures.

It appears that Christians are desperate to have a single God to represent the entire universe, but their choice of God from among Jewish fictional history, God of Israel or the Genesis God, is a serious boo-boo as well as insult to logic. Such narratives as copied herewith show clearly that the so-called God of Israel is a Jewish myth created by Moses and maintained by succeeding generations of Jewish leaders. Prophet Elijah and all other biblical prophets followed Moses' traditions of trickery, brutality, and killing of anyone who worshiped Baal and other God besides God of Israel should not surprise any reader.

GNT.

2 Kings 11

'As soon as King Ahaziah's mother Athaliah learned of her son's murder, she gave orders for all the members of ₂ only the royal family to be killed. Ahaziah's son Joash escaped. He was about to be killed with the others, but was rescued by his aunt Jehosheba, who was King Jehoram's daughter and Ahaziah's half sister. She took him and his nurse into a bedroom in the Temple and hid him from Athaliah, so that he was not killed. For six years Jehosheba took care of the boy and kept him hidden in the Temple, while Athaliah ruled as queen. ₄ But in the seventh year Jehoiada the priest sent for the officers in charge of the royal bodyguard and of the palace guards, and told them to come to the Temple, where he made them agree under oath to what he planned to do. He showed them King Ahaziah's son Joash and gave them the following orders: "When you come on duty on the Sabbath, one third of you are to guard the palace; another third are to stand guard at the Sur Gate, and the other third are to stand guard at the gate behind the other guards. The two groups that go off duty on the Sabbath are to stand guard at the Temple to protect the king. ₈ You are to guard King Joash with drawn swords and stay with him wherever he goes. Anyone who comes near you is to be killed." ₉ The officers obeyed Jehoiada's instructions and brought their men to him—those going off duty on the Sabbath and those going on duty. ₁₀ He gave the officers the spears and shields that had belonged to King David and had been kept in the Temple, 11 and he stationed the men with drawn swords all around the front of the Temple, to protect the king. ₁₂ Then Jehoiada led Joash out, placed the crown on his head, and gave him a copy of the laws governing kingship. Then Joash was anointed and proclaimed king. The people clapped their hands and shouted, "Long live the kings!"

'₁₃ Queen Athaliah heard the noise being made by the guards and the people, so she hurried to the Temple, where the crowd had gathered. ₁₄ There she saw the new king standing by the column at the entrance of the Temple, as was the custom. He was surrounded by the officers and the trumpeters, and the people were all shouting joyfully and blowing trumpets. Athaliah tore her clothes in distress and shouted, "Treason! Treason!"₁₅ Jehoiada did not want Athaliah killed in the Temple area, so he ordered the army officers: "Take her out between the rows of guards, and kill anyone who tries to rescue her." ₁₆ They seized her, took her to the palace, and there at the Horse Gate they killed her. ₁₇ The priest Jehoiada had King Joash and the people make a covenant with the Lord that they would be the Lord's people; he also made a covenant between the king and the people. ₁₈ Then the people went to the temple of Baal and tore it down; they smashed the altars and the idols, and killed Mattan, the priest of Baal, in front of the altars. Jehoiada put guards on duty at the Temple, ₁₉ and then he, the officers, the royal bodyguard, and the palace guards escorted the king from the Temple to the palace, followed by all the people. Joash entered by the Guard Gate and took his place on the throne. ₂₀ All the people were filled with happiness, and the city was quiet, now that Athaliah had been killed in the palace. ₂₁ Joash became king of Judah at the age of seven.'

Kill, kill, kill, kill, nothing but killing; self-styled kings and warmongers of ancient Jewish descendants doing nothing but destruction of life because of religious fanaticism. Can these bizarre stories of killings have anything to do with a God of the universe, if indeed, there is such a thing? Is the cosmic God a reality, that the real God sees the Jewish God using his name and image to bring misery to peace-loving people of the planet earth? Must we still go on believing there is an entity called the God? Twenty-first-century earthly people have more than enough evidence to show that Godliness is obsolete, worthless, and absolute rubbish. There is simply 'No God.' Planet earth did not need a God, does not need a God, and will never need a God. There has never been one, and there can never be one of any kind for worldly people for any reason.

Two Identical Chapters: 2 King 19 and Isaiah 37.

2 King 19:

As soon as King Hezekiah heard their report, he tore his clothes in grief, put on sackcloth, and went to the Temple of the Lord. He sent Eliakim, the official in charge of the palace, Shebna, the court secretary, and the senior priests to the prophet Isaiah son of Amoz. They also were wearing sackcloth. This is the message which he told them to give Isaiah: "Today is a day of suffering; we are being punished and are in disgrace. We are like a woman who is ready to give birth, but is too weak to do it. The Assyrian emperor has sent his chief official to insult the living God. May the Lord your God hear these insults and punish those who spoke them. So pray to God for those of our people who survive."

'When Isaiah received King Hezekiah's message, he sent back this answer: "The Lord tells you not to let the Assyrians frighten you with their claims that he cannot save you. The Lord will cause the emperor to hear a rumor that will make him go back to his own country, and the Lord will have him killed there." The Assyrian official learned that the emperor had left Lachish and was fighting against the nearby city of Libnah; so he went there to consult him. Word reached the Assyrians that the Egyptian army, led by King Tirhakah of Ethiopia, was coming to attack them. When the emperor heard this, he sent a letter to King Hezekiah of Judah to tell him, "The god you are trusting in has told you that you will not fall into my hands, but don't let that deceive you. [11] You have heard what an Assyrian emperor does to any country he decides to destroy. Do you think that you can escape? My ancestors destroyed the cities of Gozan, Haran, and Rezeph, and killed the people of Betheden who lived in Telassar, and none of their gods could save them. Where are the kings of the cities of Hamath, Arpad,

Sepharvaim, Hena, and Ivvah?" King Hezekiah took the letter from the messengers and read it. Then he went to the Temple, placed the letter there in the presence of the Lord, and prayed, "O Lord, the God of Israel, seated on your throne above the winged creatures, you alone are God, ruling all the kingdoms of the world. You created the earth and the sky. Now, Lord, look at what is happening to us. Listen to all the things that Sennacherib is saying to insult you, the living God. We all know, Lord, that the emperors of Assyria have destroyed many nations, made their lands desolate, 18 and burned up their gods—which were no gods at all, only images of wood and stone made by human hands.

'Now, Lord our God, rescue us from the Assyrians, so that all the nations of the world will know that only you, O Lord, are God."

'Then Isaiah sent a message telling King Hezekiah that in answer to the king's prayer the Lord had said, "The city of Jerusalem laughs at you, Sennacherib, and makes fun of you. 22 Whom do you think you have been insulting and ridiculing? You have been disrespectful to me, the holy God of Israel. You sent your messengers to boast to me that with all your chariots you had conquered the highest mountains of Lebanon. You boasted that there you cut down the tallest cedars and the finest cypress trees and that you reached the deepest parts of the forests. You boasted that you dug wells and drank water in foreign lands and that the feet of your soldiers tramped the Nile River dry. Have you never heard that I planned all this long ago? And now I have carried it out. I gave you the power to turn fortified cities into piles of rubble. The people who lived there were powerless; they were frightened and stunned. They were like grass in a field or weeds growing on a roof when the hot east wind blasts them. But I know everything about you, what you do and where you go. I know how you rage against me. I have received the report of that rage and that pride of yours, and now I will put a hook through your nose and a bit in your mouth, and take you back by the same road you came." Then

Isaiah said to King Hezekiah, "Here is a sign of what will happen. This year and next you will have only wild grain to eat, but the following year you will be able to plant your grain and harvest it and plant vines and eat grapes. Those in Judah who survive will flourish like plants that send roots deep into the ground and produce fruit. There will be people in Jerusalem and on Mount Zion who will survive, because the Lord is determined to make this happen. ₃₂ And this is what the Lord has said about the Assyrian emperor: 'He will not enter this city or shoot a single arrow against it. No soldiers with shields will come near the city, and no siege mounds will be built around it. ₃₃ He will go back by the same road he came, without entering this city. I, the Lord, have spoken. ₃₄ I will defend this city and protect it, for the sake of my own honor and because of the promise I made to my servant David.'" ₃₅ That night an angel of the Lord went to the Assyrian camp and killed 185,000 soldiers. At dawn the next day there they lay, all dead! Then the Assyrian emperor Sennacherib withdrew and returned to Nineveh. One day, when he was worshiping in the temple of his god Nisroch, two of his sons, Adrammelech and Sharezer, killed him with their swords and then escaped to the land of Ararat. Another of his sons, Esarhaddon, succeeded him as emperor.'

If you reread from verse 32 to 35, you will notice that for God's own honour and the promise he made to his servant David, he sent an angel to massacre an army of 185,000 Assyrians (non-Jews). 'That night an angel of the Lord went to the Assyrian camp and killed 185,000 soldiers.'

God and his angels are vicariously responsible for whatever action either of the two undertakes. It is extremely pitiful that Christians always find fictitious reason for every action of this ancient Jewish Satan who is most often painted as a blameless God. A God does no wrong. But this particular Jewish creature has said it more than 1,000 times that he is not in favour of anyone who is not a Jew, and especially worshipers of other gods. Every non-Jew is a foreigner and not under the protection of God of Israel according to this very God of Israel.

GNT.
According to Isaiah

Isaiah contains at least three separate books, written about a Jewish prophet who lived in Jerusalem at the end of the eighth BC. The book was not written by Prophet Isaiah.

Isaiah 1:
'This book contains the messages about Judah and Jerusalem which God revealed to Isaiah son of Amoz during the time when Uzziah, Jotham, Ahaz, and Hezekiah were kings of Judah.

'God Reprimands His People.

'The Lord said, "Earth and sky, listen to what I am saying! The children I brought up have rebelled against me. Cattle know who owns them, and donkeys know where their master feeds them. But that is more than my people Israel know. They don't understand at all." You are doomed, you sinful nation, you corrupt and evil people! Your sins drag you down! You have rejected the Lord, the holy God of Israel, and have turned your backs on him. Why do you keep on rebelling? Do you want to be punished even more? *Israel*, your head is already covered with wounds, and your heart and mind are sick. From head to foot there is not a healthy spot on your body. You are covered with bruises and sores and open wounds. Your wounds have not been cleaned or bandaged. No medicine has been put on them. 7 Your country has been devastated, and your cities have been burned to the ground. *While you look on, foreigners take over your land and bring everything to ruin.* Jerusalem alone is left, a city under siege—as defenseless as a guard's hut in a vineyard or a shed in a cucumber field. If the Lord Almighty had not let some of the people survive, Jerusalem would have been totally destroyed, just as Sodom and Gomorrah were. Jerusalem, your rulers and your people are like those of Sodom and Gomorrah. Listen to what the Lord is saying to you. Pay attention to what our God is teaching you. ₁₁ He says, "Do you think I want all these sacrifices you keep offering to me? I have had more than enough of the sheep you burn as sacrifices and of the fat of your fine animals. I am tired of the blood of bulls and sheep and goats. Who asked you to bring me all this when you come to worship me? Who asked you to do all this tramping around in my Temple? It's useless to bring your offerings. I am disgusted with the smell of the incense you burn. I cannot stand your New Moon Festivals, your Sabbaths, and your religious gatherings; they are all corrupted by your sins. I hate your New Moon Festivals and holy days; they are a burden that I am tired of bearing. When you lift your hands in prayer, I will not look at you. No matter how much you pray, I will not listen, for your hands are covered with blood. Wash yourselves clean. Stop all this evil that I see you doing. Yes, stop doing evil and learn to do right. See that justice is done—help those who are oppressed, give orphans their rights, and defend widows." ₁₈ The Lord says, "Now, let's settle the matter. You are stained red with sin, but I will wash you as clean as snow. Although your stains are deep red, you will be as white as wool. ¹⁹ If you will only obey me, you will eat the good things the land produces. ²⁰ But if you defy me, you are doomed to die. I, the Lord, have spoken." The Sinful City ²¹ the city that once was faithful is behaving like a whore! At one time it was filled with righteous people, but now only murderers remain.'

Is it not this very God who nurtured Israelites to be who and what they are today? How can God of Israel forget his own creation and his prescribed method of praying? The Ten Commandments he wrote on the first and the second tablets through Moses to the Israelites—the eye for eye, hand for hand, foot for foot, and the rest of all the evil moralities? Is this God suffering from amnesia, or he is not the same super perfect Spiritual one and only one Omni,

Alpha, and Omega? Worldly people are really supposed to have faith in a thing like the God Israel? Unbelievable! We really need to think seriously about these biblical dictums.

The author of the above chapter obviously has not encountered the earlier scriptures in the Pentateuch. He or she appears to be oblivious of who or what God really is supposed to be, according to the book of Genesis.

'Jerusalem, you were once like silver, but now you are worthless; you were like good wine, but now you are only water. Your leaders are rebels and friends of thieves; they are always accepting gifts and bribes. They never defend orphans in court or listen when widows present their case. So now, listen to what the Lord Almighty, Israel's powerful God, is saying: "I will take revenge on you, my enemies, and you will cause me no more trouble. I will take action against you. I will purify you the way metal is refined, and will remove all your impurity. I will give you rulers and advisers like those you had long ago. Then Jerusalem will be called the righteous, faithful city." Because the Lord is righteous, he will save Jerusalem and everyone there who repents. But he will crush everyone who sins and rebels against him; he will kill everyone who forsakes him. You will be sorry that you ever worshiped trees and planted sacred gardens. You will wither like a dying oak, like a garden that no one waters. Just as straw is set on fire by a spark, so powerful people will be destroyed by their own evil deeds, and no one will be able to stop the destruction.'

Is there any difference between the voice of the devil and the voice of God?

GNT; Isaiah 28: 'The kingdom of Israel is doomed! Its glory is fading like the crowns of flowers on the heads of its drunken leaders. Their proud heads are well perfumed, but there they lie, dead drunk. The Lord has someone strong and powerful ready to attack them, someone who will come like a hailstorm, like a torrent of rain, like a rushing, overpowering flood, and will overwhelm the land. ₃ The pride of those drunken leaders will be trampled underfoot. ₄ The fading glory of those proud leaders will disappear like the first figs of the season, picked and eaten as soon as they are ripe. ₅ A day is coming when the Lord Almighty will be like a glorious crown of flowers for his people who survive. ₆ He will give a sense of justice to those who serve as judges, and courage to those who defend the city gates from attack.

'₇ *Even the prophets and the priests are so drunk that they stagger. They have drunk so much wine and liquor that they stumble in confusion. The prophets are too drunk to understand the visions that God sends, and the priests are too drunk to decide the cases that are brought to them.* ₈ *The tables where they sit are all covered with vomit, and not a clean spot is left.* They complain about me. They say, "Who does that man think he's teaching? Who needs his message? It's only good for babies that have just stopped nursing! ₁₀ He is trying to teach us letter by letter, line by line, lesson by lesson." If you won't listen to me, then God will use foreigners speaking some strange-sounding language to teach you a lesson. ₁₂ He offered rest and comfort to all of you, but you refused to listen to him. ₁₃ That is why the Lord is going to teach you letter by letter, line by line, lesson by lesson. Then you will stumble with every step you take. You will be wounded, trapped, and taken prisoner.

'Now you arrogant leaders, who rule here in Jerusalem over this people, listen to what the Lord is saying. You boast that you have made a treaty with death and reached an agreement with the world of the dead. You are certain that disaster will spare you when it comes, because you depend on lies and deceit to keep you safe.

'This, now, is what the Sovereign Lord says: "I am placing in Zion a foundation that is firm and strong. In it I am putting a solid cornerstone on which are written the words, 'Faith that is firm is also patient.' Justice will be the measuring line for the foundation, and honesty will be its plumb line." Hailstorms will sweep away all the lies you depend on, and floods will destroy your security.

The treaty you have made with death will be abolished, and your agreement with the world of the dead will be cancelled. When disaster sweeps down, you will be overcome. It will strike you again and again, morning after morning. You will have to bear it day and night. Each new message from God will bring new terror! You will be like the person in the proverb, who tries to sleep in a bed too short to stretch out on, with a blanket too narrow to wrap himself in. The Lord will fight as he did at Mount Perazim and in the valley of Gibeon, in order to do what he intends to do—strange as his actions may seem. He will complete his work, his mysterious work. Don't laugh at the warning I am giving you! If you do, it will be even harder for you to escape. I have heard the Lord Almighty's decision to destroy the whole country. Listen to what I am saying; pay attention to what I am telling you. Farmers don't constantly plough their fields and keep getting them ready for planting. Once they have prepared the soil, they plant the seeds of herbs such as dill and cumin. They plant rows of wheat and barley, and at the edges of their fields they plant other grain. They know how to do their work, because God has taught them. They never use a heavy club to beat out dill seeds or cumin seeds; instead they use light sticks of the proper size. They do not ruin the wheat by threshing it endlessly, and they know how to thresh it by driving a cart over it without bruising the grains. All this wisdom comes from the Lord Almighty. The plans God makes are wise, and they always succeed.' Is human knowledge not the sum total of information acquired during lifetime, and therefore called 'mind,' and cannot be a God-given thing? Please, reader, think deeply about this!

GNT.

Isaiah 37

As soon as King Hezekiah heard their report, he tore his clothes in grief, put on sackcloth, and went to the Temple of the Lord. He sent Eliakim, the official in charge of the palace, Shebna, the court secretary, and the senior priests to the prophet Isaiah son of Amoz. They also were wearing sackcloth.

'This is the message which he told them to give to Isaiah: "Today is a day of suffering; we are being punished and are in disgrace. We are like a woman who is ready to give birth, but is too weak to do it. The Assyrian emperor has sent his chief official to insult the living God. May the Lord your God hear these insults and punish those who spoke them. So pray to God for those of our people who survive." When Isaiah received King Hezekiah's message, he sent back this answer: "The Lord tells you not to let the Assyrians frighten you by their claims that he cannot save you. The Lord will cause the emperor to hear a rumor that will make him go back to his own country, and the Lord will have him killed there." The Assyrian official learned that the emperor had left Lachish and was fighting against the nearby city of Libnah; so he went there to consult him. Word reached the Assyrians that the Egyptian army, led by King Tirhakah of Ethiopia, was coming to attack them. When the emperor heard this, he sent a letter to King Hezekiah of Judah to tell him: "The god you are trusting in has told you that you will not fall into my hands, but don't let that deceive you. You have heard what an Assyrian emperor does to any country he decides to destroy. Do you think that you can escape? My ancestors destroyed the cities of Gozan, Haran, and Rezeph, and killed the people of Betheden who lived in Telassar, and none of their gods could save them. Where are the kings of the cities of Hamath, Arpad, Sepharvaim, Hena, and Ivvah?" King Hezekiah took the letter from the messengers and read it. Then he went to the Temple, placed the letter there in the presence of the Lord, *15 and prayed*, [*this is the second shortest verse in the Holy Bible; Next to 'Jesus wept' John 11, 35.*] "Almighty Lord, God of Israel, seated above the winged creatures, you alone are God, ruling all the kingdoms of the world. You created the earth and the sky. Now, Lord, hear us and look at what is happening to us. Listen to all the things that Sennacherib is saying to insult you, the living God. We all know, Lord, that the emperors of Assyria have destroyed many nations, made their lands desolate, and burned up their gods—which were no gods at all, only images of wood and stone made by human hands. Now, Lord our God, rescue us from the Assyrians, so that all the nations of the world will know that you alone are God." Lord had said, "The city of Jerusalem laughs at you, Sennacherib, and makes fun of you. Whom do you think you have been insulting and ridiculing? You have been disrespectful to me, the holy God of Israel. 24 You sent your servants to boast to me that with all your chariots you had conquered the highest mountains of Lebanon. You boasted that there you cut down the tallest cedars and the finest cypress trees, and that you reached the deepest parts of the forests. 25 You boasted that you dug wells and drank water in foreign lands, and that the feet of your soldiers tramped the Nile River dry. 26. Have you ever heard that I planned all this long ago? And now I have carried it out. I gave you the power to turn fortified cities into piles of rubble. 27 The people who lived there were powerless; they were frightened and stunned. They were like grass in a field or weeds growing on a roof when the hot east wind blasts them. 28 But I know everything about you, what you do and where you go. I know how you rage against me. 29 I have received the report of that rage and that pride of yours, and now I will put a hook through your nose and a bit in your mouth and will take you back by the same road you came." 30 Then Isaiah said to King Hezekiah, "Here is a sign of what will happen. This year and next you will have only wild grain to eat, but the following year you will be able to plant grain and harvest it and plant vines and eat grapes. 31 Those in Judah who survive will flourish like plants that send roots deep into the ground and produce fruit. 32 There will be people in Jerusalem and on Mount Zion who will survive, because the Lord Almighty is determined to make this happen. 33 And this is what the Lord has said about the Assyrian emperor: 'He will not enter this city or shoot a single arrow against it. No soldiers with shields will come near the city, and no siege mounds will be built around it. ₃₄ He will go back by the same road he came, without entering this city. I, the Lord, have spoken. ₃₅ I will defend this city and protect it, for the sake of my own honour and because of the promise I made to my servant David.'" ₃₆ An angel of the Lord went to the Assyrian camp and killed 185,000 soldiers. At dawn the next day there they lay, all dead! ₃₇ Then the Assyrian emperor Sennacherib withdrew and returned to Nineveh. ₃₈ One day when he was worshiping in the temple of his god Nisroch, two of his sons, Adrammelech and Sharezer, killed him with their swords and then escaped to the land of Ararat. Another of his sons, Esarhaddon, succeeded him as emperor.'

Can there be any reason why two chapters from two separate books of the Holy Bible contain almost exact words and sentences? Although 2 King 19 contains 37 verses and Isaiah 37 has 38 verses, the two are of the same content.

Is it a printing error or a deliberate fault, or an intentional act by the initial authors of the two books?

Irenaeus, the first conductor of a search for biblical history, is known to be very meticulous in his works. He was a reader, librarian, writer, and a bishop, and it is not likely he would make such blunder. Did he probably see a need to emphasize in the two books the history of Israelites' downfall? No. Not likely. His words and sentences would have been different. If it were his, the style of writing would have matched that of the second-century literary works.

Again, Emperor Constantine 1 and his select 300 Bishops are not likely either to create this chapter duplication because their choice of books and their tiles plus chapters and verses were assigned to various meticulous bishops whose public images mattered most to them at the time.

Again, on account of the two books' histories, one cannot rule out the fourth-century bishops agreeing to assign a book title to

Prophet Isaiah because of his famous prophetic sayings about the forthcoming Messiah: the three prophecies of the coming of the 'symbol', Immanuel, 'the 'Bethlehem birth', and David ancestry' and also to title a book called '2 King,' and consciously inserting Chapter 19 with exact words, verses, and sentences of previously approved book of Isaiah chapter 37.

The two books were most likely written between eighth and fifth centuries by possibly two separate authors reporting a historical turning point of the Israelites. Both authors saw the need to tell that particular story, but why are the two chapters the same. It is known however that the book of Isaiah was written by three separate authors. The first author wrote chapters 1 to 39, and it is unlikely the same writer would copy this chapter and paste it as chapter 19 of 2 Kings.

The most logical answer to this duplication is the fact that the Bible has passed through several transformations since the third. Century AD; it is most likely to be a human error. Or indeed it can be taken as a clear indication to readers that Holy Bible is no different from other books. There is something called 'a human error'. An example of this kind of human error is Deuteronomy 14. All the verses from 13 to 18 and a few others in the same chapter and book are completely missing out of the Holy Bible. Why error? Why not intentional? In numerical counting, we count from 1, 2, 3, 4, and up, in arithmetic order, not in geometric order of jumping from 1 to 4 to 8, as it is done in the above-quoted verses. Some religious addicts loosely proudly call it a holy book.

According to Joel
GNT.

Nobody knows for certain the author of 'Joel,' the twenty-ninth book of the Holy Bible. This book is generally believed to have been written between 500 and 400 years before the birth of Christ.

The entire book contains only 3 chapters with 73 verses, and it represents one of the ancient Jewish prophets.

The author begins, 'This is the Lord's message to Joel son of Pethuel.' This first sentence tells the reader that the author is reporting a message allegedly, given by the 'Lord' to someone called Joel. The day of the Lord is coming soon. It will be a dark and gloomy day, a black and cloudy day. The great army of locusts advances like darkness spreading over the mountains. Like fire they eat up the plants. The troops that obey him are many and mighty. Do not let other nations despise us and mock us by saying, 'Where is your God? I will remove the locust army that came from the north and will drive some of them into the desert. *It was I who sent this army against you. Israel, you will know that I am among you and that I, the Lord, is your God and there is no other.'*

The author continues: 'The Lord says, "At that time I will restore the prosperity of Judah and Jerusalem. I will gather all the nations and bring them to the Valley of Judgment. There I will judge them for all they have done to my people. They have scattered the Israelites in foreign countries and divided Israel, my land. They threw dice to decide who would get the captives. They sold boys and girls into slavery to pay for prostitutes and wine. You have taken my silver and gold and carried my rich treasures into your temples. You have taken the people of Judah and Jerusalem far away from their own country and sold them to the Greeks. I will let your sons and daughters be sold to the people of Judah; they will sell them to the far-off Sabeans. I, the Lord, have spoken. Israel, you will know that I am the Lord your God. I live on Zion, my sacred hill. Jerusalem will be a sacred place. Egypt will become a desert, and Edom a ruined waste, because they attacked the land of Judah and killed its innocent people.'

Has the Lord God of Israel forgotten the instruction he gave to Moses during the Jews exodus to Canaan, to kill everyone including children, women, men, and the sick innocent people?

How can the God for Israel avenge those who were killed? This booklet is deliberately dramatized or written to sound like the author is Joel himself and that Lord God of Israel gave him the message directly to the people of Egypt, Judah, and Jerusalem. Also note the powerful mode of God's speech, the inverted quotations from God himself.

The problem with this book is that God of Israel proves clearly that he has no direct link with the individual Jews who were alive at that time; hence, all his messages must pass through a prophet or a messenger.

The most baffling question is, if God is real and had been everywhere every time with all humans, though this time with Jews only, why must he always speak through a messenger to carry out his instructions to the rest of the people? Can anyone justify God's omnipresent title? In fact, it is said in this same Holy Bible that God is with us wherever we are. He is spiritually always with us. If this is so, how come he cannot communicate directly with every human being, one on one term but rather passes through a messenger, a second person? God is definitely aware that a situation like that creates imposters who will claim to be speaking with the voice of God. Indeed, at his initial confrontation with God, Moses asked God, how he could make the people believe that he, Moses, was God's messenger. And God told Moses to perform magic with his stick. Hence, anyone who can perform wonders, such as theological magicians and tricksters, popularly known as miracle performers, can claim to be God's messengers. God's messengers, prophets, bishops, reverends, pastors, and their kind must therefore necessarily learn how to perform magic, because without that they will not be trusted as true representatives of God. This is precisely the reason why religious leaders and fanatics always try to win followers with illusions, blatant lies, and other corrupt practices.

It may be true also that Jesus Christ was persecuted by his own Jewish people with a singular charge of being an imposter, pretending to be the prophesied messiah with his magical performances. Ironically, all the illusions cited in the New Testament by Jesus are described as miracles instead of magic. Indeed they were not different from performances of other biblical magicians like Simeon and Mithras.

God's presence everywhere at all times, his infinite knowledge, and power of creation together makes one wonder when a prophet announces God's anger about certain negative human behaviour.

According to Amos
GNT.

The thirtieth book of the Holy Bible is a bit unique compared with the other prophetic books in the Bible. The *author* introduces Amos as the first Jewish prophet whose message was recorded at length. He is from Tekoa, a town in Judah. And he preached to the people of the northern kingdom of Israel during the middle of the eighth century BC. That Amos was concerned with the prevailing economic inequity among Jews at the time. That the rich had become too rich while the poor had been poorer.

In chapter 2, for instance, Amos, the most respected spiritual link between Jews and their God, is using such words as God and God of Israel to threaten his fellow Jews who were tempted to worship other gods. All possible benefits as well as punishments which all Jews will gain for obedience or suffer for disobedience are listed *by the author* and written in quotes as direct words of God. The entire chapter 2 is God's words in quotation marks. The author is not Amos but a reporter of God's message to the people of Moab, Judah, and Israel given through Amos.

Another way of understanding Amos's story is this. Amos had a dream in which God of Israel gave him a message to be delivered to the Israelites. In practical sense, Amos alone heard the message. The Jews had no way to verify the authenticity of the message except by faith in the prophet and their God. Without faith, therefore, Amos and God of Israel are irrelevant. Reason and faith are therefore necessarily incompatible. But when faith leads people to frustration and self-destruction through false hope, reason always prevails, and this has been the result in all religions and cultures.

The author continues in chapter 3 with the same pleasing voice of God of Israel to the people of Israel. The message this time is a reminder of their past and affirmation of God's infinite unique love for Jews among all the nations on earth. Jews are the only people God has known and cared for. And that is what makes their sins so terrible, and therefore must be punished.

'The houses decorated with ivory will fall in ruins; every large house will be destroyed,' so says the Lord according to Amos's dream as reported by the author of book of Amos.

Let us now introduce the God of Israel to other non-Jews and then asses if the same God can serve as a God for all. God is aware of the existence of other nations, but he himself has declared over and over that his name 'God of Israel' stands for the Israelites, the ancestors of Abraham, Isaac, and Jacob only. The Jewish prophet Micah minced no words 'That each nation worships and obeys its own god, but Israelites will worship and obey the Lord their God forever and ever. That this is what makes your sin so terrible, and that is why God must punish you for them'—very eloquent indeed!

All the prophets in the Bible are Jews, and they have preached Jewish codes of ethics for all descendants of Abraham, Isaac, and Jacob. Righteousness and sin in the Hebrew world are found in most of the sixty-six books; hence, the book of Amos is merely amplifying the already known and expected behaviour of all circumcised Jews that, first, no Jew will be exempted from punishments if God of Israel is disrespected, and second, it shall be a crime with death penalty when a Jew worships a different God besides the God of Israel.

But a critical study of the Bible shows that there is a marked behaviour difference between the God of Israelites and the Creator God in Genesis.

It is also noted that Jewish prophets consistently make their God sound and behave like the Genesis God who is supposed to be the source of all planetary knowledge. At the same time, and more often, all the prophets assign human image to the God of Israel. It is observed again in Genesis chapter 4 to chapter 10 that the author tried to mould the creator God to become a God who is solely responsible for Jewish affairs. It would have been expected that 'a know-all God, the Omnipresent' need not complain of human fault, because of this basic presumption.

In Amos 8, the following is written: 'I had another vision from the Sovereign Lord. In it I saw a basket of fruit. The Lord asked, "Amos, what do you see?" "A basket of fruit," I answered. The *Lord said to me, "The end has come for my people Israel. I will not change my mind again about punishing them."* On that day the songs in the palace will become cries of mourning. There will be dead bodies everywhere. They will be cast out in silence. Listen to this, you that trample on the needy and try to destroy the poor of the country. *"The Lord, the God of Israel, has sworn, 'I will never forget their evil deeds.'"* And so the earth will quake, and everyone in the land will be in distress. The whole country will be shaken; it will rise and falls like the Nile River. 9 The time is coming when I will make the sun go down at noon and the earth will grow dark in daytime. I, the Sovereign Lord, have spoken. I will turn your festivals into funerals and change your glad songs into cries of grief. I will make you shave your heads and wear sackcloth, and you will be like parents mourning for their only child. That day will be bitter to the end. The time is coming when I will send famine on the land. People will be hungry, but not for bread; they will be thirsty, but not for water. They will hunger and thirst for a message from the

Lord. I, the Sovereign Lord, have spoken. People will wander from the Dead Sea to the Mediterranean, and then on around from the north to the east. *They will look everywhere for a message from the Lord, but they will not find it.* Those who swear by the idols of Samaria, who say, "By the god of Dan" or "By the god of Beersheba," those people will fall and not rise again.'

Prophet Amos has spoken about his encounter with the Sovereign Lord in a dream in which there were dead bodies everywhere. In the same dream, festivals had turned into funerals and glad songs into cries of grief. This Jewish God claims to be superior in everything, and I am pretty sure prophet Amos is aware of this limitless power of the God of Israel. The question however is why should there be in existence the idol of Samaria, the God of Dan, the God of Beersheba, and the other gods? Evidently, these idols are present because the Israelites have faith in them, possibly more than God of Israel, or possibly the God of Israel is known to be impotent. The Jews appear to be terrified by some utterances of orthodox prophets, especially their promises of severe retribution when they fail to worship him. But obviously they are fed up with empty words.

But having said all these, can't we, the Bible readers, critically assess the godly ideas holistically? Ancient thinkers or knowledgeable citizens who lived in Jewish communities could predict events ahead of time because of their learned and aged experiences of their environment. Their predictions have nothing to do with spirits or any unseen power source. Some of their observations were obviously based on primitive science. When we add their inducted superstitious beliefs, prophets of the past could be what modernity terms as soothsayers, magicians, or producers of mystical ideas.

In chapter 9, Amos claims to have seen the Lord standing by the altar giving command to someone to strike the tops of the Temple columns so hard that the foundation will shake and break off and let them fall on the heads of the people. But, the question is, to whom is the Lord asking to do the damage? 'I will kill the rest of the people in war. No one will get away; not one will escape. Even if they dig their way down to the world of the dead, I will catch them. Even if they climb up to heaven, I will bring them down. If they hide on the top of Mount Carmel, I [the Lord] will search for them and catch them. If they hide from me at the bottom of the sea, I will command the sea monster to bite them. If they are taken away into captivity by their enemies, I will order them to be put to death. I am determined to destroy them, not to help them.'

This is reminiscence of twentieth-century European monster Adolf Hitler's commandment to leaders of the Weimar Republic 'heads will roll'.

In verses 2, 3, and 4, the Lord himself, using the first person singular 'I,' is doing the earthly damage himself. Note the verses 5, 6, 7. The author is reporting specific actions of the Sovereign Almighty God. He touched the earth, and it quakes; all who live there mourn. The whole world rises and falls like the Nile River. The Lord builds his home in the heavens, and over the earth he puts the dome of the sky. He calls for the waters of the sea and pours them out on the earth. His name is the Lord! The Lord says, 'People of Israel, I think as much of the people of Ethiopia as I do of you. I brought the Philistines from Crete and the Syrians from Kir, just as I brought you from Egypt. I, the Sovereign Lord, am watching this sinful kingdom of Israel, and I will destroy it from the face of the earth. But I will not destroy all the descendants of Jacob. I will give the command and shake the people of Israel like grain in a sieve. I will shake them among the nations to remove all who are worthless. The sinners among my people will be killed in war, all those who say, "God will not let any harm come near us."' The Lord says, 'A day is coming when I will restore the kingdom of David, which is like a house fallen into ruins. I will repair its walls and restore it. I will rebuild it and make it as it was long ago.

And so the people of Israel will conquer what is left of the land of Edom and all the nations that were once mine,' says the Lord, who will cause this to happen. 'The days are coming,' says the Lord, 'when grain will grow faster than it can be harvested, and grapes will grow faster than the wine can be made. The mountains will drip with sweet wine, and the hills will flow with it. I will bring my people back to their land. They will rebuild their ruined cities and live there; they will plant vineyards and drink the wine; they will plant gardens and eat what they grow. I will plant my people on the land I gave them, and they will not be pulled up again.' The Lord your God has spoken.

The entire chapter 9 of Amos sounds like a bluff from a typical human being in a leadership position who is unaware of his limited powers over his subordinates and who has been provoked by insubordination to the extent that he vows to punish offenders mercilessly. God of Israel knows he is a spirit and reliance on him by the ancient Jews for anything was based on faith. But faith is not free; it is always offered in exchange for something. The Israelites refuse to worship the God of their ancestors because the new generation found him ineffective, useless, obsolete, valueless, and completely worthless. Faith is utility-based. Faith does not depend on threats and empty words.

The most embarrassing aspect of this is the assigned spiritual sovereignty of the God of Israel. The title God and God's behaviour don't match. God's spiritual invincibility is evidently completely meaningless.

According to Jeremiah
GNT.

It is common knowledge among religious people that God actually possess endless power of creating everything in the universe. The Holy Bible, the Book of Koran and the Torah have

197

made this abundantly clear that creation is God's prerogative. But there are several chapters and verses in the three books mentioned above which contradict the infinite power idea.

In the twenty-fourth book of the Holy Bible for example, Prophet Jeremiah spoke to the people of Jerusalem that if they run through their streets and marketplaces, they would see for themselves that not a single person does what is right and tries to be faithful to God. Even though they claim to worship the Lord, they do not mean what you say. Surely the Lord looks for faithfulness. Everyone was stubborn and would not turn from their sins. They behave foolishly and did not know what their God requires or what the Lord wants them to do. The prophet decided to go to the people in power and talk with them, hoping they would succeed to persuade ordinary people to do what is right. *But all of them rejected the Lord's authority and refused to obey him, and the Lord asked himself why he should forgive the sins of his people? They have abandoned him and have worshiped gods that are not real.*

Thus according to this seventh BC prophet, worshipping other gods instead of the God of Israel is the greatest sin of all. The question we should ask God of Israel is, who made the so-called other gods? Were they also made by the same God? If they are so detestable by God himself, why were they created? And even if God made them by mistake, why can't God destroy all of them with his unlimited creative powers? He can surely eliminate all other gods or indeed make them powerless so that his jealousies of other gods would end forever. God appears to be unaware of his godly creative powers.

In frustration, the prophet continued talking, 'I fed my people until they were full, but they committed adultery and spent their time with prostitutes. They were like well-fed stallions wild with desire, each lusting for his neighbor's wife. Shouldn't I punish them for these things and take revenge on a nation such as this? I will send enemies to cut down my people's vineyards, but not to destroy them completely. I will tell them to strip away the branches, because those branches are not mine. The people of Israel and Judah have betrayed me completely. I, the Lord, have spoken. *They have said that the prophets are nothing but windbags and that they have no message from the Lord.* The Lord God Almighty said to me Jeremiah, that because these people have said such ugly things, he will turn my words into fire in my mouth, and the people will be like wood and the fire will burn them up. People of Israel the Lord is bringing a nation from far away to attack you. It is a strong and ancient nation, a nation whose language you do not know. Their archers are mighty soldiers who kill without mercy. They will devour your crops and your food; they will kill your sons and your daughters. They will slaughter your flocks and your herds and destroy your vines and fig trees. The fortified cities in which you trust will be destroyed by their army. The Lord says, 'Yet even in those days I will not completely destroy my people. When they ask why I did all these things, tell them, Jeremiah, that just as they turned away from me and served foreign gods in their own land, so they will serve strangers in a land that is not theirs.' *The Lord says, 'Tell the descendants of Jacob, tell the people of Judah: Pay attention, you foolish and stupid people, who have eyes, but cannot see, and have ears, but cannot hear. I am the Lord; why don't you fear me? Why don't you tremble before me?* You are stubborn and rebellious; you have turned aside and left me. But I, the Lord, will punish them for these things; I will take revenge on this nation.'

Jeremiah's God, the God of Israel, has demonstrated clearly through Jeremiah himself that he does not tolerate idol worshippers that the nation of Israel will be wiped out if they refuse to worship God of Israel. Again, the most perplexing question is, is the God of Israel no more responsible or no more in charge of Jews behaviour? He certainly possesses the power to make people, including Jews, do whatever he desires. Can he not command every Jew to stay hooked up to worship him alone forever? Why does God allow the Jews to be 'stupid and foolish' Jeremiah 5: 21 in the first place and then punish the people for their foolishness? Here again, the quality of God as the omnipotent and the only one who knows all at all times is evidently no more valid for the millionth time.

Jeremiah 17: 1-5: The Lord says, 'People of Judah, your sin is written with an iron pen; it is engraved on your hearts with a diamond point and carved on the corners of your altars. Your people worship at the altars and the symbols that have been set up for the goddess Asherah by every green tree and on the hilltops and on the mountains in the open country. I will have your enemies take away your wealth and your treasures because of all the sins you have committed throughout your land. You will have to give up the land I gave you, and I will make you serve your enemies in a land you know nothing about, because my anger is like a fire, and it will burn forever.' The Lord says, 'I will condemn those who turn away from me and put their trust in human beings, in the strength of mortals. Lord, you are Israel's hope; all who abandon you will be put to shame, because they have abandoned you.'

In this chapter, the Lord God of Israel seems to have forgotten that every action of people in Judah is under his control. As a God, he can switch off and on everyone's mind from worshipping any God besides himself. God of Israel is either a bad manager of human actions or he does not possess those qualities assigned to him by ancient Jews. Jeremiah, like all other ancient Jewish prophets, is obviously demonstrating his close links with God, but his godly messages conflicts with the supremacy of the all-powerful entity known as God of Israel.

If God is real, God should know he is supreme and therefore should not be worried about inferior gods and those who choose to worship them. Traditionally, Christians are forbidden to apply common sense to biblical texts as I am doing here, but I seriously wish to draw reader's attention to such commonsense issues in the Holy Bible. In the absence of that, all of us would be guilty in promoting ancient Jewish foolishness because of religious faith; Christian faith.

The enemy will surround the city and try to kill its people. The siege will be so terrible that the people inside the city will eat one another and even their own children. The Lord Almighty, the God of Israel, had said, 'I am going to bring on this city and on every nearby town all the punishment that I said I would, because you are stubborn and will not listen to what I say.' (GNT. Jer. 19: 9, 15)

Bearing in mind that Jeremiah and of course everyone in the Bible is a Jew, this Jewish prophet is saying that the God for Israelites has told him to tell everyone who worship Baal at Hinnom Valley that he is about to destroy the city, to the extent that the people inside the city will eat one another and their own children.

If the above statement was from Jeremiah himself but not from his God, it would be unfair for anyone to question it. But to say the Lord Almighty God of Israel has instructed him to say so means a lot to a critical reader. First, why would God make available other gods like Baal in any Jewish community? He can prevent other gods. And second, why would the Almighty God make his beloved humans (Jews) worship any other God besides himself? This God of Israel's power is supposed to supersede all human actions. If God is the custodian of Ultimate Power as preached by Jewish Prophets and Christian fellowship and judged by such prophetic utterances in the Holy Bible, either the said Jewish God is not aware of his powers or there is no such thing as God of any description, a Jewish, a Palestinian, a Greek, a Chinese, an Akan, a Scottish, or any cultural God. Job 15: 11 is right; religious leaders manufacture such godly names and statements for mere comfort.

It is probably noticed throughout this discourse that God's lack of awareness of his assigned unique prerogatives is repeated many times. It is so because it is unavoidable. Authors of the holy Bible are so determined to impress Bible readers that the Biblical God

possess awesome powers over all human actions, but none is backed
by action and performance.

Jeremiah 23; Lord's judgment on those rulers who destroy and
scatter his people! This is what the Lord, the God of Israel, says
about the rulers who were supposed to take care of his people 'You
have not taken care of my people; you have scattered them and
driven them away. Now I am going to punish you for the evil you
have done. I will gather the rest of my people from the countries
where I have scattered them, and I will bring them back to their
homeland. They will have many children and increase in number.
I will appoint rulers to take care of them. My people will no longer
be afraid or terrified, and I will not punish them again. I, the Lord,
have spoken. 'The Lord says, "The time is coming when I will
choose as a king a righteous descendant of David. That king will
rule wisely and do what is right and just throughout the land. When
he is king, the people of Judah will be safe, and the people of Israel
will live in peace. He will be called 'The Lord Our Salvation.'" "The
time is coming," says the Lord, "when people will no longer swear
by me as the living God who brought the people of Israel out of the
land of Egypt. Instead, they will swear by me as the living God
who brought the people of Israel out of a northern land and out of
all the other countries where I had scattered them. Then they will
live in their own land." My heart is crushed, and I am trembling.
Because of the Lord, because of his holy words, I am like a man
who is drunk, someone who has had too much wine. The land is
full of people unfaithful to the Lord; they live wicked lives and
misuse their power. Because of the Lord's curse the land mourns
and the pastures are dry. *11 The Lord says, "The prophets and the priests
are godless; I have caught them doing evil in the Temple itself. 12 The paths
they follow will be slippery and dark; I will make them stumble and fall. I
am going to bring disaster on them; the time of their punishment is coming.
I, the Lord, have spoken. 13 I have seen the sin of Samaria's prophets: they*

have spoken in the name of Baal and have led my people astray. ₁₄ *But I have seen the prophets in Jerusalem do even worse: they commit adultery and tell lies; they help people to do wrong, so that no one stops doing what is evil. To me they are all as bad as the people of Sodom and Gomorrah.* ₁₅ *So then, this is what I, the Lord Almighty, say about the prophets of Jerusalem: I will give them bitter plants to eat and poison to drink, because they have spread ungodliness throughout the land.* ₁₆ *The Lord Almighty said to the people of Jerusalem, "Do not listen to what the prophets say; they are filling you with false hopes.* They tell you what they have imagined and not what I have said. To the people who refuse to listen to what I have said, they keep saying that all will go well with them. And they tell everyone who is stubborn that disaster will never touch them." ₁₈ *I said, "None of these prophets has ever known the Lord's secret thoughts. None of them has ever heard or understood his message, or ever listened or paid attention to what he said.* His anger is a storm, a furious wind that will rage over the heads of the wicked, and it will not end until he has done everything he intends to do. In days to come his people will understand this clearly." ₂₁ *The Lord said, "I did not send these prophets, but even so they went. I did not give them any message, but still they spoke in my name.* If they had known my secret thoughts, then they could have proclaimed my message to my people and could have made them give up the evil lives they live and the wicked things they do. ₂₃ *I am a God who is everywhere and not in one place only. No one can hide where I cannot see them. Do you not know that I am everywhere in heaven and on earth? I know what those prophets have said. They speak lies in my name and claim that I have given them my messages in their dreams.* ₂₆ *How much longer will those prophets mislead my people with the lies they have invented?* They think that the dreams they tell will make my people forget me, just as their ancestors forgot me and turned to Baal. The prophet who has had a dream should say it is only a dream, but the prophet who has heard my message should proclaim that message faithfully. What good is straw compared with wheat? ₂₉ *My message is like a fire and like a hammer that breaks rocks in pieces.* ₃₀ *I am against those prophets who take each other's words and proclaim them as my message.* *31 I am also against those prophets who speak their own words and claim they came from me.*

32 Listen to what I, the Lord, say! I am against the prophets who tell their dreams that are full of lies. They tell these dreams and lead my people astray with their lies and their boasting. I did not send them or order them to go, and they are of no help at all to the people. I, the Lord, have spoken." 33 The Lord said to me, "Jeremiah, when one of my people or a prophet or a priest asks you, 'What is the Lord's message?' you are to say, 'You are a burden to the Lord, and he is going to get rid of you.' 40 I will bring on them everlasting shame and disgrace that will never be forgotten.'"

Readers of book of Jeremiah are informed by the author in its introduction that the name Jeremiah actually represents a historical person like you and me as opposed to the mere fictional characters exposed in more than 90 per cent of the entire Holy Bible. Note that Jeremiah's words are most often that of the author: they are written with Jeremiah's voice in quotes as if they are actually the prophet himself doing the talking. We should also make a note of the several statements made by God of Israel but quoted by Jeremiah are also expressed in quotation marks as if God is the one actually talking. They are written as if God actually dictated to the prophet and told them to the two Jewish religious factional groups, Judah and Israel. Most importantly, blame is labeled against rulers of Judah and Israel for destroying the two kingdoms through bad governance; hence, God of Israel vows to punish not only the kings but also the self-styled priests and prophets who falsely claim to carry God's messages.

Another interesting statement to note is in Jeremiah 23: 23-26. The Lord God of Israel is saying, 'I am "a" God who is everywhere and not in one place only. No one can hide where I cannot see them'. Really, Is God of Israel 'a' God who is everywhere? I hope the author realizes what this statement entails. By saying 'a' God means there is recognition of other gods. It is not the same as saying: 'the' God or God. A God who is everywhere is expected to know everything, before, during and after the actions of the event. A God here refers to a God whose duty is to be everywhere at all times and to see that everything is done according to that God's will. And being a God for the Israelites, he is present in all places where there is a Jew. This includes the place and time when the two rulers of Judah and Israel were misruling and destroying God's own beloved people. That God actually watched the rulers messing up his own chosen people. So, either the God of Israel behaved irresponsibly for not stopping the rulers or the rulers knew the powerlessness of their own God.

Again Jeremiah is saying the priests and prophets at the time knew perfectly well that God was present everywhere but cared less about it and that, God's name could be used to tell lies and get away with it, because the God of Israel was a mere cover up to mesmerized superstitious idol worshipers like ancient Jewish people. Surely, if that God was everywhere and no one could hide away from him according to Jeremiah, what was that God doing or thinking when the mess was going on? What is that God's reason for his inaction, and later, after the damage is done, he comes out with threatening statements of punishments? This God of Israel had been irresponsible, ungodly, and a mere imposter. The titles which make him the Almighty is unbefitting and should be told to stop bragging and shut the fuck up.

According to Psalms

GNT.

Psalms 31

Troubled Person: 'I come to you, Lord, for protection; never let me be defeated. You are a righteous God; save me, I pray! Hear me! Save me now! Be my refuge to protect me; my defense to save me. You are my refuge and defense; guide me and lead me as you have promised. Keep me safe from the trap that has been set for me; shelter me from danger. I place myself in your care. You will save me, Lord; you are a faithful God. You hate those who worship false gods, but I trust in you. I will be glad and rejoice because of your constant love. You see my suffering; you know my trouble. [Troubled Person] You have not let my enemies capture me; you have given me freedom to go where I wish. Be merciful to me, Lord, for I am in trouble; my eyes are tired from so much crying; I am completely worn out. I am exhausted by sorrow, and weeping has shortened my life. I am weak from all my troubles; even my bones are wasting away. All my enemies, and especially my neighbors, treat me with contempt. Those who know me are afraid of me; when they see me in the street, they run away. Everyone has forgotten me, as though I were dead; I am like something thrown away. I hear many enemies whispering; terror is all around me. They are making plans against me, plotting to kill me. 14 But my trust is in you, O Lord; you are my God. 15 I am always in your care; save me from my enemies, from those who persecute me. Look on your servant with kindness; save me in your constant love. I call to you, Lord; don't let me be disgraced. May the wicked be disgraced; may they go silently down to the world of the dead. Silence those liars—all the proud and arrogant who speak with contempt about the righteous. How wonderful are the good things you keep for those who honour you! Everyone knows how good you are, how securely you protect those who trust you. You hide them in the safety of your presence from the plots of others; in a safe shelter you hide them from the insults of their enemies. 21 Praise the Lord! How wonderfully he showed his love for me when I was surrounded and attacked! 22 I was afraid and thought that he had driven me out of his presence, but he heard my cry when I called to him for help. 23 Love the Lord, all his faithful people. The Lord protects the faithful, but punishes the proud as they deserve. 24 Be strong, be courageous, all you that hope in the Lord.'

A good comforting chapter: It indirectly switches human focus from self-reliance in pursuit of success to miracle source or reliance on God of Israel for spiritual assistance. There is a presumption in the following chapter that the prayer has already made an unsuccessful attempt to do something. It is hoped that God's intervention can bring success. At this point, confidence or faith of the self is abandoned. At the end of the prayers, the immediate result is a feeling of comfort, and you realise that your initial focus is either lost or frozen. And if no practical action or decision is taken after several days of prayers, it would be known that nothing useful has come out of the prayers. In the mean while, the needy person's focus is tuned to the expectation of miracle from God. If no new knowledge about your initial wish is added to your already acquired information or mind, you will recognize that you are still at the point where you were before the prayers started. The best practical action every human needs in bringing about success when everything else fails is additional quality information from those persons who know better than us. God is something you cannot see. God is therefore nothing. How can you speak to nothing and expect to get something? Out of focus out of mind! Talk to knowledgeable real persons, obtain quality understanding of your desires, make use of the new facts, and if you fail again, keep trying again and again. Every practical attempt to the wise person makes him or her wiser. You will acquire so much knowledge that your dream becomes a reality, because you had faith in yourself, not faith in something you cannot see or touch. You may keep praying daily as usual but if you don't change that unproductive habit nothing will change. We must change for the best path in order that something better can be achieved.

At the end of every exhausted effort to succeed, religious people turn to God for miracles instead of seeking better information from those who know better. Even the so-called godly miracles are not free. They are always performed at a price. You lose time and resources always. Why?

GNT.
Psalms 35

'Oppose those who oppose me, Lord, and fight those who fight against me! Take your shield and armor and come to my rescue. Lift up your spear and war axe against those who pursue me. Promise that you will save me. May those who try to kill me be defeated and disgraced! May those who plot against me be turned back and confused! May they be like straw blown by the wind as the angel of the Lord pursues them! May their path be dark and slippery while the angel of the Lord strikes them down!

'Without any reason they laid a trap for me and dug a deep hole to catch me. But destruction will catch them before they know it; they will be caught in their own trap and fall to their destruction!

'Then I will be glad because of the Lord; I will be happy because he saved me. With all my heart I will say to the Lord, "There is no one like you. You protect the weak from the strong, the poor from the oppressor." Evil people testify against me and accuse me of crimes I know nothing about. They pay me back evil for good, and I sink in despair. But when they were sick, I dressed in mourning; I deprived myself of food; I prayed with my head bowed low, as I would pray for a friend or a brother. I went around bent over in mourning, as one who mourns for his mother. But when I was in trouble, they were all glad gathered around to make fun of me; strangers beat me and kept striking me. Like those who would mock a cripple, they glared at me with hate. How much longer, Lord, will you just look on? Rescue me from their attacks; save my life from these lions! Then I will thank you in the assembly of your people; I will praise you before them all. Don't let my enemies, those liars, gloat over my defeat. Don't let those who hate me for no reason smirk with delight over my sorrow. They do not speak in a friendly way; instead they invent all kinds of lies about peace-loving people. So don't be silent, Lord; don't keep yourself far away! Rouse yourself, O Lord, and defend me; rise up, my God, and plead my cause. You are righteous, O Lord, so declare me innocent; don't let my enemies gloat over me. Don't let them say to themselves, 'We are rid of him! That's just what we wanted!' 26 May those who gloat over my suffering be completely defeated and confused; may those who claim to be better than I am be covered with shame and disgrace. 27 May those who want to see me acquitted shout for joy and say again and again, "How great is the Lord! He is pleased with the success of his servant." 28 Then I will proclaim your righteousness, and I will praise you all day long.'

Is this not what is called self-denial? Is prayers and indulgence in miracles not the mother of ignorance, decadence, and lack of human progress? Religious peoples' dependence on prayers such as Psalms 35 and 109 gives comfort and false hope and prevents them from critical thinking to solve problems. Religious people are always expecting miracles when it comes to a time when the human brain is required to be challenged critically. Religious people believe in the miracle stories narrated in the Holy Bible, and they think the biblical God can perform the same miracle for them. The miracle stories are pure Jewish myths or fable stories. Every culture has similar fantastic miracle stories too. The miracles are not real and not dependable. The only real miracle is the dream you personally have and actually working hard to achieve whatever you may have in your dream. That personal physical effort is the bottom line *not* recitation of biblical quotations, Your religious leader knows that you are expecting a miracle, and if you don't get what you are desperately looking for, he invents one for you in the name of God of Israel. We must never forget the fable of Moses, the first magician Yahweh invented for the Jews; same illusion. This has always been the deception among all the biblical heroes.

GNT.

Psalms 47 (Noise)

'₁ Clap your hands for joy, all peoples! Praise God with loud songs! ₂ The Lord, the Most High, is to be feared; he is a great king, ruling over the entire world. ₃ He gave us victory over the peoples; he made us rule over the nations. ₄ He chose for us the land where we live, the proud possession of his people, whom he loves. ₅ God goes up to his throne. There are shouts of joy and the blast of trumpets, as the Lord goes up. ₆ Sing praise to God; sing praise to our king! ₇ God is king over the entire world; praise him with songs! ₈ God sits on his sacred throne; he rules over the nations. ₉ The rulers of the nations assemble with the people of the God of Abraham. More powerful than all armies are he; he rules supreme.' You may deliberately commit a sin; then after that read this chapter and be confident that God of Israel will forgive you?

Sing praises of songs as loud as you can with your trumpets blasting out so that God in heaven hears it loud and clear. Don't even bother to think about the nuisance caused to your neighbors. God will be pleased with your noise.

The opposite of noise is silence. And it is written in several chapters of the Holy Bible to worship and pray in silence, so the choice is open. You can choose to be noisy or remain in silence. Biblical scriptures are always ambiguous. It is up to each individual to choose whatever is suitable at any given moment of how to communicate with God. The expected rationality here is not on the logic of the action; no, that will be the same as challenging God's work.

The rational will be to accept God's words in good faith regardless of its obvious effects on yourself and others. Religious practices do not go with 'common' sense or that sense which is familiar to all. Christians, for instance, are obligated to follow the laws of Abraham, Isaac, and Jacob plus of course those of Jesus

Christ. They are forbidden to question the ancient Jewish gospels even when the gospels are evidently doubtful.

GNT

Psalms 51:

Forgiveness Prayers: '$_1$ Be merciful to me, O God, because of your constant love. Because of your great mercy wipe away my sins! $_2$ Wash away all my evil and make me clean from my sin! $_3$ I recognize my faults; I am always conscious of my sins.

'$_4$ I have sinned against you—only against you—and done what you consider evil. So you are right in judging me; you are justified in condemning me. $_5$ I have been evil from the day I was born; from the time I was conceived, I have been sinful. $_6$ Sincerity and truth are what you require; fill my mind with your wisdom. $_7$ Remove my sin and I will be clean; wash me, and I will be whiter than snow.

'$_8$ Let me hear the sounds of joy and gladness; and though you have crushed me and broken me, I will be happy once again. $_9$ Close your eyes to my sins and wipe out all my evil. $_{10}$ Create a pure heart in me, O God, and put a new and loyal spirit in me. $_{11}$ Do not banish me from your presence; do not take your holy spirit away from me. $_{12}$ Give me again the joy that comes from your salvation, and make me willing to obey you. $_{13}$ Then I will teach sinners your commands, and they will turn back to you. $_{14}$ Spare my life, O God, and save me, and I will gladly proclaim your righteousness. $_{15}$ Help me to speak, Lord, and I will praise you. $_{16}$ You do not want sacrifices, or I would offer them; you are not pleased with burnt offerings. $_{17}$ My sacrifice is a humble spirit, O God; you will not reject a humble and repentant heart. $_{18}$ O God, be kind to Zion and help her; rebuild the walls of Jerusalem. $_{19}$ Then you will be pleased with proper sacrifices and with our burnt offerings; and bulls will be sacrificed on your altar.'

Every Christian is doubtlessly aware of the famous Psalms 51, the forgiveness prayers in the Holy Bible. It is in fact one of many poems used and collected by the people of ancient Israel in their worship of God of Israel. Again the poems come in many forms such as for Protection, Justice, Help, Victory, Confidence, Sadness, Praises, Thanksgiving, Sickness, Comfort, Safety, National Deliverance, Morning, Afternoon, and Evening prayers.

What makes Psalms 51 significant is the content of the nineteen verses. The sinner knows all the forbidden evil deeds which displease God. In verse 3, it is written 'I recognize my faults; I am always conscious of my sins.' The sinner intentionally performs an act which is against God's will and turns back to ask God to wipe out that deliberate sinful act, and the merciful God forgives without punishment; it is the same as permitting everyone to disrespect God's laws. This means that any Christian can willfully commit as many crimes as possible and get away with it, because God of Israel will always forgive. God is in effect promoting lawlessness and abuse of his own laws and those of mankind.

Every action, sinful or not, is known to God before the act takes place according to the Bible. God does not stop people to behave sinfully in the first instant, and when the sinner finishes the evil act, Psalms 51 is saying, no problem, tell God that you are sorry for doing what you did, and you are pardoned. No wonder many religious leaders and their institutions have used this very excuse for centuries to commit religiously serious crimes without fear of divine punishment. Can any reasonable reader tell the rest of the world why anybody should feel proud to be religious, especially Christians who worship the Bible as a Holy document, apart from using the Bible as a tool to make money without sweat? A million sins is not a big deal in the eyes of the biblical God as long as the book of Psalms remains an integral part of the Holy Bible. At the end of the day, every human action is mercifully justified by the God of Israel.

GNT.

Psalms 53

$_1$ Fools say to themselves, "There is no God." They are all corrupt, and they have done terrible things; there is no one who does what is right. $_2$ God looks down at people from heaven to see if there are any who are wise and any who worship him. $_3$ But they have all turned away; they are all equally bad. Not one of them does what is right, not a single one. $_4$ Don't they know? God asks. "Are these evildoers ignorant? They live by robbing my people, and they never pray to me." $_5$ But then they will become terrified, as they have never been before, for God will scatter the bones of the enemies of his people. God has rejected them, and so Israel will totally defeat them. $_6$ How I pray that victory will come to Israel from Zion. How happy the people of Israel will be when God makes them prosperous again!'

Fools say to themselves, there is no God: so says Psalms 53. Ordinarily, this statement would not be challenged by Bible readers, because biblical words are presumed to be God's own words. But now let us examine the key words in the first verse: 'Fool' and 'God.' In *Webster's Ninth New Collegiate Dictionary*, a fool is defined according to its historical usage starting from the time before the thirteenth century; then between thirteenth century and 1548; and, its usage from then to the present time. There are slight differences of the word's meaning during each period. Presently, the word fool simply means 'thoughtlessness,' 'aimlessness,' less than serious or less than full strength. The opposite of fool is wise.

Now let us consider 'God' as a notion, an idea, or a name given to an all-powerful spirit which human eyes cannot see or touch. God is necessarily something which exists only in the minds of some people. Being an invisible thing, its existence is possible only because an individual believes or perceives it as a real thing which actually exists. Therefore, God as an idea requires thinking. For anyone to accept or reject its plausibility, the person will need to engage the brain to review God's image. Being an idea again, therefore, it will be foolish or thoughtlessness for anyone to simply say yes there is God, because Psalms 53 says so or because many people believe in their minds that there is God.

By this logical deduction a wise person will critically naturally think seriously about the reasons why it should be accepted as a fact that there is God. The first verse as quoted above should then be formed rather as follows: a wise or intelligent people say there is no God, because with their wisdom or by careful examination of the pros-and-cons, they find insufficient evidence to support the idea that there is really a thing called God. A wise person will compare the spiritual thing with matter and conclude that the eyes cannot visually locate it or him or her at a given place at a given time. But a fool will not give a serious thought about the idea of God's existence. A fool will simply believe the existence of God without question. Proverbs 14, 8 puts it correctly as, 'Why is a clever person wise? He is wise because he knows what to do. Why is a stupid person foolish? Because he only thinks he knows.' Again, 'intelligent people want to learn, but stupid people are satisfied with ignorance or status quo' as according to Proverbs 15: 14.

We should be very careful how we think, because human life is shaped by how we think. Notwithstanding the fact that our minds are nothing more than the total information or knowledge which our brain has captured since birth. Your faith is part of your knowledge. We never stop seeking additional knowledge as humans. Knowledge is the mother of all powers. He who is stubborn whenever corrected will one day surely defeat himself or herself without recovery.

Psalms 58
GNT.

'Do you rulers ever give a just decision? Do you judge everyone fairly? ₂ No! You think only of the evil you can do, and commit

BIG QUESTION: DO HUMANS NEED GOD?

crimes of violence in the land. ₃ Evildoers go wrong all their lives; they tell lies from the day they are born. ₄ They are full of poison like snakes; they stop up their ears like a deaf cobra, ₅ which does not hear the voice of the snake charmer, or the chant of the clever magician. ₆ Break the teeth of these fierce lions, O God.

'₇ May they disappear like water draining away; may they be crushed like weeds on a path. ₈ May they be like snails that dissolve into slime; may they be like a baby born dead that never sees the light. ₉ Before they know it, they are cut down like weeds; in his fierce anger God will blow them away while they are still living.

'₁₀ The righteous will be glad when they see sinners punished; they will wade through the blood of the wicked. ₁₁ People will say, "The righteous are indeed rewarded; there is indeed a God who judges the world."'

If the world needs a universal God for all mankind, for comfort and gratification, that God must not be the sectarian spiritual God who revealed himself to Abraham, Isaac, and Jacob or the God for Israelites as invented by Moses. The world may need a God who is not biased in favour of a chosen few 'the Israelites.' The universal God should not belong to any particular or special ethnic group of people as exposed in the Holy Bible books like the Exodus, Leviticus, Numbers, Deuteronomy, Judges, and the like. The world may need a God with indisputable verifiable power credentials. The entire world surely needs a better place with mutual respect to live in peace with one another. An entity which really has the knowledge of every earthly matter and one who can be the God of the planet earth as a whole may certainly be a good idea. A just God whose origin would not be of descendants of Adam and Eve or descendants of any fantasy ethnic group is one thing that can possibly make a difference. Above all, a God who needs no worshipping, no middlemen between humans and it, one who requires no offerings of any kind, and an entity which all humans can communicate directly may be a panacea for humanity.

This brings us all to the ultimate question of 'why humans need a miracle-based super something?' Why? Sincerely, is there a real need for miracles?

GNT.

Psalms 77

Verses 1-10: '1 I cry aloud to God; I cry aloud, and he hears me. 2 In times of trouble I pray to the Lord; all night long I lift my hands in prayer, but I cannot find comfort. 3 When I think of God, I sigh; when I meditate, I feel discouraged. 4 He keeps me awake all night; I am so worried that I cannot speak. 5 I think of days gone by and remember years of long ago. 6 I spend the night in deep thought; I meditate, and this is what I ask myself: 7 "Will the Lord always reject us? Will he never again be pleased with us? 8 Has he stopped loving us? Does his promise no longer stand? 9 Has God forgotten to be merciful? Has anger taken the place of his compassion?" 10 Then I said, "What hurts me most is this—that God is no longer powerful."'

Very good observation! Has God of Israel ever been powerful? Satan and other gods would have been crushed and extinct if God really had powers of any kind.

Verses 11-14: 'I will remember your great deeds, Lord; I will recall the wonders you did in the past. 12 I will think about all that you have done; I will meditate on all your mighty acts. 13 Everything you do, O God, is holy. No god is as great as you. 14 You are the God who works miracles; you showed your might among the nations.'

As humans, do we need spiritual faith for miracles or personal faith for devoted effort to succeed? Do we really, in reality need this thing called miracle?

Verses 15-20: 'By your power you saved your people, the descendants of Jacob and of Joseph. 16 When the waters saw you, O God, they were afraid, and the depths of the sea trembled. 17 The clouds poured down rain; thunder crashed from the sky, and lightning flashed in all directions. ₁₈ The crash of your thunder rolled out, and flashes of lightning lit up the world; the earth trembled and shook. ₁₉ You walked through the waves; you crossed the deep sea, but your footprints could not be seen. ₂₀ You led your people like a shepherd, with Moses and Aaron in charge.'

You and I are alive in the year 2014, the age of advance reason, based on empirical studies; can we in actual fact relate to the above ancient Jews' fantasy written in the biblical book of Psalms, a novel which was written in about 900 years before Christ was born? It is about 3,000 years since! What is the relevance of God and miracles today? The era is past and gone forever. We cannot live in the past. The world has changed and we must all adapt to modernity in order to survive, else we shall perish. For how long can we continue to nurture our children and children's children with these fables of ancient Jews' cultural past? This process of transferring useless delusional past novels to future generation without censorship is counterproductive, self-destructive root cause of decadence and ignorance.

GNT.
Psalms 78

'₁ Listen, my people, to my teaching, and pay attention to what I say. ₂ I am going to use wise sayings and explain mysteries from the past, ₃ things we have heard and known, things that our ancestors told us. ₄ We will not keep them from our children; we will tell the next generation about the Lord's power and his great deeds and the wonderful things he has done.

'He gave laws to the people of Israel and commandments to the descendants of Jacob. He instructed our ancestors to teach his laws to their children, ₆ so that the next generation might learn them and in turn should tell their children. ₇ In this way they also will put their trust in God and not forget what he has done, but always obey his commandments. ₈ *They will not be like their ancestors, a rebellious and*

217

disobedient people, whose trust in God was never firm and who did not remain faithful to him. ₉ The Ephraimites, armed with bows and arrows, ran away on the day of battle. ₁₀ They did not keep their covenant with God; they refused to obey his law. ₁₁ They forgot what he had done, the miracles they had seen him perform. ₁₂ While their ancestors watched, God performed miracles in the plain of Zoan in the land of Egypt. ₁₃ He divided the sea and took them through it; he made the waters stand like walls. ₁₄ By day he led them with a cloud and all night long with the light of a fire. ₁₅ He split rocks open in the desert and gave them water from the depths.

'₁₆ He caused a stream to come out of the rock and made water flow like a river. ₁₇ But they continued to sin against God, and in the desert they rebelled against the Most High. ₁₈ They deliberately put God to the test by demanding the food they wanted. ₁₉ They spoke against God and said, "Can God supply food in the desert? ₂₀ It is true that he struck the rock, and water flowed out in a torrent; but can he also provide us with bread and give his people meat?" ₂₁ And so the Lord was angry when he heard them; he attacked his people with fire, and his anger against them grew, ₂₂ *because they had no faith in him and did not believe that he would save them.*

'₂₃ But he spoke to the sky above and commanded its doors to open; ₂₄ he gave them grain from heaven, by sending down manna for them to eat. ₂₅ So they ate the food of angels, and God gave them all they wanted. ₂₆ He also caused the east wind to blow, and by his power he stirred up the south wind; ₂₇ and to his people he sent down birds, as many as the grains of sand on the shore; ₂₈ they fell in the middle of the camp all around the tents. ₂₉ So the people ate and were satisfied; God gave them what they wanted. ₃₀ But they had not yet satisfied their craving and were still eating, ₃₁ when God became angry with them and killed their strongest men, the best young men of Israel. ₃₂ In spite of all this the people kept sinning; in spite of his miracles they did not trust him. ₃₃ So he ended their days like a breath and their lives with sudden disaster. ₃₄ Whenever he killed some of them, the rest would turn to him; they would repent and pray earnestly to him. 35 They remembered that God was their protector that the Almighty came to their aid. 36 But their words were all lies; nothing they said was sincere. 37 They were not loyal to him; they were not faithful to their covenant with him. 38 *But God was merciful to his people. He forgave their sin and did not destroy them. Many times he held back his anger and restrained his fury.* 39 *He remembered that they were only mortal beings, like a wind that blows by and is gone.* 40 How often they rebelled against him in the desert; how

many times they made him sad! *41 Again and again they put God to the test and brought pain to the Holy God of Israel.* 42 They forgot his great power and the day when he saved them from their enemies 43 and performed his mighty acts and miracles in the plain of Zoan in the land of Egypt. 44 He turned the rivers into blood, and the Egyptians had no water to drink. 45 He sent flies among them, that tormented them, and frogs that ruined their land. 46 He sent locusts to eat their crops and to destroy their fields. 47 He killed their grapevines with hail and their fig trees with frost. 48 He killed their cattle with hail and their flocks with lightning. 49 *He caused them great distress by pouring out his anger and fierce rage, which came as messengers of death.*

'50 *He did not restrain his anger or spare their lives, but killed them with a plague.* 51 *He killed the first-born sons of all the families of Egypt.* 52 Then he led his people out like a shepherd and guided them through the desert. 53 He led them safely, and they were not afraid; but the sea came rolling over their enemies. 54 He brought them to his holy land, to the mountains which he himself conquered. 55 He drove out the inhabitants as his people advanced; he divided their land among the tribes of Israel and gave their homes to his people. 56 But they rebelled against Almighty God and put him to the test. They did not obey his commandments, 57 but were rebellious and disloyal like their ancestors, unreliable as a crooked arrow. 58 They angered him with their heathen places of worship, and with their idols they made him furious. *59 God was angry when he saw it, so he rejected his people completely.*

'*60 He abandoned his tent in Shiloh, the home where he had lived among us. 61 He allowed our enemies to capture the Covenant Box, the symbol of his power and glory. 62 He was angry with his own people and let them be killed by their enemies. 63 Young men were killed in war, and young women had no one to marry. 64 Priests died by violence, and their widows were not allowed to mourn. 65 At last time the Lord woke up as though from sleep; he was like 66 a strong man excited by wine.* He drove his enemies back in lasting and shameful defeat. *67* But he rejected the descendants of Joseph; he did not select the tribe of Ephraim. *68* Instead he chose the tribe of Judah and Mount Zion, which he dearly loves. *69* There he built his Temple like his home in heaven; he made it firm like the earth itself, secure for all time. *70* He chose his servant David; he took him from the pastures, *71* where he looked after his flocks, and he made him king of Israel, the shepherd of the people of God. *72* David took care of them with unselfish devotion and led them with skill.' Very interesting indeed: Psalms *78* is a chapter worthy of reading by all, religious or irreligious. The entire seventy-two captivating verses sum up the relationship between two categories of Israelites. The link between ancestors of Abraham, Isaac, and Jacob on one hand and the All-Powerful God of Israel on the other hand is concisely stated. The chapter is a good literary summary of Genesis chapter 7 through to the end of the book of Judges. From verse one to verse seven, the author asks his Jewish audience to pay special attention to what he is about to tell them.

After a crisp introduction of the chapter theme, the author continued in verse 8 with a provocative statement that, 'that generation of Israelites *will not be like their ancestors* who were rebellious and disobedient people whose trust in God was never firm and who did not remain faithful to God.'

In verse 22, the author continued, 'They had no faith in God and did not believe that God would save them.' Verse 37 continues as follows; 'the Israelites were not loyal to God, and not faithful to their covenant with him.'

Are we saying that these are insignificant statements? A generation of Israelites who did not trust in God ever lived on the planet earth? Did they actually have no faith in the so-called covenant of God? Verse 56 says, they actually 'rebelled against Almighty God.' Verses 59-62 explain how God was really pissed off with his own people.

This God has become one of us, very rational like you and I. Almighty God must be completely different. Verse 65 says, 'At last time the Lord woke up as though from sleep, he was like a strong man excited by wine'. God is being compared with you and I when we are drunk and furious. Is it possible? With God's limitless access to everything, are the two entities, humans and God, comparable? My key point here is this; the author has run short of persuasive words to narrate God of Israel's power over his chosen people. The entire seventy-two verses are empty ancient Jewish religious rhetoric worthy of a Juvenile school.

GNT.

Psalms 79

'$_1$ O God, the heathen have invaded your land. They have desecrated your holy Temple and left Jerusalem in ruins. $_2$ They left the bodies of your people for the vultures, the bodies of your servants for wild animals to eat. $_3$ They shed your people's blood like water; blood flowed like water all through Jerusalem, and no one was left to bury the dead. $_4$ The surrounding nations insult us; they laugh at us and mock us. $_5$ Lord, will you be angry with us forever? Will your anger continue to burn like fire? $_6$ Turn your anger on the nations that do not worship you, on the people who do not pray to you. $_7$ For they have killed your people; they have ruined your country. $_8$ Do not punish us for the sins of our ancestors. Have mercy on us now; we have lost all hope. $_9$ Help us, O God, and save us; rescue us and forgive our sins for the sake of your own honour. $_{10}$ Why should the nations ask us, "Where is your God?" Let us see you punish the nations for shedding the blood of your servants. $_{11}$ Listen to the groans of the prisoners, and by your great power free those who are condemned to die. $_{12}$ Lord, pay the other nations back seven times for all the insults they have hurled at you. $_{13}$ Then we, your people, the sheep of your flock, will thank you forever and praise you for all time to come.'

'Do not punish us for the sins of our ancestors. Why should the nations ask us, "Where is your God?" Lord, pay the other nations back seven times for all the insults they have hurled at you. Then we, your people, the sheep of your flock, will thank you forever and praise you for all time to come.' The author is probably making reference to predecessor of Abraham, Isaac, and Jacob, or possibly to Jewish race of people as a whole. The author is definitely not referring to the entire human race. The other nations are asking or indeed mocking at the Jews, 'Where is your God, the God of Israel you have so much confidence or faith?' Why is he not coming to deliver you out of your present difficulties?

I like to draw the reader's attention to such clauses as 'your God' and 'other nations', because throughout the biblical scriptures, all the authors use of such sayings to show that the God of Israel is *not* a God for the whole universe. According to Jewish traditions, God of Israel has always remained their God, Jews' God. Those of you non-Jews who keep borrowing that entity to be yours are making terrible mistakes. If you need a God for yourself or your race, please go somewhere else, or certainly look for it from within your particular culture or ancient traditional history. If you are lucky to find one, by all means worship him or her or it. Then after this exercise, ask yourself, 'Is there or can there really be a God of any kind or any type or any image?' And if so, why must there be a God? Why can't we cast away these old-fashioned ideas and rather create confidence or faith in ourselves that we can actually live happily without God, or, that we have indeed lived without one all these years, because there is really no such thing as God as ancient Jews perceived it? All the Godly images we have are mere biblical fantasies or mere human imaginations.

GNT.
Psalms 82

'$_1$ God presides in the heavenly council; in the assembly of the gods he gives his decision: $_2$ "You must stop judging unjustly; you must no longer be partial to the wicked! $_3$ Defend the rights of the poor and the orphans; be fair to the needy and the helpless. $_4$ Rescue them from the power of evil people. $_5$ How ignorant you are! How stupid! You are completely corrupt, and justice has disappeared from the world. $_6$ 'You are gods,' I said; 'all of you are children of the Most High.' $_7$ But you will die like mortals; your life will end like that of any prince." $_8$ Come, O God, and rule the world; all the nations are yours.'

I wonder if the reader can sniff out the fantasy element of Psalms 82 given above. 'God presides in the heavenly council; in the assembly of the gods he gives his decision'. May we know precisely which gods assembly he presides: God of France, God of Britain, God of Russia, God of Pakistan, God of Ghana, God of Cuba, or God of what, of who or of where? Is this in reference to the God who emphatically declares himself as God of Israel in the previous chapters; presiding in the Jewish heavenly council of gods?

It is very necessary to think about these statements in the Holy Bible. We cannot simply let them pass without critically thinking about them. Book of Genesis is telling us there is only one God who created the universe and humans plus every natural matter. The book of Exodus tells us there is a God called 'I AM', who later became known as God of Israel for Israelites only. Books of Matthew, Mark, Luke, and John are also telling us about another

God who was half-human and half-ghost, formally called Jesus the Christ, the son of God, and God himself.

The question is which of these gods is Psalms 82 verse one, making reference to? 'God presides in the heavenly council in the assembly of gods.' Which of these principal gods is the chairman of the council, and who are the rest of the assembly of gods' members?

GNT.

Psalms 89

'₁ O Lord, I will always sing of your constant love; I will proclaim your faithfulness forever. ₂ I know that your love will last for all time, that your faithfulness is as permanent as the sky. ₃ You said, "I have made a covenant with the man I chose; I have promised my servant David, ₄ 'A descendant of yours will always be king; I will preserve your dynasty forever.'" ₅ The heavens sing of the wonderful things you do; the holy ones sing of your faithfulness, Lord. ₆ No one in heaven is like you, Lord; none of the heavenly beings is your equal. ₇ You are feared in the council of the holy ones; they all stand in awe of you. ₈ Lord God Almighty, none is as mighty as you; in all things you are faithful, O Lord. ₉ You rule over the powerful sea; you calm its angry waves. ₁₀ You crushed the monster Rahab and killed it; with your mighty strength you defeated *your enemies.* ₁₁ Heaven is yours, the earth also; you made the world and everything in it. ₁₂ You created the north and the south; Mount Tabor and Mount Hermon sing to you for joy.

'₁₃ How powerful you are! How great is your strength! ₁₄ Your kingdom is founded on righteousness and justice; love and faithfulness are shown in all you do. ₁₅ How happy are the people who worship you with songs, who live in the light of your kindness! ₁₆ Because of you they rejoice all day long, and they praise you for your goodness. ₁₇ You give us great victories; in your love you make us triumphant. ₁₈ You, O Lord, chose our protector; you, the Holy God of Israel, gave us our king. ₁₉

In a vision long ago you said to your faithful servants, "I have given help to a famous soldier; I have given the throne to one I chose from the people. [20] I have made my servant David king by anointing him with holy oil. [21] My strength will always be with him, my power will make him strong. [22] His enemies will never succeed against him; the wicked will not defeat him. [23] I will crush his foes and kill everyone who hates him. [24] I will love him and be loyal to him; I will make him always victorious. [25] I will extend his kingdom from the Mediterranean to the Euphrates River. [26] He will say to me, 'you are my father and my God; you are my protector and saviour.' [27] I will make him my first- born son, the greatest of all kings. [28] I will always keep my promise to him, and my covenant with him will last forever. [29] His dynasty will be as permanent as the sky; a descendant of his will always be king. [30] But *if* his descendants disobey my law and do not live according to my commands, [31] *if* they disregard my instructions and do not keep my commandments, [32] then I will punish them for their sins; I will make them suffer for their wrongs. [33] But I will not stop loving David or fail to keep my promise to him. [34] I will not break my covenant with him or take back even one promise I made him. 'Once and for all I have promised by my holy name: I will never lie to David. [36] He will always have descendants, and I will watch over his kingdom as long as the sun shines. [37] It will be as permanent as the moon that faithful witness in the sky." [38] But you are angry with your chosen king; you have deserted and rejected him. [39] You have broken your covenant with your servant and thrown his crown in the dirt. [40] You have torn down the walls of his city and left his forts in ruins. [41] All who pass by steal his belongings; all his neighbours laugh at him. [42] You have given the victory to his enemies; you have made them all happy. [43] You have made his weapons useless and let him be defeated in battle. [44] You have taken away his royal sceptre and knocked his throne to the ground. [45] You have made him old before his time and covered him with disgrace. 46 Lord, will you hide yourself forever? How long will your anger burn like fire? 47 Remember how short my life is; remember that you created all of us mortal! 48 Who can live and never die? How can we humans keep ourselves from the grave?

' 49 Lord, where are the former proofs of your love? Where are the promises you made to David? 50 Don't forget how I, your servant, am insulted, how I endure all the curses of the heathen. 51 Your enemies insult your chosen king, O Lord! They insult him wherever he goes. 52 Praise the Lord forever! Amen! Amen!'

GNT.

Psalms 91

' 1 Whoever goes to the Lord for safety, whoever remains under the protection of the Almighty, 2 can say to him, "You are my defender and protector. You are my God; in you I trust." 3 He will keep you safe from all hidden dangers and from all deadly diseases.

' 4 He will cover you with his wings; you will be safe in his care; his faithfulness will protect and defend you. 5 You need not fear any dangers at night or sudden attacks during the day 6 or the plagues that strike in the dark or the evils that kill in daylight. 7 A thousand may fall dead beside you, ten thousand all around you, but you will not be harmed. 8 You will look and see how the wicked are punished. 9 You have made the Lord your defender, the Most High your protector, 10 and so no disaster will strike you, no violence will come near your home. 11 God will put his angels in charge of you to protect you wherever you go. 12 They will hold you up with their hands to keep you from hurting your feet on the stones. 13 You will trample down lions and snakes, fierce lions and poisonous snakes.

' 14 God says, "I will save those who love me and will protect those who acknowledge me as Lord. 15 When they call to me, I will answer them; when they are in trouble, I will be with them. I will rescue them and honour them. ₁₆ I will reward them with long life; I will save them."

Here is another chapter with wishful ideas of a frustrated faithful individual. O Lord 'you are feared in the council of the holy ones'. 'I, your Lord, the Holy God of Israel will always keep my promises and my covenant. But if the descendants disobey my laws and disregard my instructions and commandments, I will punish them for their sins'. 'Once and for all I have promised by my holy name: I will never lie to David.' Psalms 89: 35: 'God promises by his holy name that he will never lie to David.' Where did the author get this information? How can rational readers of the Holy Bible ignore these quotations and go about bragging about the existence of a spiritual thing called God?

These man-made notions were formed thousands of years ago because of ignorance, superstitions, and a need for reasons to explain causes and effects of natural phenomena. In the twenty-first century, human knowledge has expanded to the extent that such godly ideas in this chapter and indeed most chapters of the revered book are irrelevant. Those who see a need for them say so because they make decent living out of the scriptures, particularly in poor and superstitious communities. All religious leaders depend on financial contributions from their followers. As long as one can read and interpret Bible quotations to match current life event, superstitious ignorant and mostly illiterate followers will share their meager income with their leaders. They are gullible and ignorant because they believe there is something called miracles. And the Holy Bible talks about miracles and nothing but miracles. The Holy Bible is therefore a tool used by brilliant crooks for cheating superstitious people. Believers of miracles will forever remain gullible people. There are many swindlers out there whose agenda in religion is to manufacture miraculous ideas, similar to those in the Holy Bible and sell them for money.

GNT

Psalms 105

$_1$ Give thanks to the Lord, proclaim his greatness; tell the nations what he has done. $_2$ Sing praise to the Lord; tell the wonderful things he has done. $_3$ Be glad that we belong to him; let all who worship him rejoice. $_4$ Go to the Lord for help; and worship him continually. $_5$ You descendants of Abraham, his servant; you descendants of Jacob, the man he chose: remember the miracles that God performed and the judgments that he gave. [Verse 6 is missing.] $_7$ The Lord is our God; his commands are for the entire world. $_8$ He will keep his covenant forever, his promises for a thousand generations. $_9$ He will keep the agreement he made with Abraham and his promise to Isaac. $_{10}$ The Lord made a covenant with Jacob, one that will last forever. $_{11}$ "I will give you the land of Canaan," he said. "It will be your own possession." $_{12}$ God's people were few in number, strangers in the land of Canaan. $_{13}$ They wandered from country to country, from one kingdom to another. $_{14}$ But God let no one oppress them; to protect them, he warned the kings: $_{15}$ "Don't harm my chosen servants; do not touch my prophets." $_{16}$ The Lord sent famine to their country and took away all their food. $_{17}$ But he sent a man ahead of them, Joseph, who had been sold as a slave. $_{18}$ His feet were kept in chains, and an iron collar was around his neck, $_{19}$ until what he had predicted came true. The word of the Lord proved him right. $_{20}$ Then the king of Egypt had him released; the ruler of nations set him free. $_{21}$ He put him in charge of his government and made him ruler over all the land, $_{22}$ with power over the king's officials and authority to instruct his advisers. $_{23}$ Then Jacob went to Egypt and settled in that country. $_{24}$ The Lord gave many children to his people and made them stronger than their enemies. $_{25}$ He made the Egyptians hate his people and treat his servants with deceit. $_{26}$ Then he sent his servant Moses, and Aaron, whom he had chosen. $_{27}$ They did God's mighty acts and performed miracles in Egypt. $_{28}$ God sent darkness on the country, but the Egyptians did not obey his command. 29 He turned their rivers into blood and killed all their fish. $_{30}$ Their country was overrun with frogs; even the palace was filled with them. $_{31}$ God commanded, and flies and gnats swarmed throughout the whole country. $_{32}$ He sent hail and lightning on their land instead of rain; $_{33}$ he destroyed their grapevines and fig trees and broke down all the trees. $_{34}$ He commanded, and the locusts came, countless millions of them; $_{35}$ they ate all the plants in the land; they ate all the crops. $_{36}$ He killed the first-born sons of all the families of Egypt. $_{37}$ Then he led the Israelites out; they carried silver and gold, and all of them were healthy and strong. $_{38}$ The Egyptians were afraid of them and were glad when they left. $_{39}$ God put a cloud over his people and a fire at night to give them light. $_{40}$ They asked, and he sent quails; he gave them food from heaven to satisfy them. $_{41}$ He opened a rock, and water gushed out, flowing through the desert like a river. $_{42}$ He remembered his sacred promise to Abraham his servant. $_{43}$ So he led his chosen people out, and they sang and shouted for joy. $_{44}$ He gave them the lands of other peoples and let them take over their fields, $_{45}$ so that his people would obey his laws and keep all his commands. Praise the Lord!'

Chapter 105 extracts of the book of Psalms. It is headed as '*In praise of the creator*'. Verse 5 begins, 'You descendants of Abraham, his servants; you descendants of Jacob, the man he chose; remember the miracles that God performed and the judgments that he gave.' Verse 7: 'The Lord is our God; his commands are for the entire world.'

No wonder authors of the New Testament quoted Psalms more than any book of the Old Testament. The chapter heading is quite misleading. The word 'creator' as used here appears to be the same as used by the author of the book of Genesis, the supposed originator of the universe. But the entire content of chapter 105 is dedicated to God of Abraham and of Jacob or God for the twelve nations of Israel. These gods are not the same. There were surely other people besides the Israelites at the time of the event; there were the people of Canaan, people of Egypt, and the rest of worldly people. The Holy Bible repeatedly announces that God of Israel is for Israelites only. In verse 12, it is written, 'God's people are few in number, strangers in the land of Canaan.' In Deuteronomy 32: 9, it is written, 'He assigned to each nation a god, but Jacob's descendants he chose for himself.' Micah: 4: 5 says, 'each nation worships and obeys its own god, but we Israelites will worship and obey the Lord our god forever and ever'.

From verse 42 to 45 of this chapter, the author explicitly states, 'He remembered his sacred promise to Abraham his servant; so he led his chosen people out and shouted for joy. He gave them the lands of other people and let them take over their fields, so that his people will obey his laws and keep all his commandments.' The God of Israel is a different character from the fictionalized God who created the planet earth. A God for all mankind will not steal or take by force the property of one of his creation and give to another group of people just because the God made a promise to someone in the past. A God for 'all,' will love 'all,' regardless of race or religion. The God of Israel is noticeably a satanic God and unworthy of anything to anyone.

The authors of the 150 chapters of the book of Psalms are definitely Jews and therefore promote nothing but the image of their God character as a wonder-performer to Jewish audience. But notice that this character's promotion is based mainly on miracles performed in the past. And even then we are told in other chapters that the people of the past did not believe or trust the God of Israel. Remember also that this God made himself a God for the Israelites. He was not chosen or appointed or nominated by the Jews.

Notice again that Psalms: 106: 16-36 is devoted to the extent to which God of Israel's destructive powers are projected on the Egyptians. Devastating punishment of all kinds is inflicted on

Egyptians for refusing to let the Jews leave Egypt. Are Egyptians not God's children too? They were punished because they are not part of Abraham and Jacob's descendants. They are not Jews and therefore not under the protection of God of Israel. God of Israel is absolutely different from God of all mankind, if indeed there is such a thing. In fact, both gods are ancient Jewish fictional characters. None is worth anything in contemporary societies. It is self-destructive to maintain faith in any of them. Faith in biblical God exposes people's vulnerability to miracle inventor exploits.

GNT.

Psalms 109

Troubled Person: 'I praise you, God; don't remain silent! Wicked people and liars have attacked me. They tell lies about me and they say evil things about me, attacking me for no reason. They oppose me, even though I love them and have prayed for them. They pay me back evil for good and hatred for love. Choose some corrupt judge to try my enemy, and let one of his own enemies accuse him.

'May he be tried and found guilty; may even his prayer be considered a crime! May his life soon be ended; may someone else take his job! May his children become orphans, and his wife a widow! May his children be homeless beggars; may they be driven from the ruins they live in! May his creditors take away all his property, and may strangers get everything he worked for. $_{12}$. May no one ever be kind to him or care for the orphans he leaves behind. $_{13}$ May all his descendants die, and may his name be forgotten in the next generation. $_{14}$ May the Lord remember the evil of his ancestors and never forgive his mother's sins. $_{15}$ May the Lord always remember their sins, but may they themselves be completely forgotten! $_{16}$ That man never thought of being kind; he persecuted and killed the poor, the needy, and the helpless. $_{17}$ He loved to curse—may he be cursed! He hated to give blessings—may no one bless him! $_{18}$. He cursed as naturally as he dressed himself;

may his own curses soak into his body like water and into his bones like oil! [19] May they cover him like clothes and always be around him like a belt! [20] Lord, punish my enemies in that way—those who say such evil things against me! [21] But my Sovereign Lord, help me as you have promised, and rescue me because of the goodness of your love. [22] I am poor and needy; I am hurt to the depths of my heart. Troubled person: [23] Like an evening shadow I am about to vanish; I am blown away like an insect. [24]. My knees are weak from lack of food; I am nothing but skin and bones. [25]. When people see me, they laugh at me; they shake their heads in scorn. [26]. Help me, O Lord my God; because of your constant love, save me! [27] Make my enemies know that you are the one who saves me. [28]. They may curse me, but you will bless me. May my persecutors be defeated, and may I, your servant, be glad. [29] May my enemies be covered with disgrace; may they wear their shame like a robe. [30]. I will give loud thanks to the Lord; I will praise him in the assembly of the people, [31] because he defends the poor and saves them from those who condemn them to death.'

What do you think about the above chapter? Should God really accept the plea to condemn and to destroy another on behalf of a petitioner? Must God act on such petitions? Should there be a God, should he or she really listen to humans with all these ungodly expectations? Is the idea of God not simply a mere human wish for certain action or inaction which is seemingly beyond human capacity? Are these not mere words for comfort? Is it really worth living with godly notions?

I wish all readers will pose critical account of these observations seriously.

GNT.
Psalms 115

'[1] To you alone, O Lord, to you alone, and not to us, must glory be given because of your constant love and faithfulness? [2] Why should the nations ask us, "Where is your God?" $_3$ Our God is in heaven; he does whatever he wishes. $_4$ Their gods are made of silver and gold, formed by human hands. $_5$ They have mouths, but cannot speak, and eyes, but cannot see. $_6$ They have ears, but cannot hear, and noses, but cannot smell. $_7$ They have hands, but cannot feel, and feet, but cannot walk; they cannot make a sound. $_8$ May all who made them and who trust in them become like the idols they have made. $_9$ Trust in the Lord, you people of Israel. He helps you and protects you. $_{10}$ Trust in the Lord, you priests of God. He helps you and protects you. $_{11}$ Trust in the Lord, all you that worship him. He helps you and protects you. $_{12}$ The Lord remembers us and will bless us; he will bless the people of Israel and all the priests of God. $_{13}$ He will bless everyone who honors him, the great and the small alike. $_{14}$ May the Lord give you children—you and your descendants! $_{15}$ May you be blessed by the Lord, who made heaven and earth! $_{16}$ Heaven belongs to the Lord alone, but he gave the earth to us humans. $_{17}$ The Lord is not praised by the dead, by any who go down to the land of silence. $_{18}$ But we, the living, will give thanks to him now and forever. Praise the Lord!'

This is pure ancient Jewish baloney; believable only by superstitious primitive minds. Read Psalms 115: 2: 'Why should the nations ask us, "where is your God?"' The answer is in verse 3: 'Our God is in heaven; he does whatever he wishes.' Really, in the year 2014! Please let us stop kidding ourselves. Read 1Cor. 14; 20.

In 950 years before Christ was born; or in 2,963 years ago, if the Jews at the time sang praises to their God, it should be perfectly understood without question, because human knowledge then and human knowledge now are not comparable. At that time, every inexplicable event or thing was a mystery or something caused by a cultural deity. And according to ancient Jews, the source of all mysteries was God of Israel who accordingly lived in heaven or some place in the sky. This was the Jewish belief about 2,963 years past. The size of planet earth remains the same, but the people and planetary matter in general are constantly changing. There are about 8 billion people now as compared to about 8 million people then. This is a fact. And the Jews are one amongst the worlds over 7,000 cultures. The Holy Bible contains information about Jews and their understanding of their world at that time; I mean the ancient time of not less than 2,000 years ago. Jews of today don't depend on biblical stories. They have changed and adapted to modern ideas. How about you the reader, a non-Jew, have you changed or still chained to the ancient Jews' ideas?

There is a new world order. Everything is a million times different now. Even a Jew of today cannot look into the sky and talk to the sky or God of Israel for miracles as his forefathers did over 2,000 years ago. Today, and indeed, as well as then, that which makes everything possible has always been quality information stored in the human brain organ. Humans must use and depend on modern quality knowledge to survive, to progress and to succeed in life. God of any culture is obsolete. They are *not* part of modern scientific world.

GNT.

Psalms 148

$_1$ Praise the Lord! Praise the Lord from heaven, you that live in the heights above. $_2$ Praise him, all his angels, and all his heavenly armies. $_3$ Praise him, sun and moon; praise him, shining stars. $_4$ Praise him, highest heavens, and the waters above the sky. $_5$ Let them all praise the name of the Lord! He commanded, and they were created; $_6$ by his command they were fixed in their places forever, and they cannot disobey. $_7$ Praise the Lord from the earth, sea monsters and all ocean depths; $_8$ lightning and hail, snow and clouds, strong winds that obey his command. $_9$ Praise him, hills and mountains, fruit trees and forests; $_{10}$ all animals, tame and wild, reptiles and birds. $_{11}$ Praise him, kings and all peoples, princes and all other rulers; $_{12}$ young women and young men, old people and children too. ₁₃ Let them all praise the name of the Lord! His name is greater than all others; his glory is above earth and heaven. ₁₄ He made his nation strong, so that all his people praise him—the people of Israel, so dear to him. Praise the Lord!'

If the nature of God is true, what would be the importance of praising God, as the author of Psalms 148 is asking all worldly matter to practice. Why 'Praises?' What does honour or respect do for God? God is supposed to be the Almighty; he has everything and has infinite access to everything including praises. Praises should be a meaningless baseless fallacy to such an incredible character called God. Praises shouldn't make sense to God. God should be beyond admiration, because the knowledge of being admired is already in his procession. Humans need praises because we are not as perfect as God. Humans are fallible and vulnerable to all earthly temptations. Humans need praises when we perform better beyond all expectations. Praises energises us to continue functioning better than normal. We should rather praise ourselves not God.

Or shall we say this God in question is the God of Israel and not necessarily the Omni Universal creator? Oh yes, the answer must be nothing but yes! A fallible God would need to be praised for being careful in avoiding all faults. A perfect God is expected to be infinitely perfect. It must be an obligation for God to show perfection every second, every minute, every hour, and every day endlessly. Any description of God that falls short of this is phony.

In the book of Exodus, the God of Israel once asked for Moses' advice. Yes, God of Israel swears. Yes, God of Israel most often lost control of his temper. God of Israel, many times, forgot his awesome infinite powers. He automatically disqualifies himself from godly praises and unworthy of an Almighty Supreme title.

PART 4

The Apostle Paul
1Timothy and 2 Timothy
1 Corinthians
Proverbs
GNT.

The Gospel According to Apostle Paul

PAUL WAS A Jew, born in Turkey. He was the founder of Christianity and was beheaded in AD 66 in Rome according to the 'Easton's Bible Dictionary'. By quick glance of the Holy Bible, many readers may conclude that all the twenty-seven books of the New Testament were written by the Apostle Paul, because most of them appear to be so. Many expert theologians, however, do accept that at least seventeen of the twenty-seven books were written by Paul. Again some eminent biblical scholars hold the view that thirteen books out of the known published New Testament can be authenticated as Pauline, judged by their biblical textual contents.

In recent years, however, researchers of Christological studies have concluded that seven out of the entire twenty-seven New Testament books can actually be assigned to Paul, himself, as the author. These seven books are Romans, 1 and 2 Corinthians, 1 and 2 Timothy, Philemon, Galatians, Philippians, and Thessalonians. It ought to be noted here that besides the Holy Bible, there is no historical record to support any of the above claims. In fact, apart from biblical history, no recorded *human* history exists that can completely support the *biblical stories* of both Jesus Christ, Mark, Matthew, Luke, John, Peter, James, and Jude: even Paul's history is full of conjectures. We shall, however, examine Paul's acclaimed significance in Christianity at a later time. The acclaimed Pauline books are as follows:

1   Romans contains 16 chapters

2 a. Corinthians contains 16 chapters (First Letter)

2 b. Corinthians contains 13 chapters (Second Letter)

3 a. 1Timothy contains 6 chapters (First Letter)

3 b. 2 Timothy contains 4 chapters (Second Letter)

4.   Philemon contains 25 verses only

5.   Galatians contains 6 chapters

6.   Philippians contains 4 chapters

7 a. 1 Thessalonians contains 5 chapters (First Letter)

7 b. 2 Thessalonians contains 3 chapters (Second Letter)

The total number of books written by Paul in the Holy Bible that are generally accepted by theologians and historians are ten, but since three are of two parts (first and second book), it is normally considered as seven books.

There is a very important caveat which all readers must know about Saul/Paul and his works as recorded in the book of Acts: 'Credibility question.' 'The men who were traveling with Saul had stopped, not saying a word; *they heard the voice* but could not see anyone' (Acts 9: 7). 'The men with me saw the light, but *did not* hear the voice of the one who was speaking to me' (Acts 22: 9).

The two statements contradict each other.

Again, the first chapter of the book of Acts and the first chapter of the book of Luke begin with the same salutation as follows: 'Dear Theophilus.' Readers of Acts are informed at the introduction that 'Acts' is a continuation of Luke and hence, the two books should be considered as written by the same unknown author. It is believed by many that Luke was written in about seventy to eighty years after Christ's death. At that time, it is known that there was no identifiable group of Jews or Gentiles in the Palestine Peninsular who called themselves Christians during Paul's time or before AD 67.

In Acts 26: 28, it is written, 'Agrippa said to Paul, in this short time do you think you will make me a Christian?' Please note that 'Christian' as a word which represents a group of followers of Christ was not possible until after 325 years of Christ's death. The quotation is obviously the author's own invention. These and several narratives of Paul in the New Testament must therefore be read with caution. They contain too many obvious chronological distortions and religious inconstancies.

According to 1 Timothy

GNT

1 Timothy 2

₁ Church Worship; First of all, then, I urge that petitions, prayers, requests, and thanksgivings be offered to God for all people; [2] for kings and all others who are in authority, that we may live a quiet and peaceful life with all reverence toward God and with proper conduct. [3] This is good and it pleases God our Saviour, [4] who wants everyone to be saved and to come to know the truth. [5] For there is one God, and there is one who brings God and human beings together, the man Christ Jesus, [6] who gave himself to redeem the whole human race. That was the proof at the right time that God wants everyone to be saved, [7] and that is why I was sent as an apostle and teacher of the Gentiles, to proclaim the message of faith and truth. I am not lying; I am telling the truth! [8] In every church service I want the men to pray, men who are dedicated to God and can lift up their hands in prayer without anger or argument. [9] I also want the women to be modest and sensible about their clothes and to dress properly; not with fancy hair styles or with gold ornaments or pearls or expensive dresses, [10] but with good deeds, as is proper for women who claim to be religious. [11] Women should learn in silence and all humility. [12] I do not allow them to teach or to have authority over men; they must keep quiet. [13] For Adam was created first, and then Eve. [14] And it was not Adam who was deceived; it was the woman who was deceived and broke God's law. [15] But a woman will be saved through having children, if she perseveres in faith and love and holiness, with modesty.'

If we can accept Paul as a fellow human with a recorded human history, as opposed to the fictional characters of the Old Testament whose histories are generally biblical tales, there are a few questions we would like to have clear answers from Paul if he was alive today.

1. Where did Paul get to know that Jesus the Christ was the one who linked God and humans?
2. Is Paul's perception of 'God' the same as the Old Testament 'God of Israel,' the God who emphasized in several books that he is *not* a God for foreigners but for Jews only?
3. How did Paul know that Jesus redeemed himself for the whole human race, rather than the Jewish race; when Jesus himself in Luke 12: 49-53 said he did not come to earth to redeem earthly people.
4. Is this person, Saul or Paul, the same proud-self-confessed terrorist, the anti-Christ, the daydreamer, anti-feminist women hater?

5. Who is Paul kidding?

From the first day after Christ's supposed resurrection from death to over thirty years after Christ's death: all news about the Christ had vanished from the then Jewish world: none other than Satan's own advocate [Saul or Paul] suddenly comes to the scene and projects himself as the clean messenger of God, destined to save both Jews and Gentiles, or Jews and non-Jews.

6. Paul, please tell me, I like to know what happened to Isaiah's prophesied 'young woman' who is pregnant and who will have a son and name him 'Immanuel' (Isa. 7: 14). And please, Senior Paul, how do you reconcile the above with the following: Matthew 1: 23, 'A virgin will become pregnant' and have a son, and he will be called Immanuel.' How come Joseph named Mary's son Jesus and not Immanuel as prophetically expected? Again, is a young woman necessarily a virgin?

According to 2 Timothy

2 Timothy 1

'From Paul, an apostle of Christ Jesus by God's will, sent to proclaim the promised life which we have in union with Christ Jesus—[2] To Timothy, my dear son: May God the Father and Christ Jesus our Lord give you grace, mercy, and peace. [3] I give thanks to God, whom I serve with a clear conscience, as my ancestors did. I thank him as I remember you always in my prayers night and day. [4] I remember your tears, and I want to see you very much, so that I may be filled with joy. [5] I remember the sincere faith you have, the kind of faith that your grandmother Lois and your mother Eunice also had. I am sure that you have it also. [6] For this reason I remind you to keep alive the gift that God gave you when I laid my hands on you. [7] For the Spirit that God has given us does not make us timid; instead, his Spirit fills us with power, love, and self-control. [8] Do not be ashamed, then, of witnessing for our Lord; neither be ashamed of me, a prisoner for Christ's sake. Instead, take your part in suffering for the Good News, as God gives you the strength for it. [9] He saved us and called us to be his own people, not because of what we have done, but because of his own purpose and grace. He gave us this grace by means of Christ Jesus before the beginning of time, [10] but now it has been revealed to us through the coming of our Savior, Christ Jesus. He has ended the power of death and through the gospel has revealed immortal life. [11] God has appointed me as an apostle and teacher to proclaim the Good News, [12] and it is for this reason that I suffer these things. But I am still full of confidence, because I know whom I have trusted, and I am sure that he is able to keep safe until that Day what he has entrusted to me. [13] Hold firmly to the true words that I taught you, as the example for you to follow, and remain in the faith and love that are ours in union with Christ Jesus. [14] Through the power of the Holy Spirit, who lives in us, keep the good things that have been entrusted to you. [15] You know that everyone in the province of Asia, including Phygelus and Hermogenes, has deserted me. [16] May the Lord show mercy to the family of Onesiphorus, because he cheered me up many times. He was not ashamed that I am in prison, [17] but as soon as he arrived in Rome, he started looking for me until he found me. [18] May the Lord grant him his mercy on that Day! And you know very well how much he did for me in Ephesus.'

My interest here is not the chapter content but its overall purpose. 2 Timothy is considered one of the sixty-six books in Christians' most famous sacred document, the Holy Bible—the fifty-fifth book.

Readers are informed at the introduction that the four-chaptered book with eighty-three verses is a second letter of advice and warning written by Apostle Paul to a young evangelist called Timothy.

Question: can a letter or a short note be considered a book? What is the difference between 'a book' and 'a letter'?

Paul is known to have written two separate letters to this young Jewish follower of Paul himself and, of course, Christ the divine, and they are correctly titled epistles, and therefore could have been joined together as most of the earlier books in the Old Testament. For instance, Genesis is the compilation of 11 books joined; Deuteronomy is the compilation of 11 books joined; Isaiah is compilation of 3 books joined; Song of Songs is a collection of poems or love letters; Psalms is a collection of aged-old hymns and prayers; and indeed, much more separated than the two letters written by Paul to Timothy: so why are the two letters not joined together to form a single book? I do not see any theological literary sense to classify each letter by Paul to Timothy as separate books.

The same thing applies to the first and second books of Corinthians, Thessalonians, Peter, and John. They are letters from Paul and therefore not necessarily books. Besides, the contents of the books are advisory, warnings, and encouragements to his followers regarding dangers and pleasures of preaching Jesus Christ's gospels.

According to 1 Corinthians

GNT

1 Corinthians 5

'Immorality in the Church: Now, it is actually being said that there is sexual immorality among you so terrible that not even the heathen would be guilty of *it. I am told that a man is sleeping with his stepmother!* [2] How, then, can you be proud? On the contrary, you should be filled with sadness, and the man who has done such a thing should be expelled from your fellowship. [3-4] And even though I am far away from you in body, still I am there with you in spirit; and as though I were there with you, I have in the name of our

Lord Jesus already passed judgment on the man who has done this terrible thing. As you meet together, and I meet with you in my spirit, by the power of our Lord Jesus present with us, [5] you are to hand this man over to Satan for his body to be destroyed, so that his spirit may be saved in the Day of the Lord. [6] It is not right for you to be proud! You know the saying, "A little bit of yeast makes the whole batch of dough rise." [7] You must remove the old yeast of sin so that you will be entirely pure. Then you will be like a new batch of dough without any yeast, as indeed I know you actually are. For our Passover Festival is ready, now that Christ, our Passover lamb, has been sacrificed. [8] Let us celebrate our Passover, then, not with bread having the old yeast of sin and wickedness, but with the bread that has no yeast, the bread of purity and truth. [9] *In the letter that I wrote you I told you not to associate with immoral people.* [10] Now I did not mean pagans who are immoral or greedy or are thieves, or who worship idols. To avoid them you would have to get out of the world completely. [11] What I meant *was that you should not associate with a person who calls himself a believer but is immoral or greedy or worships idols or is a slanderer or a drunkard or a thief. Don't even sit down to eat with such a person.* [12-13] After all, it is none of my business to judge outsiders. God will judge them. But should you not judge the members of your own fellowship? As the scripture says, "Remove the evil person from your group."'

The Lord Jesus Christ's followers are warned by Apostle Paul to stay away from sexual immorality. He cites a case where a man had sexual intercourse with his stepmother.

1 Corinthians 7

'Questions about Marriage: Now, to deal with the matters you wrote about. A man does well not to marry. [2] But because there is so much immorality, every man should have his own wife, and every woman should have her own husband. [3] A man should fulfill his duty as a husband, and a woman should fulfill her duty as a wife, and each should satisfy the other's needs. [4] A wife is not the master of her own body, but her husband is; in the same way a husband is not the master of his own body, but his wife is. [5] Do not deny yourselves to each other, unless you first agree to do so for a while in order to spend your time in prayer; but then resume normal marital relations. In this way you will be kept from giving in to Satan's temptation because of your lack of self-control. [6] I tell you this not as an order, but simply as permission. [7] Actually I would prefer that all of you were as I am; but each one has a special gift from God, one person this gift, another one that gift. [8] Now, to the unmarried and to *the widows I say that it would be better for you to continue to live alone as I do.* [9] But if you cannot restrain your desires, go ahead and marry—it is better to marry than to burn with passion. [10] *For married people I have a command which is not my own but the Lord's: a wife must not leave her husband;* [11] *but if she does, she must remain single or else be reconciled to her husband; and a husband must not divorce his wife.* [12] To the others I say (I, myself, not the Lord): if a *Christian* man has a wife who is an unbeliever and she agrees to go on living with him, he must not divorce her. [13] And if a *Christian* woman is married to a man who is an unbeliever and he agrees to go on living with her, she must not divorce him. [14] For the unbelieving husband is made acceptable to God by being united to his wife, and the unbelieving wife is made acceptable to God by being united to her *Christian* husband. If this were not so, their children would be like pagan children; but as it is, they are acceptable to God. [15] However, if the one who is not a believer wishes to leave the *Christian* partner, let it be so. In such cases the *Christian* partner, whether husband or wife, is free to act. God has called you to live in peace.

[16] How can you be sure, *Christian* wife, that you will not save[b] your husband? Or how can you be sure, *Christian* husband, that you will not save[c] your wife?

'Live As God Called You: [17]*each* of you should go on living according to the Lord's gift to you, and as you were when God called you. This is the rule I teach in all the churches. [18] If a circumcised man has accepted God's call, he should not try to remove the marks of circumcision; if an uncircumcised man has accepted God's call, he should not get circumcised. [19] For whether or not a man is circumcised means nothing; what matters is to obey God's commandments. [20] Each of you should remain as you were when you accepted God's call. [21] Were you a slave when God called you? Well, never mind; but if you have a chance to become free, use it. [22] For a slave who has been called by the Lord is the Lord's free person; in the same way a free person who has been called by Christ is his slave. [23] God bought you for a price; so do not become slaves of people. [24] My friends, each of you should remain in fellowship with God in the same condition that you were when you were called.

'Questions about the Unmarried and the Widows: [25] Now, concerning what you wrote about unmarried people: I do not have a command from the Lord, but *I give my opinion* as one who by the Lord's mercy is worthy of trust. [26] Considering the present distress, I think it is better for a man to stay as he is. [27] Do you have a wife? Then don't try to get rid of her. Are you unmarried? Then don't look for a wife. [28] But if you do marry, you haven't committed a sin; and if an unmarried woman marries, she hasn't committed a sin. But I would rather spare you the everyday troubles that married people will have. [29] What I mean, my friends, is this: there is not much time left, and from now on married people should live as though they were not married; [30] those who weep, as though they were not sad; those who laugh, as though they were not happy; those who buy, as though they did not own what they bought; [31] those who deal in material goods, as though they were not fully occupied with them. For this world as it is now will not last much longer. [32] I would like you to be free from worry. *An unmarried man concerns himself with the Lord's work, because he is trying to please the Lord.* [33] *But a married man concerns himself with worldly matters, because he wants to please his wife;* [34] *and so he is pulled in two directions. An unmarried woman or a virgin concerns herself with the Lord's work, because she wants to be dedicated both in body and spirit; but a married woman concerns herself with worldly matters, because she wants to please her husband.* [35] I am saying this because I want to help you. I am not trying to put restrictions on you. Instead, I want you to do what is right and proper, and to give yourselves completely to the Lord's service without any reservation. [36] In the case of an engaged couple who have decided not to marry: if the man feels that he is not acting properly toward the young woman and if his passions are too strong and he feels that they ought to marry, then they should get married, as he wants to. There is no sin in this. [37] But if a man, without being forced to do so, has firmly made up his mind not to marry, and if he has his will under complete control and has already decided in his own mind what to do—then he does well not to marry the young woman. [38] So the man who marries does well, but the one who doesn't marry does even better. [39] A married woman is not free as long as her husband lives; but if her husband dies, then she is free to be married to any man she wishes, but only if he is a *Christian.* [40] She will be happier, however, if she stays as she is. That is my opinion, and I think that I too have God's Spirit.'

There are two very relevant ideas in 1 Corinthians chapter 7 which are worthy of particular attention. These are (a) the word 'Christian' and (b) Paul's personal opinions.

The Apostle Paul was beheaded in AD 67 and therefore all his letters and indeed his works were done before the above date. This means that Paul's letters were written during the first thirty years *after* Christ's death. At that period, there was no group of religious people who were identified as Christians. Historically, at the time of Jesus Christ's crucifixion, Saul/Paul was about five or seven years old or an infant; hence, Saul/Paul's knowledge of Jesus Christ can be said to be insignificant.

In the book of Acts, Saul/Paul declared that he was personally among the murderers of Stephen in a Jewish Temple in Jerusalem and indeed, committed several wicked deeds in communities where Christ's theological ideas were practiced from time to time. The prevailing Jewish religion at the time, first century to the fourth century, was based on the Laws of Moses (written laws) and traditional (unwritten) Jewish or Judaic customary laws.

The word Christians was not used to describe any single religious faction, because Christ's followers were minor unorganized rival groups and almost non-existent when Paul was alive. Indeed, it was Saul/Paul himself who initiated Jesus' pioneering gospels during Christ Era early years. Paul was beheaded about AD 67 because of his teaching of deviant Christ ideas. There were certainly no Christians during the first hundred years after the crucifixion. Even during the rule of Emperor Constance 1, through to Constantius (337-361), the Christos was insignificant splinter groups operating within the umbrella of the age-old Judaic structure according to *The Oxford History of the Biblical World,* pages 564-590.

Paul's letters to the Corinthians could not contain the word 'Christians' as it is seen used eight times in 1 Corinthians chapter 7. This implies that Paul's letters were transcribed at a later period, by someone other than Paul, definitely between CE 150 and CE 500 when 'Christians' as an organized group or as a word had began to emerge.

Paul's opinion, distinct from that of Lord God of Israel, appeared to be made clear. If you read verses 12-16, you will notice that the author begins with a statement, 'I say, I myself not the Lord', followed by what is expected of a Christian according to Paul himself. Again in verse 25, the echo of Paul is clear: 'I do not have a command from the Lord, but I give my opinion as one who by the Lord's mercy is worthy of trust.'

The style and the tone of speeches in the six verses match the religious events of CE 324 through to CE 500. At the period, Orthodox (circumcised) Jews and the emerging minority (uncircumcised) Christ Jewish followers were bitter rivals. A

Decree known as Edict of Milan had been passed to prevent conversion of one to the other, although together they had obtained Roman Emperor's recognition as a single official religion in all Roman territories. The two Jewish religious communities were far apart. Intermarriage problems were serious concerns of both sects and almost forbidden. Paul would have shown concern if he were alive then.

The New Testament as we know today was compiled at that period. Thus Paul's letters, written about 300 years earlier, were either modified or invented to show or to reflect what Paul would have said in those circumstances if he was alive then.

Indeed Bishop Athanasius of Alexandria had then completed his compilation of the twenty-seven books of the New Testaments in AD 367. And there is no doubt that he was the one who wove the word 'Christian' into Paul's religious ideas; ref. page 579, ibid.[1]

My point here is this: readers of the Holy Bible must be cautioned with quotation marks when reading the Holy Bible. All the quotes represent the type of words, sentences, or opinions which the characters concerned would have used or said. None was original voice.

1 Corinthians 9

'Rights and Duties of an Apostle: Am I not a free man? Am I not an apostle? Haven't I seen Jesus our Lord? And aren't you the result of my work for the Lord? [2] Even if others do not accept me as an apostle, surely you do! Because of your life in union with the Lord you yourselves are proof of the fact that I am an apostle. [3] When people criticize me, this is how I defend myself:

[4] Don't I have the right to be given food and drink for my work? [5] Don't I have the right to follow the example of the other apostles and the Lord's brothers and Peter, by taking a Christian wife with me on my trips? [6] Or are Barnabas and I the only ones who have to work for our living? [7] What soldiers ever have to

pay their own expenses in the army? What farmers do not eat the grapes from their own vineyard? What shepherds do not use the milk from their own sheep? ⁸ I don't have to limit myself to these everyday examples, because the Law says the same thing. ⁹ We read in the Law of Moses, "Do not muzzle an ox when you are using it to thresh grain." Now, is God concerned about oxen? ¹⁰ Didn't he really mean us when he said that? Of course that was written for us. Anyone who ploughs and anyone who reaps should do their work in the hope of getting a share of the crop. *¹¹ We have sown spiritual seed among you. Is it too much if we reap material benefits from you?* ¹² If others have the right to expect this from you, don't we have an even greater right? But we haven't made use of this right. Instead, we have endured everything in order not to put any obstacle in the way of the Good News about Christ. ¹³ Surely you know that the men who work in the Temple get their food from the Temple and that those who offer the sacrifices on the altar get a share of the sacrifices. *¹⁴ In the same way, the Lord has ordered that those who preach the gospel should get their living from it.* ¹⁵ But I haven't made use of any of these rights, nor am I writing this now in order to claim such rights for myself. I would rather die first! Nobody is going to turn my rightful boast into empty words!

¹⁶ I have no right to boast just because I preach the gospel. After all, I am under orders to do so. And how terrible it would be for me if I did not preach the gospel! *¹⁷ If I did my work as a matter of free choice, then I could expect to be paid; but I do it as a matter of duty, because God has entrusted me with this task. ¹⁸ What pay do I get, then? It is the privilege of preaching the Good News without charging for it, without claiming my rights in my work for the gospel. ¹⁹ I am a free man, nobody's slave; but I make myself everybody's slave in order to win as many people as possible. ²⁰ While working with the Jews, I live like a Jew in order to win them; and even though I myself am not subject to the Law of Moses, I live as though I were when working with those who are, in order to win them. ²¹ In the same way, when working with Gentiles, I live like a Gentile, outside*

the Jewish Law, in order to win Gentiles. This does not mean that I don't obey God's law; I am really under Christ's law. [22] *Among the weak in faith I become weak like one of them, in order to win them. So I become all things to all people, that I may save some of them* **by whatever means are possible.** [23] *All this I do for the gospel's sake, in order to share in its blessings.* [24] Surely you know that many runners take part in a race, but only one of them wins the prize. Run, then, in such a way as to win the prize. [25] Every athlete in training submits to strict discipline, in order to be crowned with a wreath that will not last; but we do it for one that will last forever. [26] That is why I run straight for the finish line; that is why I am like a boxer who does not waste his punches. [27] I harden my body with blows and bring it under complete control, to keep myself from being disqualified after having called others to the contest.'

The Apostle Paul is stating the rights and duties of an apostle. He asks a question, *'Are you not the result of my work for the Lord?'* Being the pioneer teacher of the *Good News about Jesus Christ,* Paul wanted the people of Corinth, especially his new recruits, to know that he deserves to be recognized as a prophet, because his duties were prophetic.

He also mentioned the roles played by Jesus' brothers, Peter and Barnabas, to make a point in verse 11. 'We have sown spiritual seed among you. Is it too much if we reap material benefits from you?' Verse 14: 'The Lord has ordered that those who preach the Gospel should get their living from it.'

Now let us read verse 20-23 again and see exactly what Paul means. 'While working with the Jews, I live like a Jew in order to win them; and even though I myself am not subject to the Law of Moses, I live as though I were when working with those who are, in order to win them. In the same way, when working with Gentiles, I live like a Gentile, outside the Jewish Law, in order to win Gentiles. This does not mean that I don't obey God's law; I am really under Christ's law. Among the weak in faith I become weak like one of them, in order to win them. So I become all things to all people, that I may save some of them *by whatever means possible*. All this I do for the gospel's sake, in order to share in its blessings.'

As a matter of duty, God has entrusted him to preach the '**Good News**' to all without pay and by every means possible, although he is aware that he is entitled to be rewarded materially.

My problem with this chapter is 'the **Good News**' clause in verse 18. Why not just 'the News', because 'good' presupposes the availability or knowledge of the 'bad' or the not so good news. Good News means good deeds of Jesus Christ. This excludes those deeds which are not so good. Implicitly, Paul knows all the news about the man Jesus, but he is willing to talk about *the good ones only*. Paul is, however, not saying that Jesus did no wrong. Paul is just saying that he is not willing to discuss the other news about Jesus. Paul is definitely aware of the purposes of baptism and also aware that Jesus Christ submitted himself to be baptized or cleansed by John the Baptist. He who is clean and pure needs no refinement and purification. The public is therefore entitled to hear from Paul the other human story of Mary's first son, Jesus the Christ, especially during his teenage years (13-19) plus, of course, his primary adolescence (20-29) years. It is obvious that these deleted-out years of Jesus Christ is full of bad news that readers may vomit when they are exposed in any form. The forty-first book of the Holy Bible gives a hint of Jesus Christ's other news: 'Why do you call me good?' Jesus asked him, 'No one is good except God alone.' (Mark 10: 18). This is obviously Christ' own sin confession.

1 Corinthians 11

'Imitate me, then, just as I imitate Christ, Covering the Head in Worship: [2] I praise you because you always remember me and follow the teachings that I have handed on to you. [3] But I want you to understand that Christ is supreme over every man, *the husband is supreme over his wife, and God is supreme over Christ.* [4] So a man who prays or proclaims God's message in public worship with his head covered disgraces Christ. [5] And any woman who prays or proclaims God's message in public worship with nothing on her head disgraces her husband; there is no difference between her and a woman whose head has been shaved. [6] If the woman does not cover her head, she might as well cut her hair. And since it is a shameful thing for a woman to shave her head or cut her hair, she should cover her head. [7] A man has no need to cover his head, because he reflects the image and glory of God. But *woman reflects the glory of man*; [8] for man was not created from woman, but woman from man. [9] Nor was man created for woman's sake, but *woman was created for man's sake*. [10] On account of the angels, then, a woman should have a covering over her head to show that she is under her husband's authority. [11] In our life in the Lord, however, woman is not independent of man, nor is man independent of woman. [12] For as woman was made from man, in the same way man is born of woman; and it is God who brings everything into existence. [13] Judge for yourselves whether it is proper for a woman to pray to God in public worship with nothing on her head. [14] Why, nature itself teaches you that long hair on a man is a disgrace, [15] but on a woman it is a thing of beauty. Her long hair has been given her to serve as a covering. [16] But if anyone wants to argue about it, all I have to say is that neither we nor the churches of God have any other custom in worship.'

Apostle Paul is a classic Jew. Paul propagates throughout the New Testament that a woman was created out of man, woman was made for man, woman was created for man's sake, that woman has no independent mind, etc. Verse 12 establishes another Jewish religious anomaly: 'For as woman was made from man, in the same way man is born of woman.' Paul has used every possible verb in the action dictionary to show that female human species is nonentity. But here Paul seems to be loosely saying that man is born out of woman. Is this supposed loose talk, not the most serious commonest phenomena known to every race of people on planet earth, except ancient Jew; Is it not a fact all human beings are products of the woman's womb?

Can humanity deny the woman her natural role of producing a child? I am sure the reader is yearning to ask how woman entered the planet earth to begin with. This question is certainly important. But you will equally agree with me that the Jewish Genesis answer to this question is too loose, too weak, too infantile, illogical, and unsatisfactory to any reasonable person.

No one knows for sure 'If' there was, ever, the first man or the first woman or the first in everything natural on our planet. And because we lack indisputable evidence to support 'firstly' ideas of Genesis, we should not stop searching for clues that can reasonably explain the 'first' concept in creation. Personally, I don't believe there was ever such a time or such an entity called God who designed nature. If you still believe in Genesis or the Holy Bible's explanation of the beginning or creation, I would ask you to reread your book of Genesis again, but this time meticulously and not with a religious spectacles.

I know that diehard religious people are not comfortable when the wisdom of their God is challenged. But sincerely speaking, wouldn't it be convincing if the biblical God had created a single unit of every living organism on each of the seven different continents? If indeed God was the designer of the universe, would he or she not know that there are different climatic temperatures and geographical conditions, and therefore necessary to design people according to each area's natural conditions rather than just Adam and Eve in Palestine to procreate and then spread to the rest of the universe? God of Israel, God of France, God of Africa, God of Australia, God of America, God of Pakistan; yes, why not? Why God of Israel but not God of any of the above places?

Why would God of Israel originate in the Palestine peninsular area and not in China, India, Australia, Africa, Europe, or the

Americas? Why was the first human being on planet earth not a Chinese, an Indian, Japanese, an African, a Caucasian, or any other ethnicity? I wish such prominent church leaders of the first and second centuries as Irenaeus, Hippolytus, Origen, Justin Martyr, and Apostle Paul would be around today to answer these questions.

1 Corinthians 14

'More about Gifts from the Spirit. It is love, then, that you should strive for. Set your hearts on spiritual gifts, especially the gift of proclaiming God's message. [2] Those who speak in strange tongues do not speak to others but to God, because no one understands them. They are speaking secret truths by the power of the Spirit. [3] But those who proclaim God's message speak to people and give them help, encouragement, and comfort. [4] Those who speak in strange tongues help only themselves, but those who proclaim God's message help the whole church. [5] I would like for all of you to speak in strange tongues; but I would rather that you had the gift of proclaiming God's message. For the person who proclaims God's message is of greater value than the one who speaks in strange tongues—unless there is someone present who can explain what is said, so that the whole church may be helped. [6] So when I come to you, my friends, what use will I be to you if I speak in strange tongues? Not a bit, unless I bring you some revelation from God or some knowledge or some inspired message or some teaching. [7] Take such lifeless musical instruments as the flute or the harp—how will anyone know the tune that is being played unless the notes are sounded distinctly? [8] And if the one who plays the bugle does not sound a clear call, who will prepare for battle? [9] In the same way, how will anyone understand what you are talking about if your message given in strange tongues is not clear? Your words will vanish in the air! [10] There are many different languages in the world, yet none of them is without meaning. [11] But if I do not know the language being spoken, those who use it will be foreigners to me and I will be a foreigner to them. [12] Since you are eager to have the gifts of the Spirit, you must try above everything else to make greater use of those which help to build up the church [13] the person who speaks in strange tongues, then, must pray for the gift to explain what is said. [14] For if I pray in this way, my spirit prays indeed, but my mind has no part in it. [15] What should I do, then? I will pray with my spirit, but I will pray also with my mind; I will sing with my spirit, but I will sing also with my mind. [16] When you give thanks to God in spirit only, how can ordinary people taking part in the meeting say "Amen" to your prayer of thanksgiving? They have no way of knowing what you are saying.

[17] Even if your prayer of thanks to God is quite good, other people are not helped at all. [18] I thank God that I speak in strange tongues much more than any of you. [19] But in church worship I would rather speak five words that can be understood, in order to teach others, than speak thousands of words in strange tongues. [20] Do not be like children in your thinking, my friends; be children so far as evil is concerned, but be grown up in your thinking. [21] In the Scriptures it is written, "By means of people speaking strange languages I will speak to my people, says the Lord. I will speak through lips of foreigners, but even then my people will not listen to me." [22.] So then, the gift of speaking in strange tongues is proof for unbelievers, not for believers, while the gift of proclaiming God's message is proof for believers, not for unbelievers. [23] If, then, the whole church meets together and everyone starts speaking in strange tongues—and if some ordinary people or unbelievers come in, won't they say that you are all crazy? [24] But if everyone is proclaiming God's message when some unbelievers or ordinary people come in, they will be convinced of their sin by what they hear. They will be judged by all they hear, [25] their secret thoughts will be brought into the open, and they will bow down and worship God, confessing, 'Truly, God is here among you!' Order in the Church;

26. This is what I mean, my friends. When you meet for worship, one person has a hymn, another teaching, another revelation from God, another a message in strange tongues, and still another the explanation of what is said. Everything must be of help to the church. 27 If someone is going to speak in strange tongues, two or three at the most should speak, one after the other, and someone else must explain what is being said. 28 But if no one is there who can explain, then the one who speaks in strange tongues must be quiet and speak only to himself and to God. 29 Two or three who are given God's message should speak, while the others are to judge what they say. 30 But if someone sitting in the meeting receives a message from God, the one who is speaking should stop. 31 All of you may proclaim God's message, one by one, so that everyone will learn and be encouraged. 32 The gift of proclaiming God's message should be under the speaker's control, 33 because God does not want us to be in disorder but in harmony and peace. As in all the churches of God's people, 34 the women should keep quiet in the meetings. They are not allowed to speak; as the Jewish Law says, they must not be in charge. 35 If they want to find out about something, they should ask their husbands at home. It is a disgraceful thing for a woman to speak in a church meeting.

'36 Or could it be that the word of God came from you? Or are you the only ones to whom it came? 37 If anyone supposes he is God's messenger or has a spiritual gift, he must realize that what I am writing to you is the Lord's command. 38 But if he does not pay attention to this, pay no attention to him. 39 So then, my friends, set your heart on proclaiming God's message, but do not forbid the speaking in strange tongues. 40 Everything must be done in a proper and orderly way.'

This is obviously the voice of the famous Turkish Jew, Paul, speaking to Jewish audience, in a form of a letter written somewhere around AD 57; and as narrated by Jewish Rabbis somewhere around AD 500: or possibly narrated by late medieval followers of Christ around AD 1300. The choice of words and sentences used are distinctly different from the first century style of writing.

Paul himself confessed that he was a terrorist and an evil-minded person according to the book of Acts 22: 19-20; 26: 9-11. As a classic ancient chauvinist Jew, he had no value for women and would have preferred if marriages never existed, because it prevents focus on preaching the so-called Good News. He failed to realize that over 60 per cent of all world population, at any given time, had been women. To ignore them as insignificant humans is a very sad mistake and ungodly. And here is a man who Christian's worldwide sing praises to, as the God-appointed messenger or an apostle appointed by God to unite Jews and Gentiles with 'the good news' 'only' about Christ whom he never met personally when both were alive as real humans.

In verse 34, this crazy individual from nowhere claims to be a specialist in Jewish customary laws, Laws of Moses, as well as righteousness according to Christ, who supposedly died about thirty something years earlier. There is no record that Paul ever met Jesus in person when both were alive. It is known, however, that Paul was about five or seven years old when Christ died.

Well, then, apart from dreams, or Paul's supposed encounter with the spirit of Christ when he was going to Damascus with his companions, his knowledge of Jesus Christ was essentially his own invention. We are told of Paul's encounter with James, Barnabas, and Peter who were presumed to be among Jesus' followers with very few evidential records in the book of Acts.

Paul appears to be educating his Jewish audience the customary laws and the laws according to Jesus Christ.

Again, elsewhere in other books, Apostle Paul found women as domesticated humans. In his Letter to Timothy, 1 Timothy 2: 12, he writes, 'I do not allow women to have authority over men; they must keep quiet'. From verse 15, we can realize that he believed women shall be saved only by giving birth to children. Here is a man who confessed to be the worse among all sinners, 1 Timothy 1: 15, and at the same time exhibiting himself as the holiest of all mankind. A man who preferred to remain single and unmarried (1 Cor. 7: 8) and probably knew nothing about women, yet about seventeen books of the Holy Bible are assigned to him as their author. How can we ignore his gender pronouncements? Or indeed, all biblical authors' gender bias against women. Paul, in particular, has become a successful umbrella under which are hidden modern-day repentant hardcore social deviants. Yes, if a character such as Paul can become a prophet, why not his kind: murderers, rapist, drug dealers and thieves?

Most Bible readers are aware that the entire book is Jewish; hence, all customary laws therein stated are essentially Jewish. And if Bible readers fail to recognize this crucial aspect of Christian scriptures, the snobbery of women who have always represented majority of human population throughout human earthly experience, and simply universalize the book as a holy unquestionable document, then there is a problem with what they read and teach.

According to Proverbs

GNT.

Proverbs 8

'Wisdom: ₁ Listen! Wisdom is calling out. Reason is making herself heard. ₂ On the hilltops near the road and at the crossroads she stands. ₃ At the entrance to the city, beside the gates, she calls:

This is the voice of wisdom: ₄"I appeal to all of you; I call to everyone on earth. ₅ Are you immature? Learn to be mature. Are you foolish? Learn to have sense. ₆ Listen to my excellent words; all I tell you is right. ₇ What I say is the truth; lies are hateful to me.

₈Everything I say is true; nothing is false or misleading. ₉ To those with insight, it is all clear; to the well-informed, it is all plain. ₁₀Choose my instruction instead of silver; choose knowledge rather than the finest gold. ₁₁I am Wisdom, I am better than jewels; nothing you want can compare with me. ₁₂I am Wisdom, and I have insight; I have knowledge and sound judgment. ₁₃To honour the Lord is to hate evil; I hate pride and arrogance, evil ways and false words. ₁₄I make plans and carry them out. I have understanding, and I am strong. ₁₅I help kings to govern and rulers to make good laws. ₁₆Every ruler on earth governs with my help, officials and nobles alike. ₁₇I love those who love me; whoever looks for me can find me. ₁₈I have riches and honour to give, prosperity and success.

₁₉What you get from me is better than the finest gold, better than the purest silver. ₂₀I walk the way of righteousness; I follow the paths of justice, ₂₁giving wealth to those who love me, filling their houses with treasures. ₂₂"The Lord created me first of all, the first of his works, long ago. ₂₃*I was made in the very beginning, at the first, before the world began.*

₂₄I was born before the oceans, when there were no springs of water. ₂₅I was born before the mountains, before the hills were set in place, ₂₆before God made the earth and its fields or even the first handful of soil. ₂₇I was there when he set the sky in place, when he stretched the horizon across the ocean, ₂₈when he placed the clouds in the sky, when he opened the springs of the ocean ₂₉ and ordered the waters of the sea to rise no further than he said. I was there when he laid the earth's foundations. ₃₀I was beside him like an architect, I was his daily source of joy, always happy in his presence ₃₁happy with the world and pleased with the human race.

₃₂"Now; young people, listen to me. Do as I say and you will be happy. ₃₃Listen to what you are taught. Be wise; do not neglect it.

₃₄Those that listen to me will be happy—those who stay at my door every day, waiting at the entrance to my home. ₃₅Those who find me find life, and the Lord will be pleased with them. ₃₆Those who do not find me hurt themselves; anyone who hates me loves death."' Proverbs chapter 8 above sums up everything regarding knowledge or wisdom. You may ignore the use of the words 'Lord' and 'God' in the chapter because they are used to represent the human brain organ. The bottom line of life, as humans, is the size or the weight of information stored in our brain tissue. It is not Lord God or any entity outside the brain. Your failure or success, your happiness or sadness, your progress or decadence, your richness or poverty, your foolishness or intelligence are totally dependent on quality information captured by your individual brain organ. None of the above has anything to do with Lord God of Israel, God in Heaven, Satan, Evil Spirit, or any spirit of any kind. Spirits can exist in your mind if you give them space in your brain lobes. They are nothing but illusions.

BIBLIOGRAPHY

The Oxford History of the Biblical World,
Edited by Michael D. Coogan.
Oxford University Press.
Oxford. 1998.

The Holy Bible.
The British & Foreign Bible Society.
Cambridge University Press,
London. 1934

GNT
The Good News Bible;
Today's English Version
American Bible Society. British Edition
United Bible Society: 21st. Print.
London:. 1986.

APPENDIX

Good News Bible
INTENTIONAL MISQUOTATIONS OF some Old Testament
statements in the New Testament books:

Old Testament	New Testament
Isaiah 7: 14	Matthew 1: 23
Isaiah 40: 3	Matthew 3: 3
Isaiah 6: 9-10	Matthew13:14,15
Isaiah 29: 13	Matthew 15: 8-9
Psalms 8: 2	Matthew 21: 16
Isaiah 40: 3	Mark 1: 3
Isaiah 6: 9-10	Mark 4: 12
Isaiah 29: 13	Mark 7: 6-7
Isaiah 40: 3-5	Luke 3: 4-6
Isaiah 61: 1	Luke 4: 18
Isaiah 6: 9	Luke 8: 10
Isaiah 40: 3	John 1: 23
Isaiah 53: 1	John 12: 38
Isaiah 6: 10	John 12: 40

Exodus 20: 13. 'Thou shall not kill.'
Ecclesiastes 3: 3. 'A time for killing.'

Reference Source: Good News Bible

Lightning Source UK Ltd.
Milton Keynes UK
UKHW040747191022
410730UK00001B/31